Greenhill Books

# Rommel's Year of Victory

Motto:

Den gefallenen Kameraden
zum Gedächtnis,
den Lebenden zur Erinnerung,
der Heimat eine Brücke zum Verstehen!

Walther Nehring
General der Panzer

A memorial to the fallen comrades
A reminder to the living
A bridge, so that the Homeland can understand

Walther Nehring
General der Panzertruppe

# Rommel's Year of Victory

## The Wartime Illustrations of the Afrika Korps by Kurt Caesar

Text by James Lucas

Foreword by Erwin Rommel

Preface by Barrie Pitt

**Greenhill Books, London**

**Stackpole Books, Pennsylvania**

*Rommel's Year of Victory*
first published 1998 by Greenhill Books,
Lionel Leventhal Limited, Park House, 1 Russell Gardens,
London NW11 9NN and Stackpole Books, 5067 Ritter
Road, Mechanicsburg, PA 17055, USA



*British Library Cataloguing in Publication Data*
A catalogue record for this book is available from the British Library

ISBN 1-85367-302-1

*Library of Congress Cataloging-in-Publication Data available*

*Publishing History*
The illustrations on pages 10, 15–18, 32–4, 40–3, 48–74, 78–87, 90, 94–105, 108, 114–24, 128–35, 138, 142–52, 156, 160–5 and 168–74 by Kurt Caesar, the Dedication and the Foreword were originally published in 1943 by Carl Röhrig Verlag, München. The present German edition containing these and other illustrations was published in 1994 by Verlag E.S. Mittler & Sohn Gmbh, 32052 Herford (Germany), under the title *Marsch und Kampf des deutschen Afrikakorps*, copyright E.S. Mittler & Sohn Gmbh, Herford.

Illustrations on pages 6–9, 12, 22–30, 36–8, 44, 76, 88–9, 92, 106–7, 110–12, 127, 136, 140, 154, 157–8, 166 and 176 by Kurt Caesar, intended for a second volume of the original German edition that was never produced, are published here for the first time.

The text by James Lucas is published here for the first time.

Design by John Anastasio, Creative Line
Printed in Hong Kong by Midas Printing Ltd.

# Contents

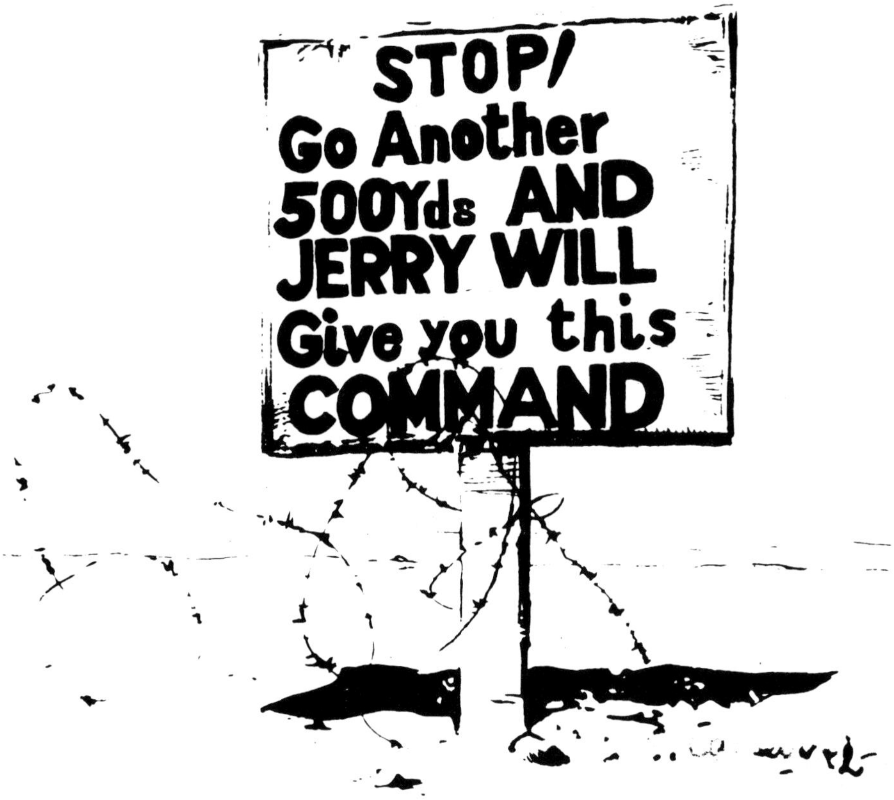
STOP/
Go Another
500Yds AND
JERRY WILL
Give you this
COMMAND

# List of Illustrations

# PREFACE

It is always interesting to come across views 'from the other side of the hill', and for those who recall the days of the Desert War the views from the other side of that particular barren, stony, bush-bespattered wilderness can be both awful and awe-inspiring. Did we all, British, Germans, Poles and Italians, really live for months in that arid hell – and fight each other across it when battle couldn't be avoided?

James Lucas has brought back memories so vivid as to make us automatically check bedsheets for sand every evening and slippers and shoes for lurking spiders in the morning.

And remember the dust!

Could anyone who had been there during those days ever forget the dust at Tobruk? Or the reek of cordite everywhere and the taste of chlorine in everything?

This text and Kurt Caesar's illustrations paint the picture ... for some, too damn clearly.

Barrie Pitt, 1998

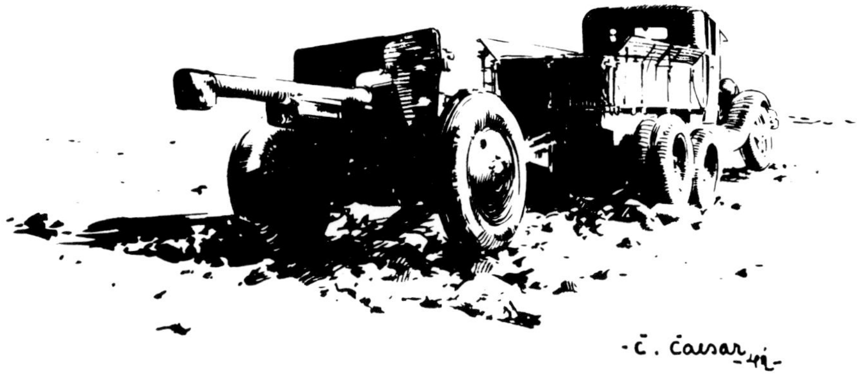

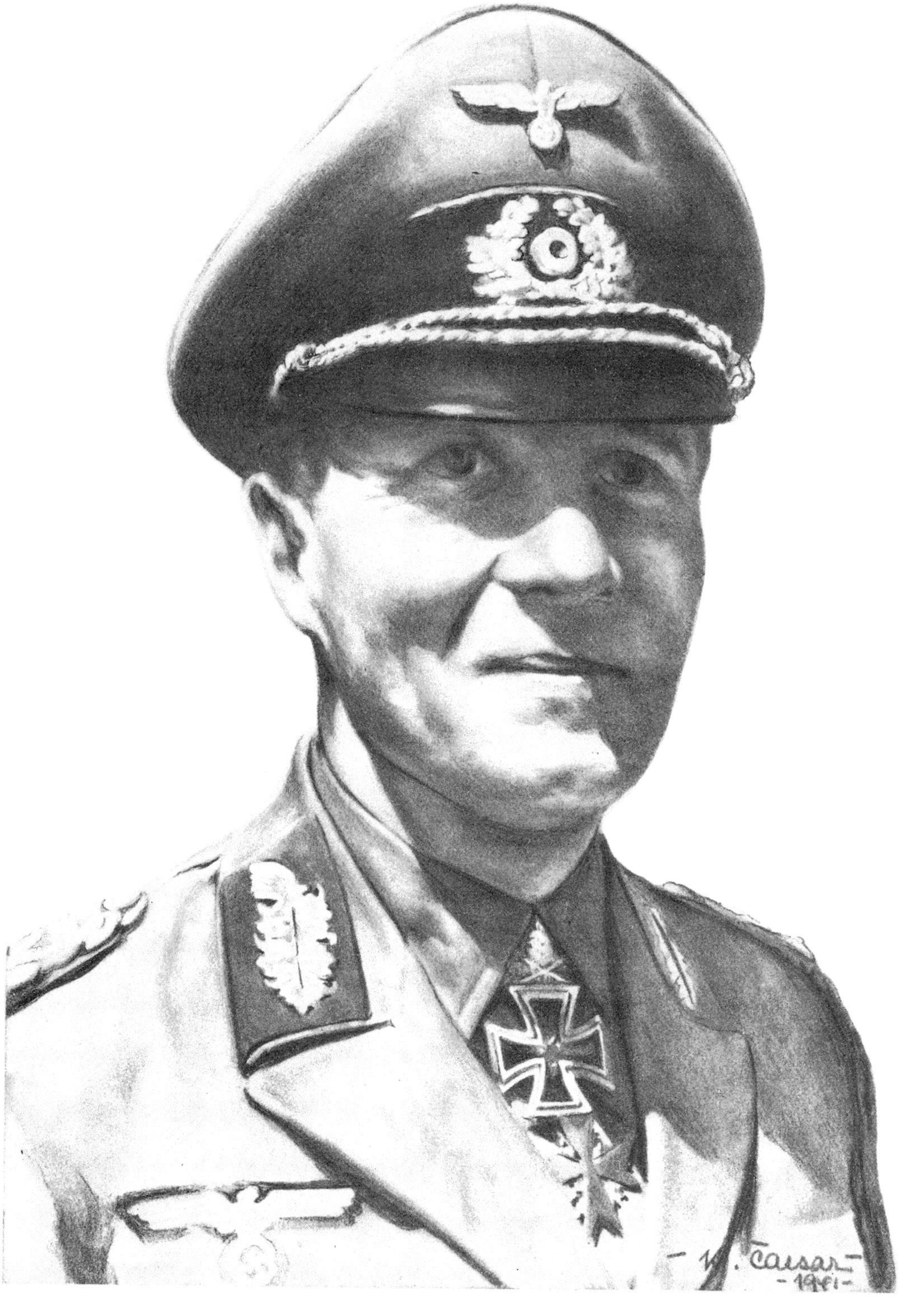


Field Marshal Rommel. He is shown here decorated with the Oak Leaf and Swords to the Knight's Cross as well as the *Pour le Mérite.*

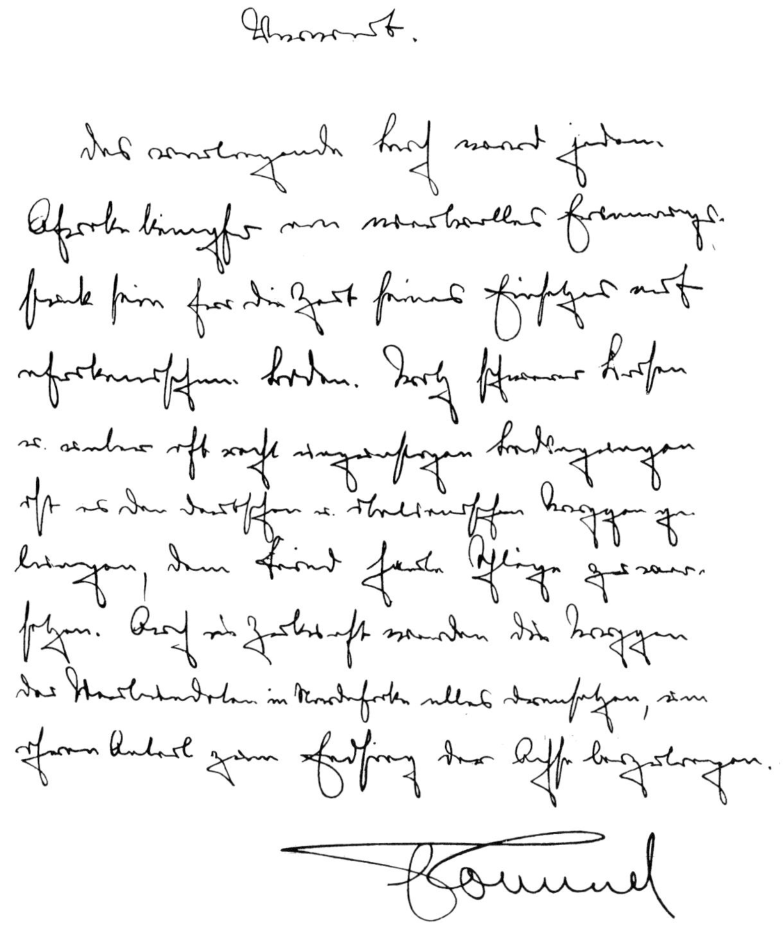

Geleitwort.

Das vorliegende Buch wird jedem Afrikakämpfer ein wertvolles Erinnerungsstück sein für die Zeit seines Einsatzes auf afrikanischem Boden. Trotz schwerer Krisen u. unter oft recht ungünstigen Bedingungen ist es den deutschen u. italienischen Truppen gelungen, dem Feind harte Schläge zu versetzen. Auch in Zukunft werden die Truppen der Verbündeten in Nordafrika alles daransetzen, um ihren Anteil zum Endsieg der Achse beizutragen.

Rommel

General der Panzertruppe
und Befehlshaber der
Panzergruppe Afrika

# Foreword

To every soldier who took part in the battles on African soil, this book will be a valuable record of his service. Despite many crises and often under the most difficult conditions, German and Italian troops dealt the enemy hard blows. In the days to come the allied soldiers in North Africa will make every effort to contribute to the final victory of the Axis Powers.

Erwin Rommel, 1943

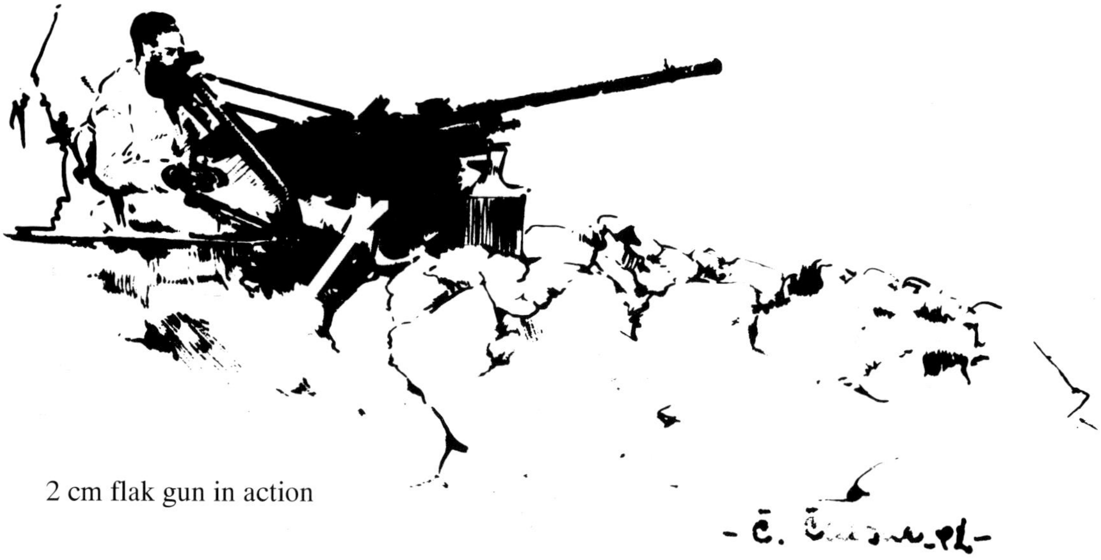

2 cm flak gun in action

# CHRONOLOGY

**12 November 1940** OKW issues Instruction No 18: 'A force is to be raised to support the Italians in North Africa for an autumn attack upon Egypt.' That Instruction is later countermanded.

**16 January 1941** The outstanding British victory over the Italians in December 1940 compels Hitler to reconsider his plans and he decides that the purpose of a German intervention in Libya is to prevent the collapse of the Italians. A German force is ordered to be raised and despatched.

**6 February 1941** Erwin Rommel is named as commander of German troops in Africa and arrives in Tripoli.

**12 February 1941** The first German air raid on Benghazi.

**19 February 1941** German Afrika Korps is given its official title.

**24 February 1941** The first clash between British and German patrols.

**22/24 March 1941** German forces capture El Agheila.

**2 April 1941** Agedabia captured by German detachments.

**8 April 1941** The Battle of Mechili.

**10 April 1941** Under the pressure of Rommel's assault the Western Desert Force withdraws on Tobruk.

**11 April 1941** Panzer forces cut the Tobruk–El Adem road and take 3000 prisoners, including three Generals.

**12 April 1941** The opening moves of the offensive to capture Tobruk fail to seize the fortress, but Rommel throws a cordon of infantry around the place. Bardia and Sollum on the Egyptian frontier are attacked so as to give the Italo-German forces an eastern outpost.

**27 April 1941** Halfaya Pass captured. Sollum falls on the 28th.

**15 June 1941** A British attempt to recapture Halfaya fails with heavy losses.

**5 August 1941** Panzer Group Africa formed.

**18 November 1941** Opening of Eighth Army's 'Operation Crusader', to raise the siege of Tobruk.

**21 November 1941** The Tobruk garrison makes a sortie to link up with the relieving force.

**23 November 1941** In confused fighting British 7th Armoured Division is scattered in the Battle of Sidi Rezegh, part of the 'Crusader' operation.

**24 November 1941** Believing Eighth Army around Tobruk to be defeated, Rommel makes an abortive 'dash for the wire' in order to destroy the British forces around Halfaya.

**2 December 1941** 'Operation Crusader' ends with a local German tactical victory.

**7 December 1941** The reinforced Eighth Army renews its assaults, forcing Rommel to withdraw Axis forces to positions at Gazala.

**17 January 1942** The Italo-German garrison of Halfaya surrenders.

**21 January 1942** Rommel opens a new offensive to recapture Cyrenaica.

**28 January 1942** Benghazi falls to Axis forces in Rommel's new offensive.

**30 January 1942** Panzer Army Africa (the German/Italian panzer army) formed.

**4 February 1942** Rommel's advance outruns its supplies and stalls at the Gazala positions.

**26 May 1942** Following retraining and massive preparations, Rommel opens his summer offensive.

**2 June 1942** The Free French defensive 'box' at the southern end of the Gazala line comes under attack as Rommel attempts to turn the British southern flank.

**20 June 1942** During the German offensive panzer forces destroy the British armour and go on to capture Tobruk.

**22 June 1942** Axis forces advance into Egypt with the aim of reaching the Suez canal.

**1 July 1942** The First Battle of El Alamein opens but the Axis forces are too weak to break through the British defences. Rommel breaks off the battle.

**31 August 1942** The Battle of Alam el Halfa (called Second Alamein by the Germans) opens.

**2 September 1942** The German offensive at Alam el Halfa fails and Montgomery halts British operations in order to build up the strength of Eighth Army. Rommel's forces regroup to the west of the British positions at El Alamein.

**23 October 1942** Montgomery's offensive opens the 'third' Battle of El Alamein and this ends with the Axis forces retreating through Libya and into Tunisia.

**12 May 1943** The war in Africa ends with the surrender of the Panzer Army Africa.

# Prologue

'A German and an English motorised reconnaissance patrol clashed during the morning of 24th February at a point on the Libyan coast, to the south-east of Agedabia. A number of English vehicles, including several armoured cars, were destroyed and some prisoners taken. There were no losses on the German side.'

*– OKW communiqué, dated 26 February 1941*

'To OKW. All ammunition has been fired off. All weapons and military equipment destroyed. The Afrika Korps has carried out the orders given to it and has fought to the end...'

*– The last signal sent by Cramer, Commander Afrika Korps, 12 May 1943*

Between the first communiqué announcing the action of 24 February 1941, and the last signal sent out on 12 May 1943, lies the period during which was fought the campaign in North Africa. This volume covers the first year of German operations in the Italian colony of Libya – Rommel's year of victory.

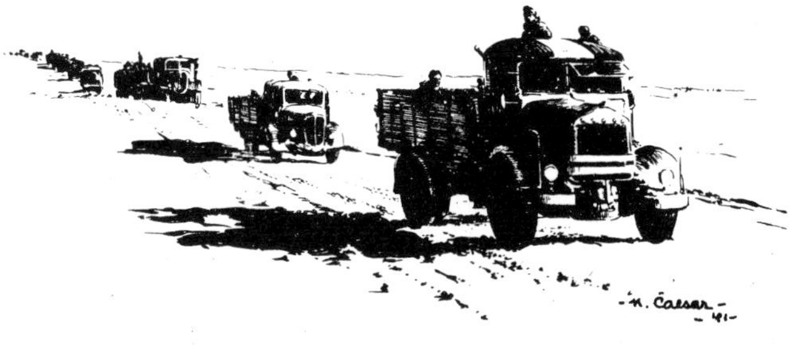

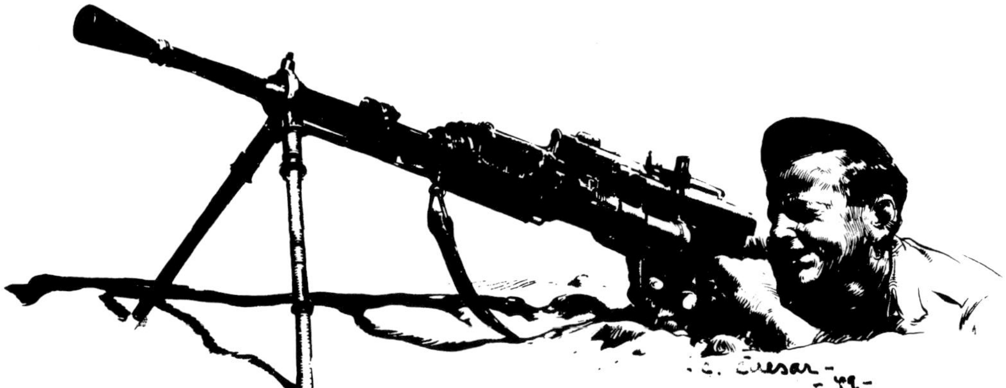

An Italian light machine-gun ('Breda') in action.

# The Historical Background

Although German involvement in the fighting in Africa dated only from the early Spring of 1941, her Axis partner, Italy, had been engaged in operations against the British since September 1940. Mussolini, the Italian leader, had ambitions to increase the size of the Fascist empire in Africa and intended to achieve this by attacking those neighbouring states which constituted part of Britain's overseas possessions.

The first step in achieving this territorial expansion was taken when Mussolini ordered Graziani's 10th Army to open an attack on Egypt, which began in mid-September. The weak British forces positioned along the Libyan–Egyptian frontier wire fought a defensive battle against the assault of six Italian infantry divisions and eight tank battalions, withdrawing slowly and allowing the Italian thrust to reach Sidi Barrani, some 18 km inside Egypt. There Graziani's army halted and remained inactive until, on 7 December, General Wavell's Western Desert Force (7th Armoured and 4th Indian Infantry Divisions) opened a counter-offensive which not only drove the Italians back across the frontier wire, but pursued them westwards through their own Imperial territory. By 12 January 1941 the British had not only destroyed much of Graziani's army, but had also captured the fortress of Bardia and the strategically important harbour of Tobruk, and had opened an advance upon Tripoli, the capital of Libya.

This crisis in the desert was not the only one confronting Italy. She was already facing defeat in Greece, which she had invaded in autumn 1940. The Italian attack here had presented Winston Churchill, the British Prime Minister, with the opportunity of re-establishing a British presence in Europe by aiding the Greeks in the defence of their homeland. Churchill acted promptly, ordering that an expeditionary force, made up of the major part of Wavell's Western Desert Force, be sent to Greece. The Prime Minister's decision was based on the belief that the Italians in Africa were all but beaten and

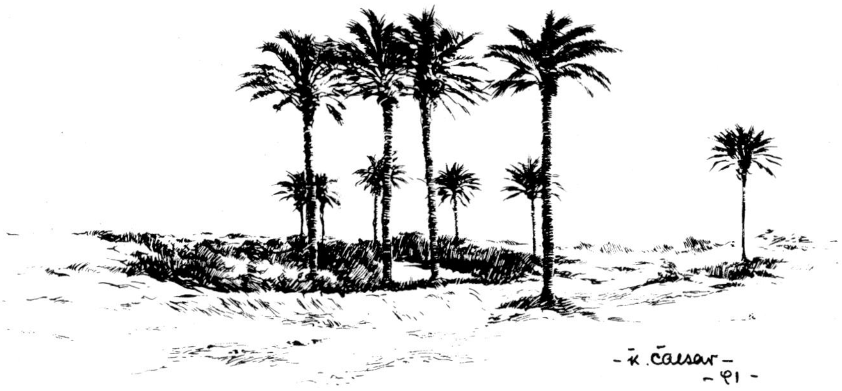

that British troops could be spared from that continent to fight in Europe. Churchill had not foreseen that Hitler would despatch German troops to support the fascist Empire in Africa.

The genesis of German involvement in North Africa can be said to lie with the Army High Command (OKH) initiative of July 1940. In considering operations in the Mediterranean, OKH offered Hitler five options, including one for the despatch of a German panzer corps to aid the Italian Army in Libya. In September 1940, when Graziani's 10th Army invaded Egypt, it seemed that the need was no longer there, and the first elements raised for the embryo panzer corps were stood down. Wavell's swift and seemingly unstoppable advance into Libya reactivated the German plan, and Hitler's Directive No. 22, dated 11 January 1940, laid down that 'Germany must give assistance [to Italy]. I order that a blocking force be raised ... capable of supporting our allies ... in their defence of Tripolitania'. Lengthy discussions led to delays, but it was eventually confirmed that the German contingent would be in corps strength, and plans were drawn up to ship the first detachments of 5th Light Division and to follow those with the fighting echelons of 5th Panzer Regiment (15th Panzer Division). At a later date the other formations of 15th Panzer would be shipped to Libya. There, the whole German corps was to take up a blocking position in the Sirte desert.

On 11 February, when the first German troops disembarked in Tripoli, Rommel flew first to Rome for discussions with Mussolini, and then to Sicily for a briefing by General Geissler, commanding the German X Air Corps. One day later he flew to Tripoli for discussions with the Italian commanders, before going on to Germany to lay before Hitler his plan of campaign. Receiving the Führer's approval of his operational plan, Rommel returned to Tripoli. He and the first elements of what was to become the Afrika Korps, *das deutsche Afrika Korps,* were ready to go into action.

Of the three major combatant nations which fought the Libyan campaign the British had the most experience of tropical conditions. They had ruled a colonial Empire for more than two centuries. The Italians became involved in Africa in the late-19th century but did not colonise Libya until 1912. By comparison, Germany came very late to the 'race for Africa', and those few colonies which she had gained before the First World War had been taken from her at the end of it.

Having thus little or no experience of warfare in tropical regions, the German military mind was not dominated by the dogma which cluttered the thinking of the British and Italian military and ignored accounts of difficulties associated with campaigning in desert conditions. The Germans disregarded many of the rules insisted on in the British Army and not only worked shirtless in the hottest sun but soon discarded the sun helmet formerly considered essential in other armies. Most important of all, they mingled freely and without feelings of superiority among the Arab people, and were popular with the natives as a consequence.

The German soldier in Africa adapted quickly to the primitive conditions of desert life, no thanks to the supply branches of the High Command, which failed to equip him for tropical service. The desert uniform, designed by the Tropical Institute in Hamburg in 1940, consisted of a tightly buttoned jacket, breeches, high boots of canvas and leather and a sun helmet. The harsh conditions of active service life and the high temperatures met with in Libya forced unofficial changes to that standard dress, leading in time to the adoption of a distinctive style of uniform with which the German soldier in Africa

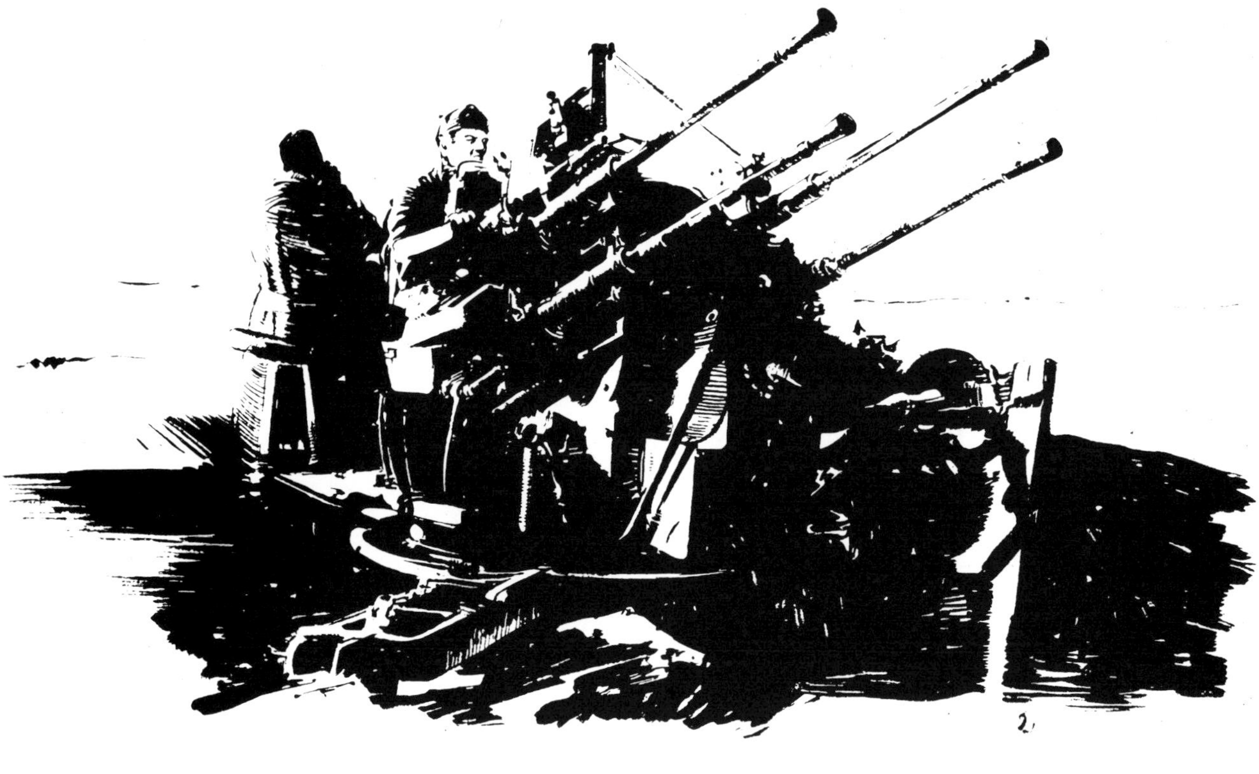

A Vierling (four-barrel) 2 cm
calibre flak gun action. It is
mounted on a turntable to give
it a 360 degree traverse.

is closely identified: a long-peaked linen cap, shorts or wide-legged trousers of paratroop pattern, and boots. Shorts were the most comfortable trouser type, but those who wore them risked suffering cuts or grazes which usually deteriorated into painful ulcers. The tight jacket was often discarded in favour of shirt-sleeve order, and the impractical sun helmet was not worn in the front line, and was seldom worn anywhere else.

As a reward for the privations that the officers and soldiers were enduring, Führer Hauptquartier authorised, in 1941, the cuff band 'Afrika', to be worn by those with a minimum of two months service. Later, in 1942, an Italo-German war medal was also issued. There were no other visible marks of distinction specific to the Afrika Korps, although the song *Panzer rollen in Afrika vor* ('Panzers are rolling forward in Africa') was added to the German Army's song book, and a new verb, *rommeln,* meaning a move so swift that it caused confusion to the enemy, found its way into the German language, albeit briefly.

Given the fact that the Italians and the Germans had a political relationship, known as the Axis, it might have been expected that the Italians, with their knowledge of desert conditions, would have offered their allies advice on a great many things. But they did not. As a result of their hasty departure the first German soft-skin vehicles to come to Africa arrived in European camouflage colours. Because German stores did not have paint of the required shade for desert camouflage, a short-term solution was to spray the outside of vehicles with oil and then to cover the oil with sand. Nor were the Germans warned about the harsh, scouring effect of desert dust on the engines of vehicles which were not fitted with special filters. Until they were, the life of a German motor engine was short – between 1000 and 1500 km, or half that of an engine fitted with a filter. Although the Italians had developed a special tropical-pattern diesel engine for use in their own vehicles, they did not advise their allies of this; nor did they point out the superiority of diesel over petrol engines in desert conditions. Many of the first German lorries to arrive were fitted with

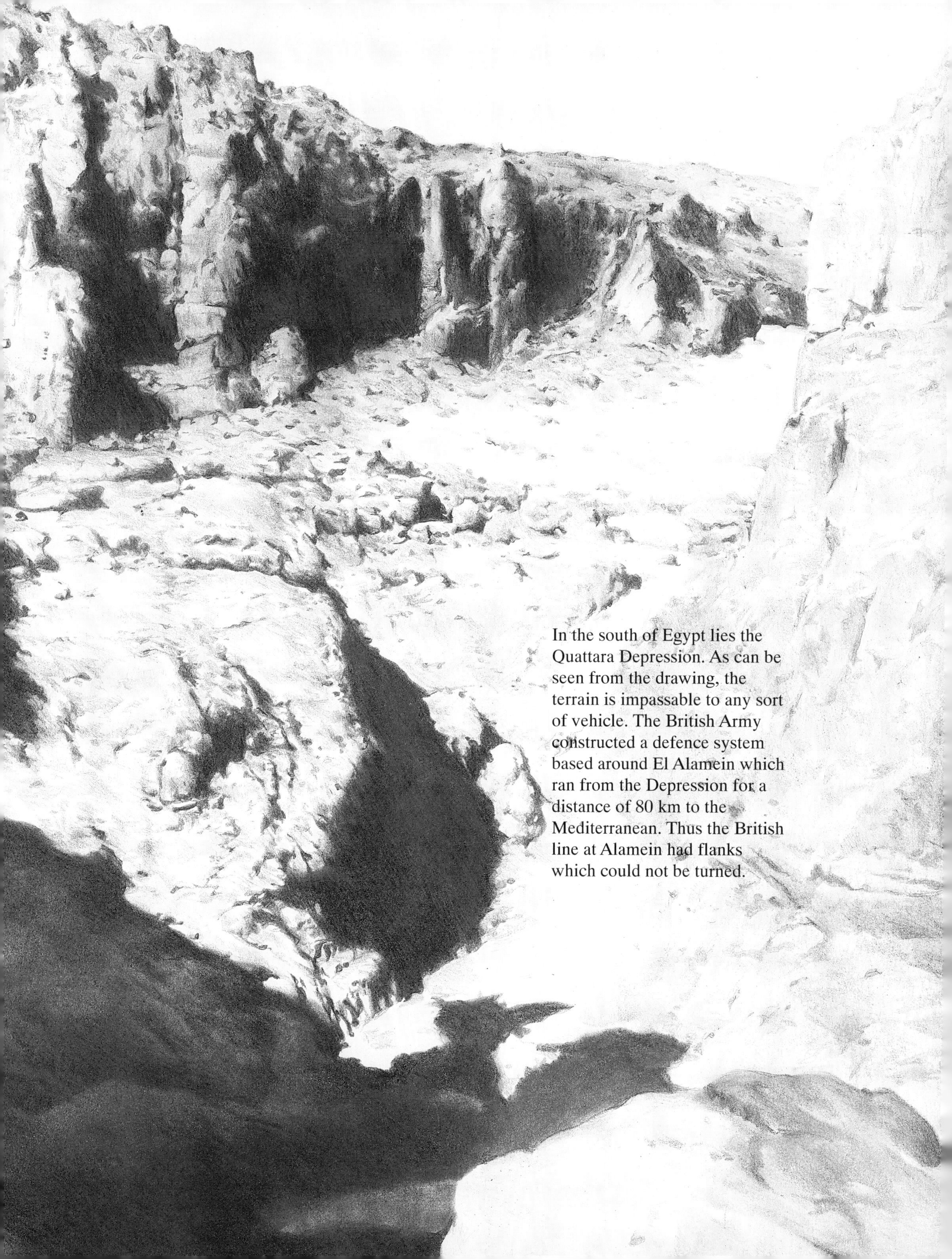

In the south of Egypt lies the Quattara Depression. As can be seen from the drawing, the terrain is impassable to any sort of vehicle. The British Army constructed a defence system based around El Alamein which ran from the Depression for a distance of 80 km to the Mediterranean. Thus the British line at Alamein had flanks which could not be turned.

double sets of tyres, in the belief that these would provide greater traction across the dunes. However, much of the landscape consisted of small pieces of rock rather than sand-dunes, and these worked their way between the double tyres and resulted in frequent punctures.

In the matter of rations and cooking, the German planners showed themselves lamentably short-sighted. German Army rations were cooked in wood-fuelled field kitchens, and the desert was, of course, a treeless waste. German rations did not include potatoes, a staple of military diet, because, in the opinion of nutrition experts, the great heat would cause raw vegetables to deteriorate quickly. The British Army had overcome this problem by putting the vegetables into tins and cooking them, a solution which did not occur to the Germans. Their first detachments were also issued with *Knackebrot* – a form of pumpernickel biscuit – instead of bread, until properly equipped kitchens capable of baking bread were sent to Africa. Only in the matter of containers did the Germans have a piece of non-combat equipment that was superior to the British issue, and even today the term 'Jerrican' refers to a sturdy, upright and robust tin capable of withstanding the harshest treatment. British locally-made containers were known as 'flimsies', which described them exactly...

Because of the great distances between Libyan towns – distances which were greatly increased when the armies of both sides moved away from the coast road and into the empty desert – both sides set up forward supply depots, which contained such basic necessities as water, fuel, spare parts, and dry rations. Such depots had to be well concealed and strongly guarded, otherwise the Arabs or the enemy might find them and either destroy their contents or pilfer them. Supplies on the German side were always short. When unit quartermasters complained of lack of supplies, Rommel would advise them to steal what they needed from the British, who 'always had plenty'. This was true. Although the British line of communication was longer than the Axis one, it was better protected by the Royal Navy, and the supplies sent out from Britain to its only

Heavy lorries driving along the highway near Buk Buk.
The Italian soldiers in the leading truck are probably
Bersaglieri anti-tank gunners.

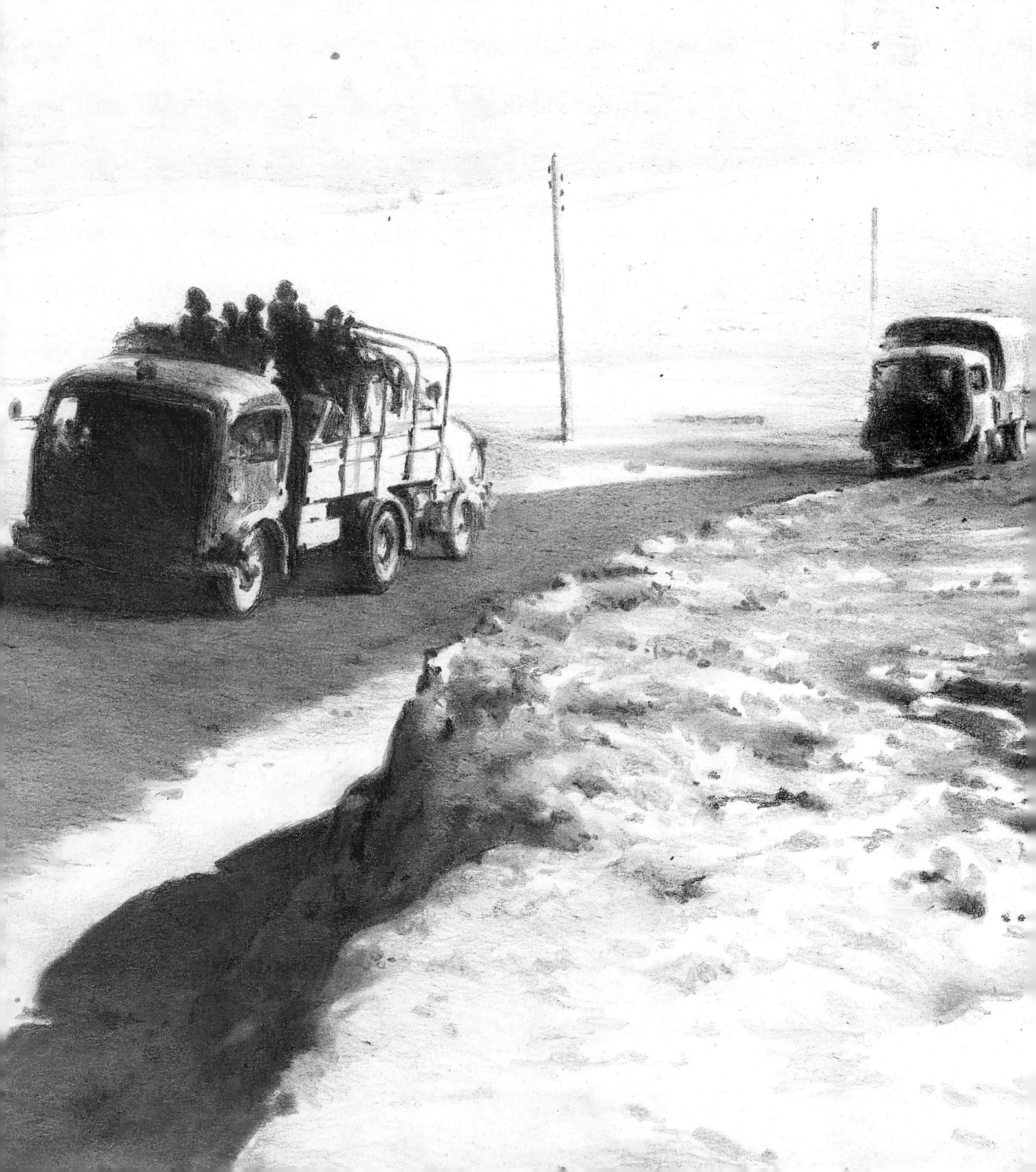

theatre of war were, if not lavish, certainly ample. By contrast, Rommel and the Afrika Korps had to compete for supplies, equipment and, above all, fuel, with the almost insatiable demands of the enormous Russian Front.

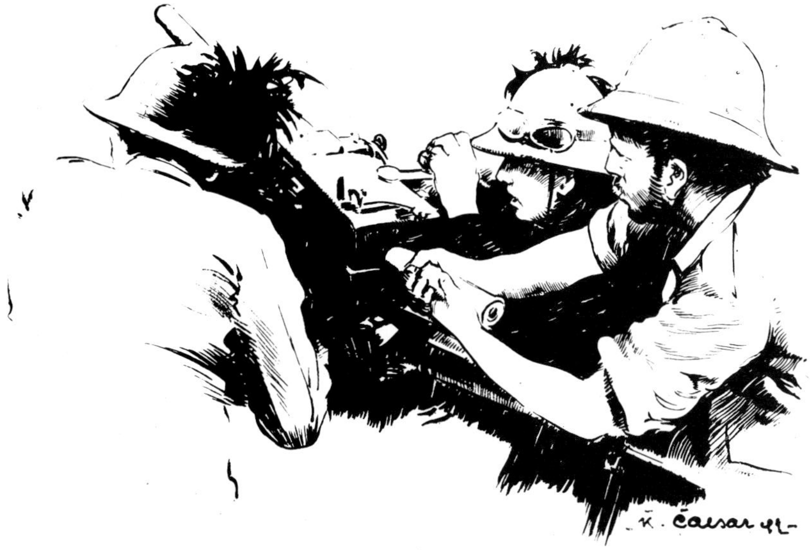

Probably a group of German command vehicles during the battle of Gazala, May – June 1942. The nearest one is a Panzer III and by its side is a reconnaissance half-track. Behind that is a soft-top Volkswagen staff car. Burning vehicles litter the horizon.

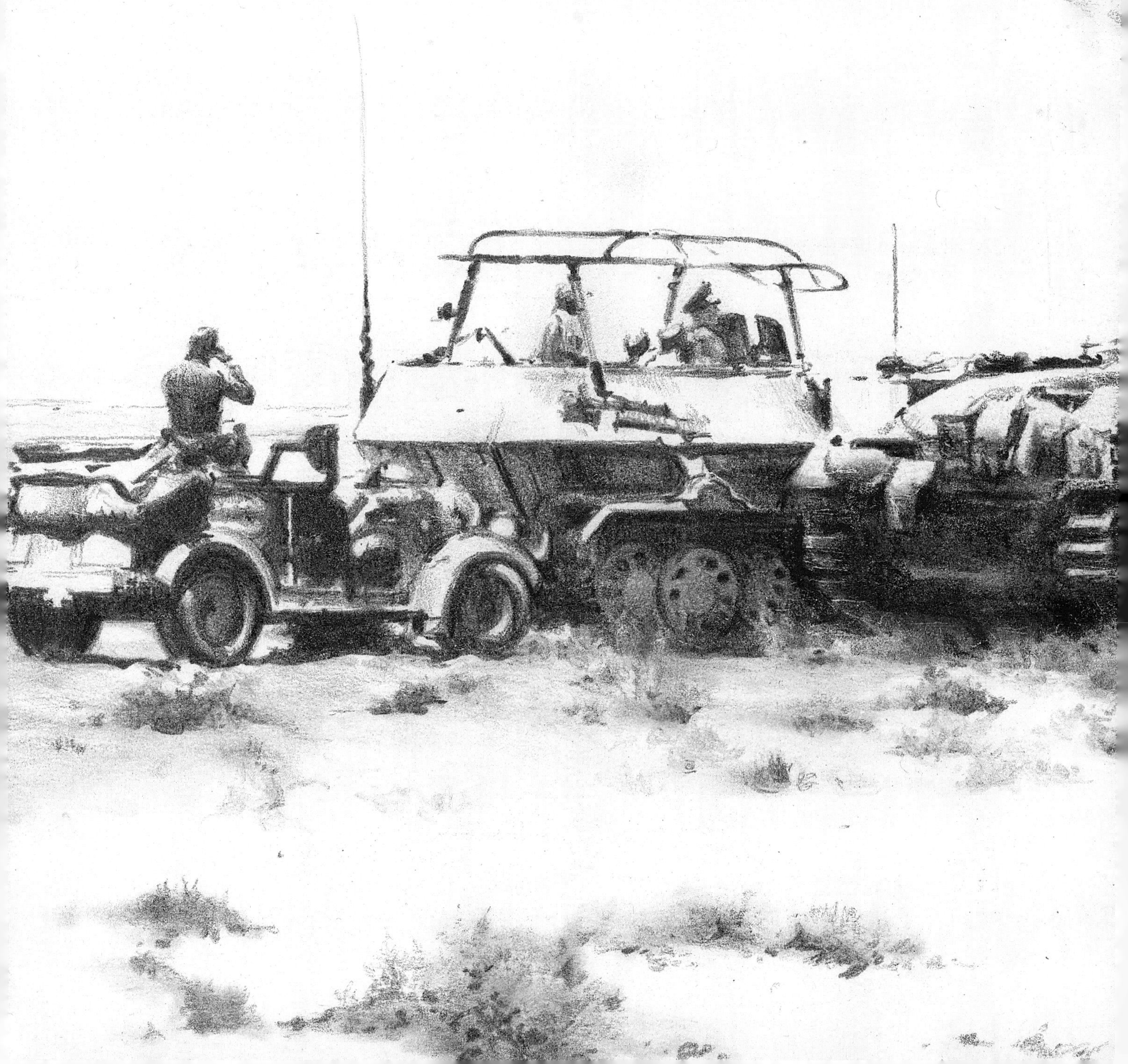

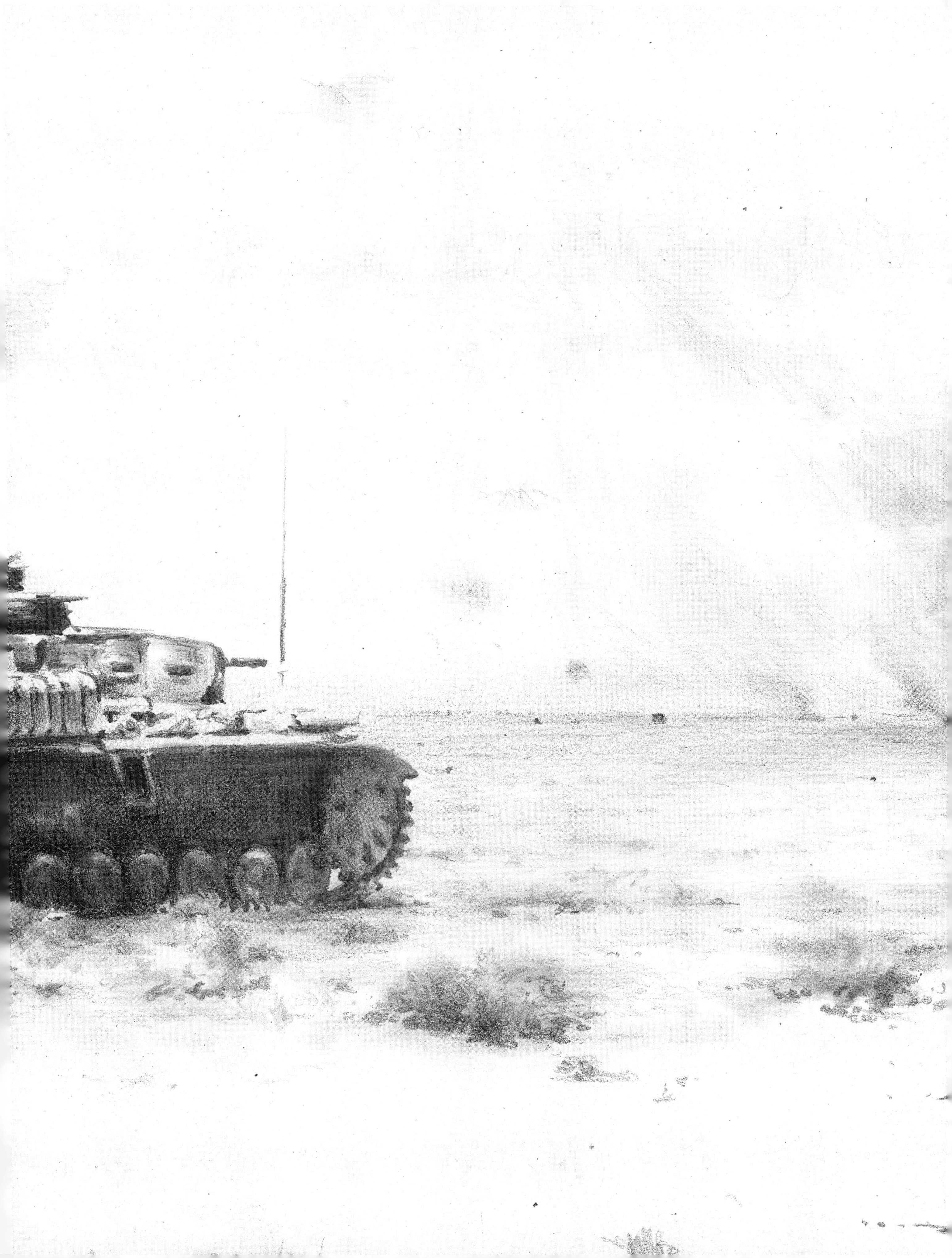

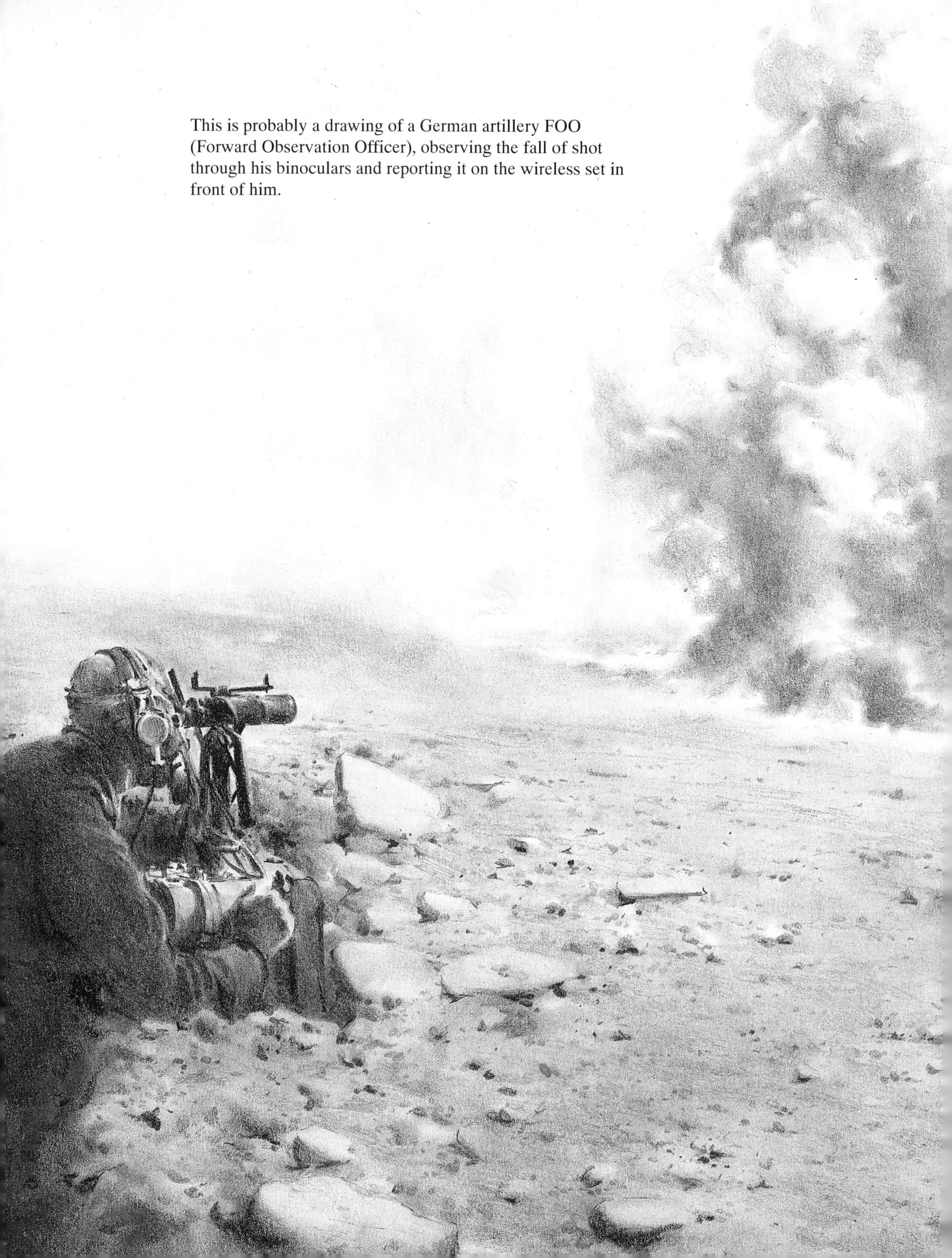

This is probably a drawing of a German artillery FOO (Forward Observation Officer), observing the fall of shot through his binoculars and reporting it on the wireless set in front of him.

# STRATEGY

Mussolini's strategy was to exploit Britain's supposed weakness in the Middle East, by capturing those of her Imperial possessions which bordered on Italy's own African colonies. The victories which those invasions were expected to produce would increase the economic and strategic position of the Italian Empire. It was in pursuit of this strategy that the Italian armed forces launched a short-lived invasion of Egypt in September 1940. The successful British counter-offensive in December that year drove the Italians back almost to Tripoli, and it was the fear that their Axis partner might be forced out of the war which brought the Germans to the desert on a rescue mission.

Initially Hitler's Third Reich had no grand strategical plan for Africa, but when, in autumn 1942, the German forces in Russia gained swift and, so it seemed, decisive victories, a strategy was formulated. This proposed a giant pincer movement, one arm of which was to drive through the south of Russia and into the Caucasus, while the other, made up of the Axis forces in Libya, was to thrust through Palestine and into the Middle East. The meeting of those pincers would bring together a great mass of German armour, artillery, and infantry which would then advance towards India, there to join hands with the Japanese forces which would be emerging from the jungles of Burma.

In the German 'pincer' plan it was vital that the port of Tobruk be seized and held, for it was the largest port in Libya and would form one of the advanced supply depots to nourish the German/Italian desert forces as they drove through the Middle East. Another supply depot would be Alexandria, in Egypt. The island of Malta constituted a third possible naval and supply base, but Axis plans for an airborne assault to capture it were aborted when Tobruk was finally captured in the summer of 1942. In Rommel's own words, 'We have Tobruk. We do not need Malta.'

In the spring of 1941, Africa was the only land theatre of operations in which the British Army was fighting. It followed, then, that it was to this single theatre that the bulk of British arms production was sent. British

British 25-pdr artillery piece in action. The kneeling figure is wearing a leather jerkin, and the man standing to the right of the gun wears a pullover.

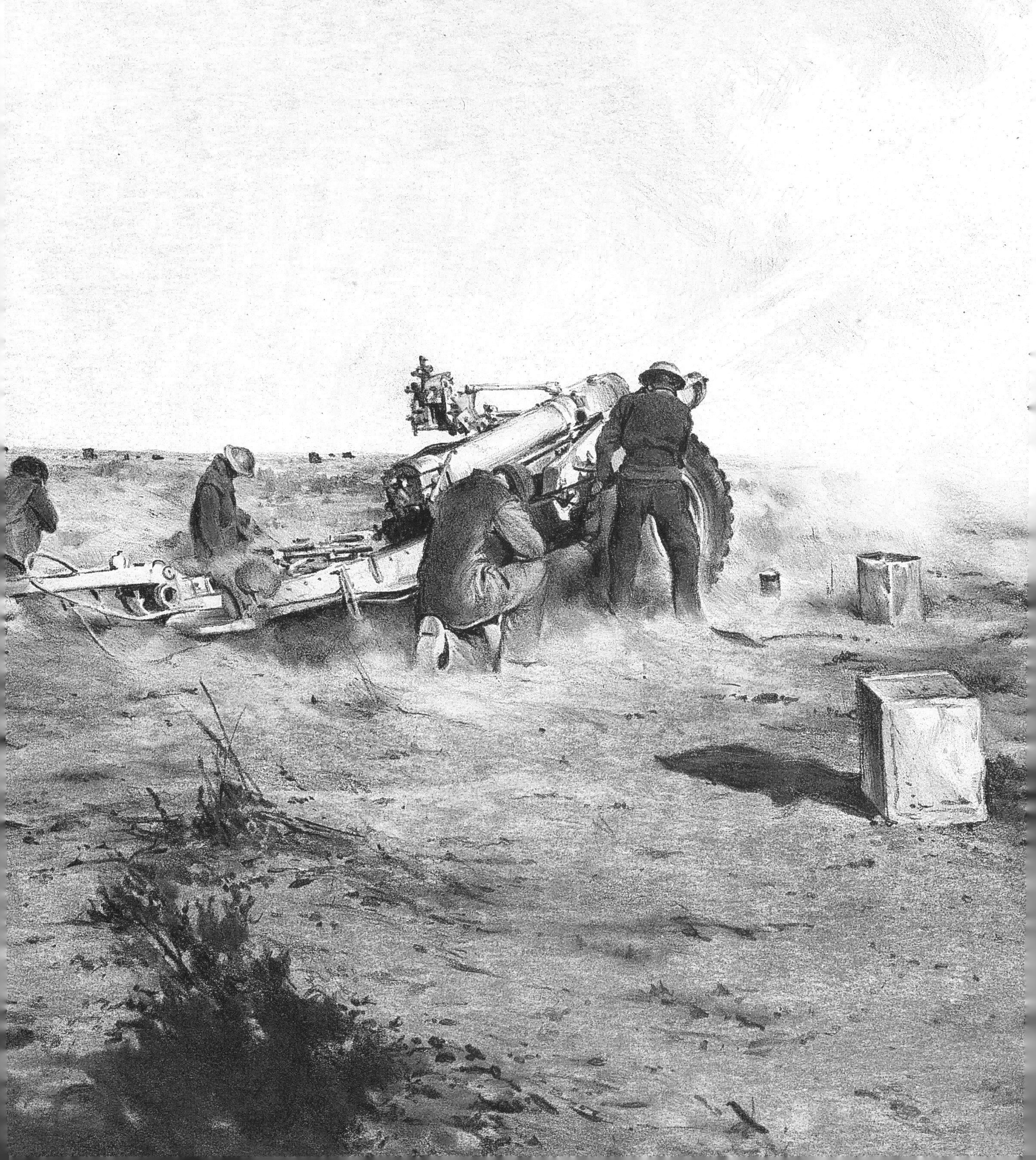

strategy was to retain its Imperial possessions by defeating the Axis armies in the desert. The British forces, having cleaned up one continent, could then move forward to the invasion of Europe, there to bring the war to a close.

Tactics are the junior companions of strategy. In the desert war only the Germans developed tactical ideas that were new. Rommel, accepting the definition that the North African battlefield was 'a tactician's paradise but a quartermaster's hell', evolved battle drills to meet a given tactical situation. When 15th Panzer Division disembarked he trained it quickly and thoroughly in those drills. Essentially, they were an improved version of standard German Army European tactics, but Rommel was deeply aware that the Axis armies in Africa would always lack supplies and believed that he could partly overcome this deficiency and gain victories through his style of intensive training. He was determined to achieve the closest collaboration between all branches of the Army as well as between the Army and the other arms of service: the Luftwaffe and the Navy. He insisted that the sister services did not fight battles in isolation but as part of an overall strategic plan. Rommel demanded the closest collaboration between units and trained them until they had perfected this. He also adapted to desert conditions a tactic he had used in France in 1940 – a gun-line of 88s. These weapons had originally been designed for anti-aircraft duties, but when used in an anti-tank role their high muzzle velocity enabled them to 'kill' Allied armoured vehicles at distances in excess of three kilometres. Highly mobile, the fast-firing and accurate 88s could quickly form a gun-line to meet a British tank charge or to give local and powerful support to a faltering German attack.

Battle tactics will be described in the chapters dealing with the campaigns, but since weapons often determine tactics it should be pointed out that the weapons used by the German Army in Libya were all standard pattern. No new weapons were designed or produced especially for the Desert War.

A dead British soldier in the desert. The body carries no divisional markings, so it is not possible to give an identification.

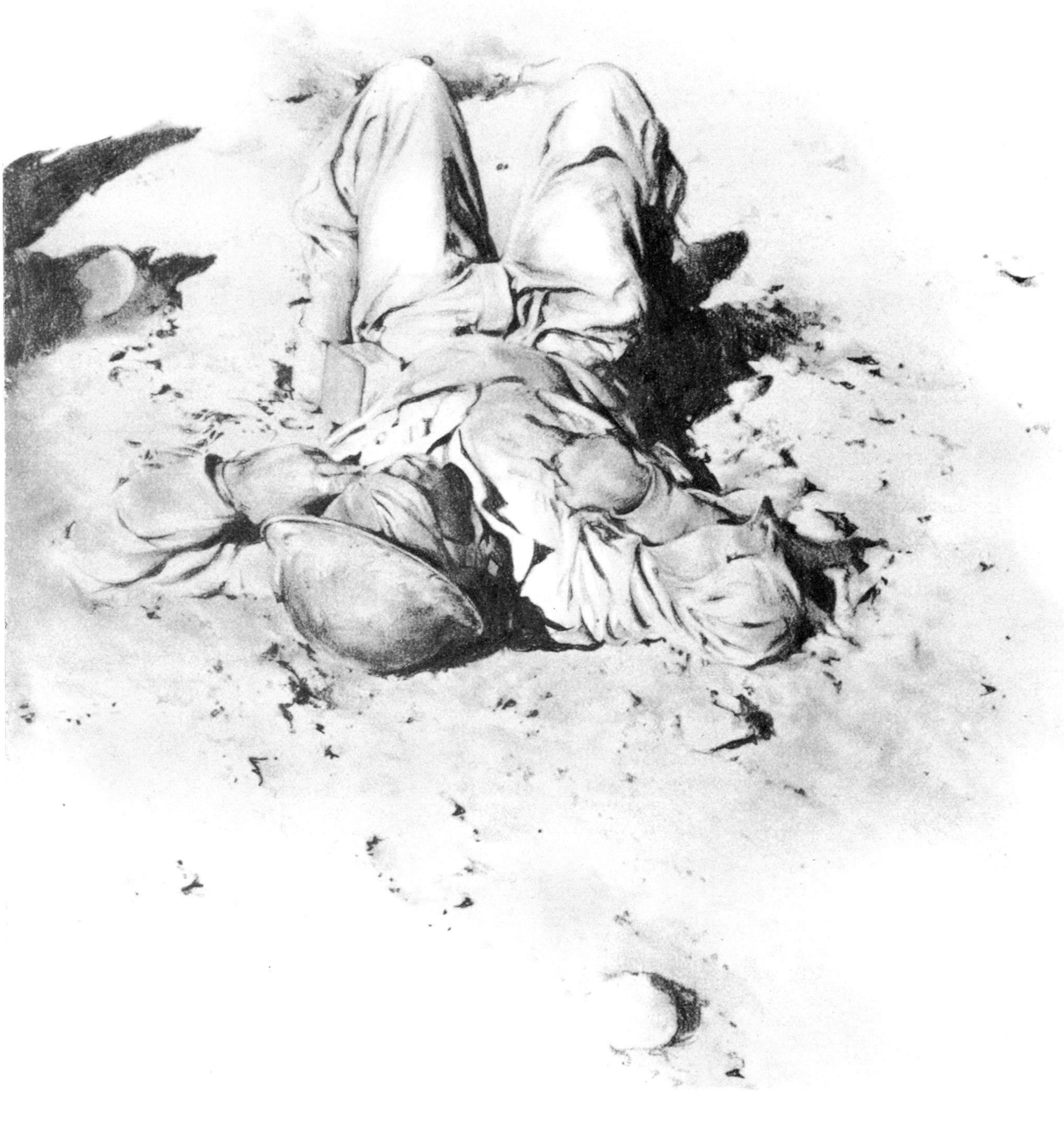

# The Battlefield

The principal battlefield referred to in this book extended across twenty degrees of longitude, and was made up of a terrain which was mostly barren desert. The fighting was carried out in the Italian colony of Libya, although there were shallow Axis incursions into western Egypt as well as a whole six-month campaign in the French colony of Tunisia, whose conclusion brought the war in Africa to a close and ended the life of the Afrika Korps. As a generalisation, it can be said that the principal fighting took place in a small area, confined on a north-south line to a space between the Mediterranean and a point about 80 km into the desert. On the east-west axis, although operations were carried out across the whole length of Libya they were chiefly concentrated in an area east of the Cyrenaican peninsula and west of the Egyptian frontier.

The desert was not the vast expanse of sand-dunes of popular imagination, although these were found in some places. As mentioned above, much of the desert was actually made of pieces of rock resting on a deep layer of gritty, grey dust which had such penetrative power that it could abrade vehicle engines unless these were protected by dust filters. This dust was scoured from the bedrock by the action of fierce winds – the *khamsin* and the *ghibli* – and was able to affect the shape of hills to such an extent that during the battle of El Alamein, officers of one of the regiments of the 51st Highland Division could not agree which piece of high ground was their objective.

Little lived in the desert, and little grew there. There was a thin strip of fertile land bordering the Mediterranean, but this soon petered out into a wasteland which was in most places difficult going for vehicles. There were some areas which were completely impassable, one such being a vast bowl in the ground in western Egypt known as the Quattara Depression. This formed a barrier in the south of the country below which no military operations were carried out. In its battles at El Alamein the British Army relied upon the impassable Quattara Depression as a flank which could not be turned. Even the surface of the desert itself was not all

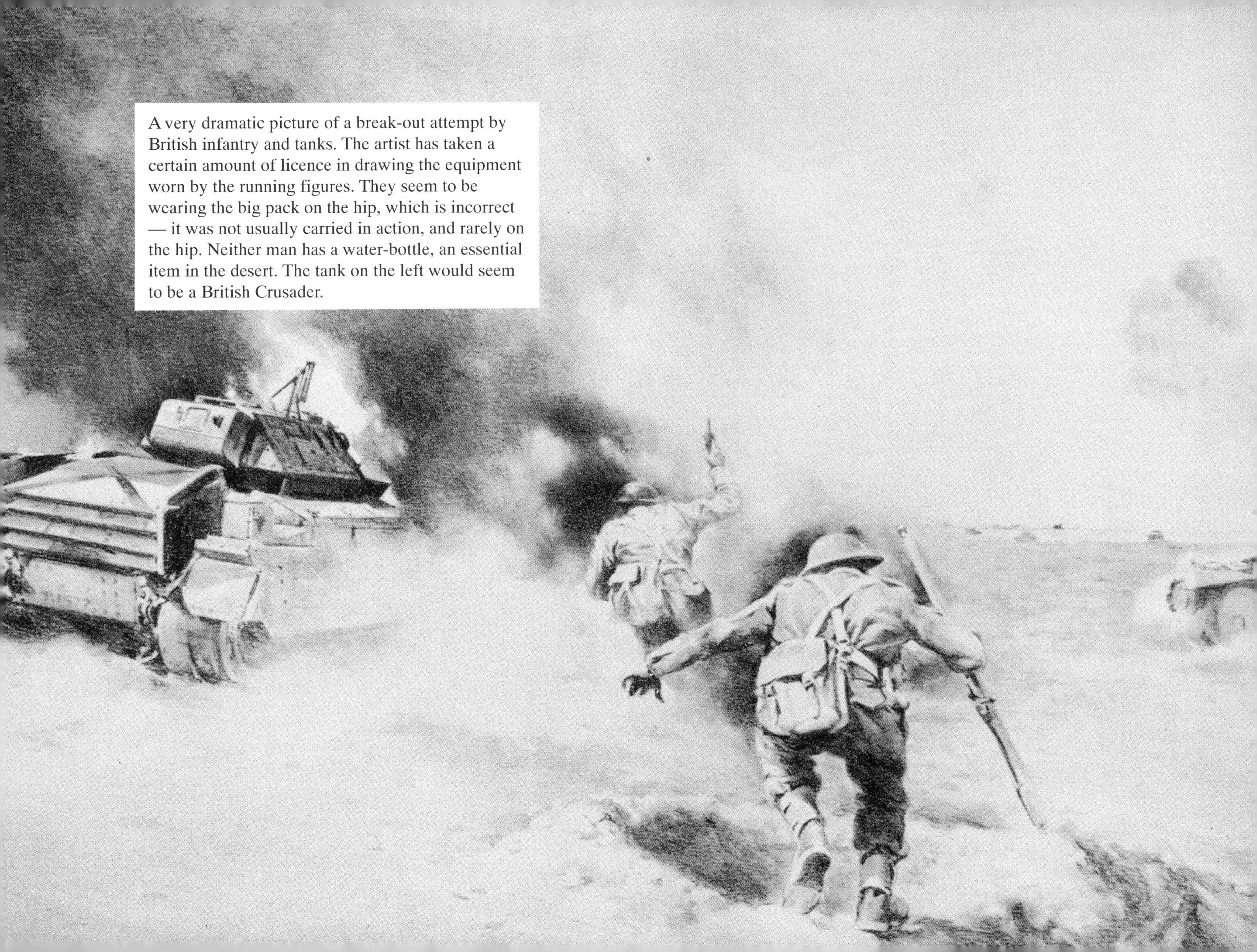

A very dramatic picture of a break-out attempt by British infantry and tanks. The artist has taken a certain amount of licence in drawing the equipment worn by the running figures. They seem to be wearing the big pack on the hip, which is incorrect — it was not usually carried in action, and rarely on the hip. Neither man has a water-bottle, an essential item in the desert. The tank on the left would seem to be a British Crusader.

bedrock and dust, but contained salt seas and quicksand into which even small vehicles could sink without trace. There were also vast areas of rock and large boulders, which were impassable even to tracked vehicles.

In summer the weather was blindingly hot in the day and cool by night; and in the winter cold by day and bitterly cold by night. Sandstorms could blow at any season of the year, these being usually accompanied by a sharp rise in temperature so that high humidity accompanied the flying sand. Any attack coming out of a sandstorm gained complete surprise, because the dense cloud of dust and sand cut visibility almost to zero, thereby cloaking the attacking troops. A sandstorm frayed the nerves with its dust and howling wind, and it was widely believed that a *khamsin* which lasted for more than five days justified murder. Both sides wore British anti-gas goggles and scarves to protect the eyes, nose and mouth against the penetrating dust during a *khamsin.*

Rain was an unusual phenomenon, but when it fell it often did so with such intensity that the ground could not absorb it all at once. The unabsorbed surface water raced across the gritty, rocky ground carving out channels, known as wadis, some of which, having been created over years or even decades, were of very great depth. Infantry soldiers often dug into the walls of a dry, shallow wadi to make scrape holes in which to live and find shelter from the intensely hot sun. A wadi could also be used as a natural defensive position or a ready-made anti-tank ditch. In 1941, when rain of monsoon proportions fell and caused considerable flooding, a number of German soldiers sheltering in wadis were drowned.

Torrential rain had other disadvantages, chief among which was that it washed away the surfaces of the *trigh* or native tracks. In the whole of Libya there was only one first-class, all-weather main road – the Via Balbia. This ran for more than 1000 km, from the capital, Tripoli, as far as the Egyptian border, and linked all the principal coastal towns of the Italian colony. There were no all-weather roads leading from the sea into the desert, because the Italians had not built any towns in the interior. That government's rationale was that since nobody would want to drive down into the empty and inhospitable desert regions there was no point in building settlements or roads. The only people who usually went into the

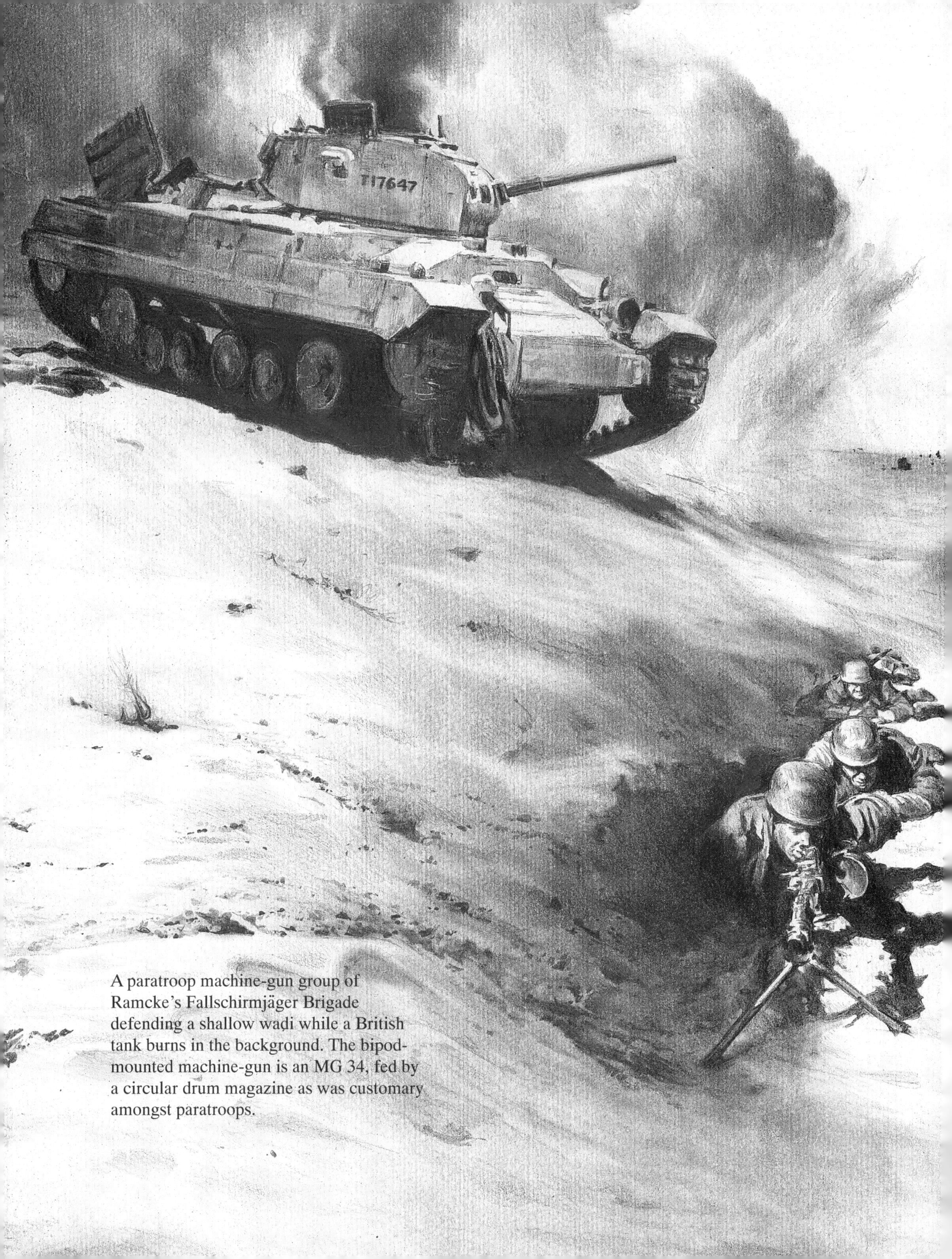


A paratroop machine-gun group of Ramcke's Fallschirmjäger Brigade defending a shallow wadi while a British tank burns in the background. The bipod-mounted machine-gun is an MG 34, fed by a circular drum magazine as was customary amongst paratroops.

southern wasteland were Arabs, who walked or rode along the *trigh* which criss-crossed the country. Human and animal traffic had given these a firm surface which was, nevertheless, at best only semi-permanent, and it took time for a surface once destroyed by rain to be restored by the pressure of travellers' feet. The most frequently used *trigh* were robust enough to bear a limited amount of armoured traffic, but if subjected to too heavy a volume the fragile surface crumbled. Where two or more *trigh* converged there was usually a local landmark, perhaps a shrine (*marabut*), or a well (*bir*). In a countryside totally devoid of any other distinctive features, these junctions were essential as landmarks or points of reference, to both the local population, walking or travelling across country, and the armies of both sides, which either garrisoned them or used them as supply depots or watering points.

Some of the major *trigh* bore names given to them by the Arab population. One of these was Trigh Capuzzo, the main track in the north, which led from deep in the interior to the fort of that name, built almost on the Egyptian frontier. On its way Trigh Capuzzo linked Sidi Rezegh and El Adem. The main track in the south was the Trigh el Abd, which extended south from Halfaya to Sidi Omar before turning westwards to pass through Gabr el Saleh and Bir el Gobi and then on into Cyrenaica.

Among the terrain features which influenced military operations were ridges of high ground or escarpments. These ran on a generally east–west line, and one particular piece of high ground ran almost without a break from Tobruk in the west to Sollum in the east. Farther south from this coastal ridge was a second escarpment, running on a line from Bardia to El Adem, with a third one, shorter in length, between El Adem and Capuzzo. No attempt had been made by the Italians to build roads across this series of escarpments and any movement in a north–south direction was certain to be obstructed by ground sufficiently high to force a traveller to make a long detour. The escarpments dominated the lower ground, as for example that near the Trigh Capuzzo, which overlooked the airfield at Sidi Rezegh. In the north of Libya, where the high ground ran down to the sea, the coastal plain was reduced in width so that it formed a narrow pass, and thus an ideal defensive position. All in all the broken nature of the desert terrain made it 'a paradise for tacticians', and it was the ability of panzer commanders to use it so skilfully which brought them the successes they enjoyed.

A final point about communications in Libya is that the Italians had not constructed a full-length railway from Tripoli to the Egyptian frontier, although there were a few short, local lines leading into and from the major coastal cities. By contrast, the British in Egypt had built one major railroad leading westward towards the Italian colony, as well as a number of other tracks southward into the Sudan and eastward into Palestine. These railways were supplemented by a network of well-constructed, permanent roads, so that the British forces enjoyed an extensive communications network denied to the Italians.

# German Orders of Battle

In most armies of the world 'corps' or 'army corps' is the accepted term used to describe the grouping of two divisions, either infantry or armoured or one of each, into a single major formation. Although the number of divisions constituting a corps is usually two this is not a fixed quota: there have been some occasions when a corps has comprised only a single division, and others where it has consisted of five or more. During the period covered by this book the 'Afrika Korps' usually consisted of the 15th and 21st Panzer Divisions, though there was a period during which the 90th Light Division also served on its strength.

The first German formation to fight in Libya was the 5th Light or Motorised Division, which was upgraded in status on 1 October 1941 to become 21st Panzer Division. Its initial order of battle was the 5th Panzer Regiment, 104th (Motorised) Infantry Regiment, and 3rd (Motorised) Reconnaissance Battalion. Later the 200th Infantry Regiment also served as part of the 5th for time.

Between April and June 1941, the 15th Panzer Division disembarked in Tripoli. When it reached full establishment it was made up of the 8th Panzer Regiment, 115th Infantry Regiment, 8th (Motorised) Machine-Gun Battalion, 15th (Motorised) Motor Cycle Battalion, and 13th (Motorised) Reconnaissance Battalion.

The final German unit to be raised and fielded as a division in 1941 was the 90th Light (Africa) Division. This was created out of supernumerary formations which had no divisional affiliation. Its date of birth was August 1941, and it received its official number and description on 28 November that year The principal component of the 90th Light was two motorised regiments: the 155th and 361st, although the 200th Infantry Regiment also served on its strength for a while. Also on the divisional strength was the Panzer Grenadier Regiment (Africa), one of whose battalions was made up of Arab volunteers recruited from the local population. The 90th Light's 361st (Motorised) Regiment was another

A British column of soft-skin vehicles, probably 3-tonners, being shot up by Panzer IIIs. In contrast to the Axis vehicles depicted on page 67, the headlights of the British trucks can be seen to be fitted with black-out masks.

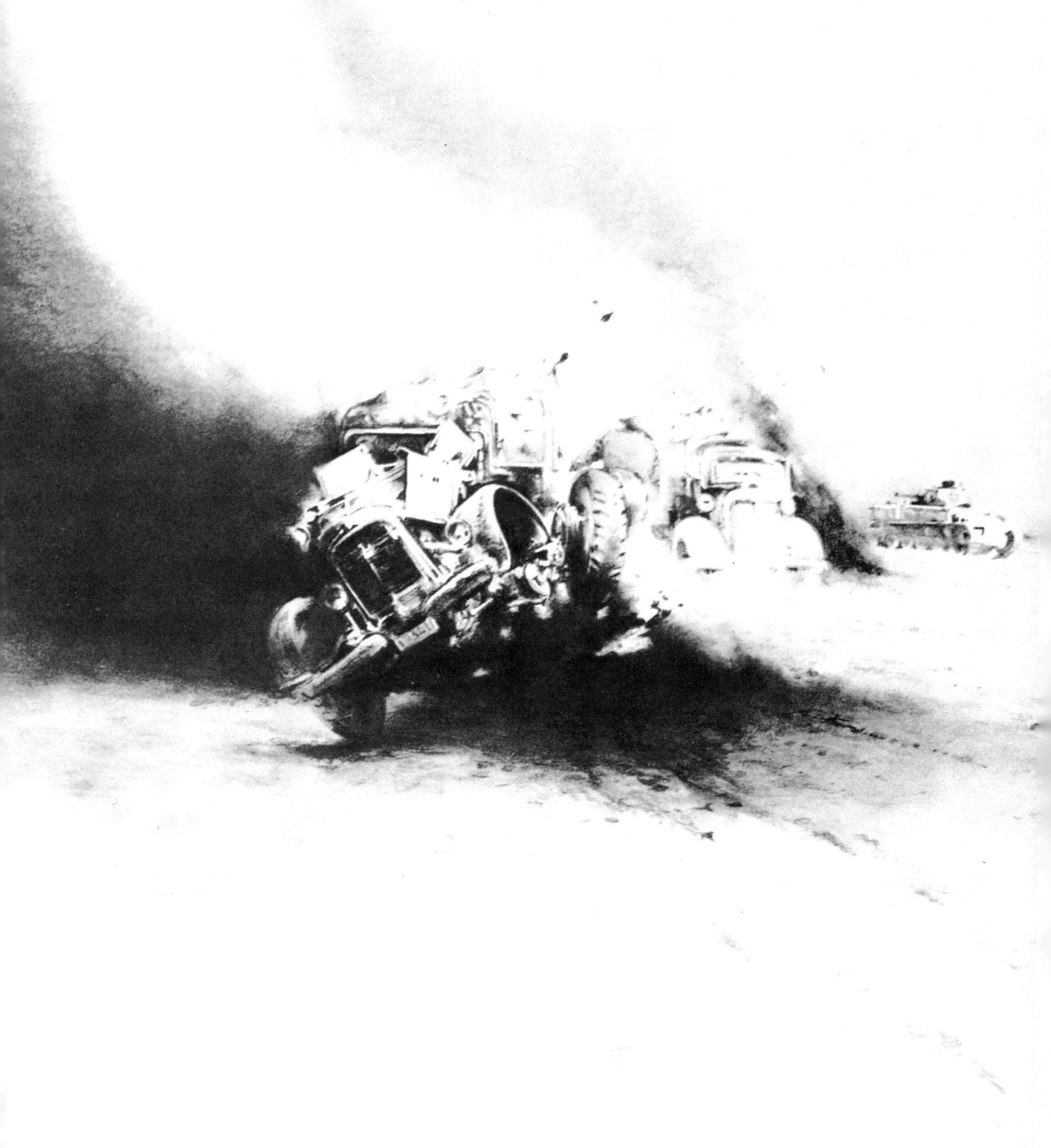

unusual unit, containing a high proportion of Germans who had served with the Foreign Legion and were therefore technically French citizens.

These were not the only unusual formations to serve in Panzer Group Africa. Detachments from the Brandenburg Regiment, fielded by Abwehr, were also active in this theatre of war. Abwehr was the German intelligence/counter-intelligence organisation, whose active service units often dressed in native or civilian clothes to carry out their deep penetration reconnaissance missions, or to attack and destroy important targets. At other times, disguised in the uniforms of the enemy, they were used as infantry groups to spearhead military assaults. It follows, therefore, that each Brandenburger had to be fluent in the language of the country in which he was operating. Most of those who served in Africa were not only fluent in Arabic, but also proficient in Swahili or some other local tongue and conversant with other Middle Eastern or African languages. One of my German friends who served in the Brandenburg Regiment numbered among his linguistic accomplishments Farsi, the language spoken in Afghanistan, where he had operated during the war.

In the matter of wearing disguise or enemy uniforms, although British commando units – many of them led by German-speaking Palestinian Jewish soldiers – often operated while dressed in Afrika Korps clothing, Rommel forbade his military units from operating in like fashion. However, his ban could not extend to cover the Brandenburg units for, being under the Abwehr – which was a state organisation – these were not, strictly speaking, service personnel.

It was the headquarters group of the 200th Special Services Regiment, *ie* the Brandenburgers, under the command of Lieutenant-Colonel von Schwerin, which led the advance of Streich's division to Mugda in 1941. Later that year Brandenburg strength rose when Lieutenant von Könen, a former explorer, raised and led an Afrika Kompanie. It is known that the Brandenburg Regiment carried out at least one assault landing from the sea early in 1942, and when the Eighth Army was in retreat during June/July of that year as a result of the disastrous Gazala battle, all available Brandenburg detachments were briefed on a very deep penetration/demolition operation which they were to undertake. Disguised as British servicemen, they were to penetrate the Eighth Army's battle line at El Alamein and reach the Suez Canal and the Nile. There they were to seize the bridges across these waterways and to hold them until relieved. Rommel's failure to win the battle of Alam Halfa meant that the preconditions to launch the operation were never met and it was therefore aborted.

Several attempts were made to 'drop' secret agents or spies. Included among such infiltration missions in 1942 was 'Operation Salam', in which the spies, who were dressed in Luftwaffe khaki-drill when they passed through British checkpoints but later changed into civilian clothes, were successfully 'dropped' in Egypt, only to be immediately arrested by British Intelligence officers who had been waiting for them. One bizarre Brandenburg mission was mounted early the same year because OKW was convinced that British convoys were not sailing as far as the Cape but were discharging their cargoes at Lagos, on the west coast of Africa, and were then bringing the supplies and vehicles by road convoy to Egypt. A Brandenburg group was ordered to determine the location of the suspected road in order that a second group could blow up sections of it and halt the flow of supplies. This operation involved the first Brandenburg group in a round journey of more that 5000 km, carried out in enemy territory and through terrain which was barren, arid and hostile. When the group returned to base in autumn 1942, armed with the intelligence details it had gathered, Rommel had more to worry about than the location of a road thousands of kilometres away. He was at that time fighting and losing the battle of Alam Halfa.

Earlier than that, in the summer of 1942, the result of Rommel's successful Gazala offensive had made it seem likely that Panzer Group Africa might soon advance to the Suez Canal. However, it was soon realised at Group headquarters that the troops on the ground had been fighting for weeks without pause and might be too exhausted to make a thrust that would take them to the canal. OKW therefore ordered a reinforcement of experienced but rested troops to be sent to Libya, and a group of paratroops in brigade strength was flown to Tripoli and taken up the line, where they were to be used to smash a way through Eighth

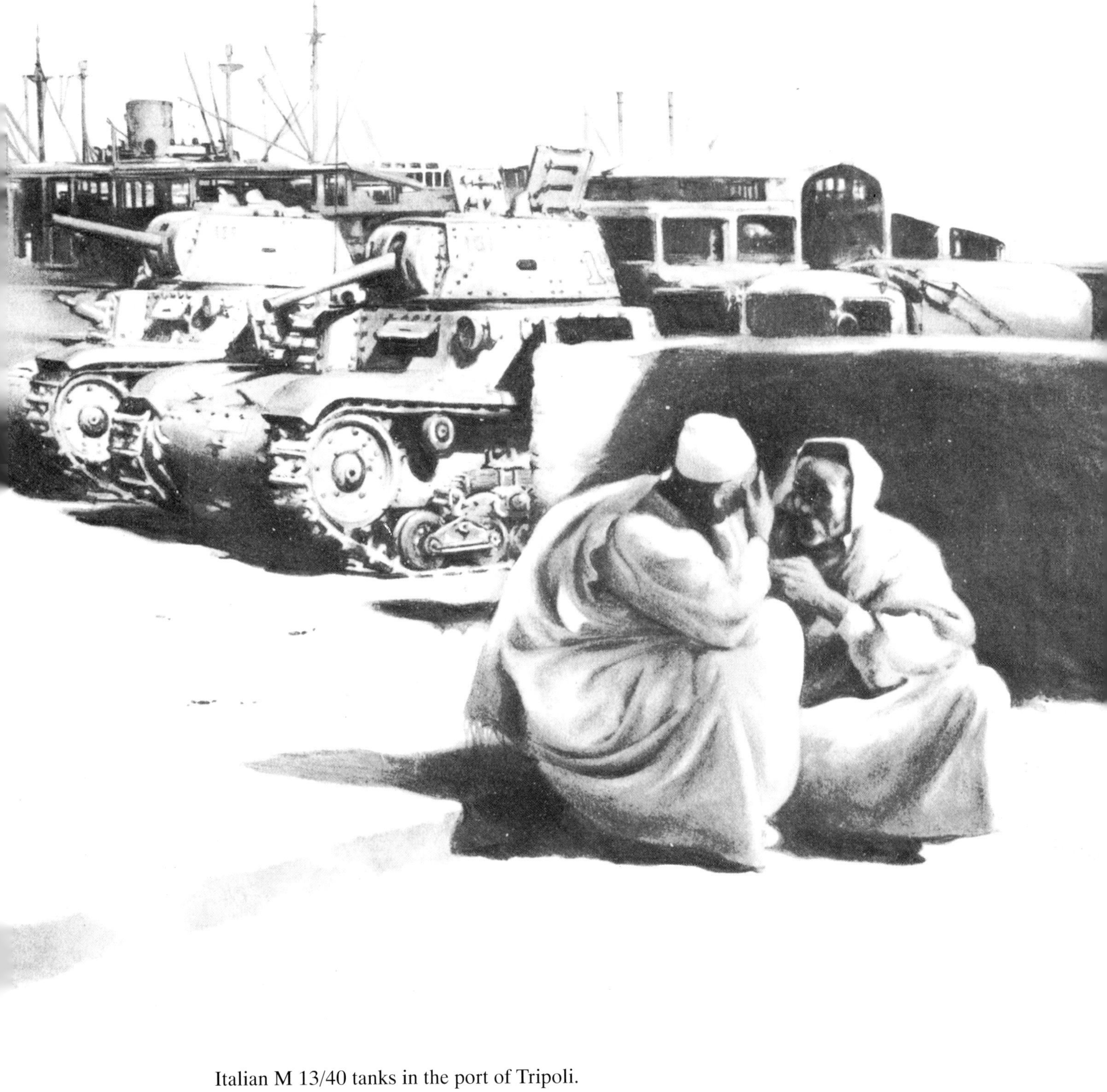

Italian M 13/40 tanks in the port of Tripoli.

This drawing shows the serpentine road along the top of the Sollum escarpment, and one of the steep gradients which were a feature of this stretch of the highway.

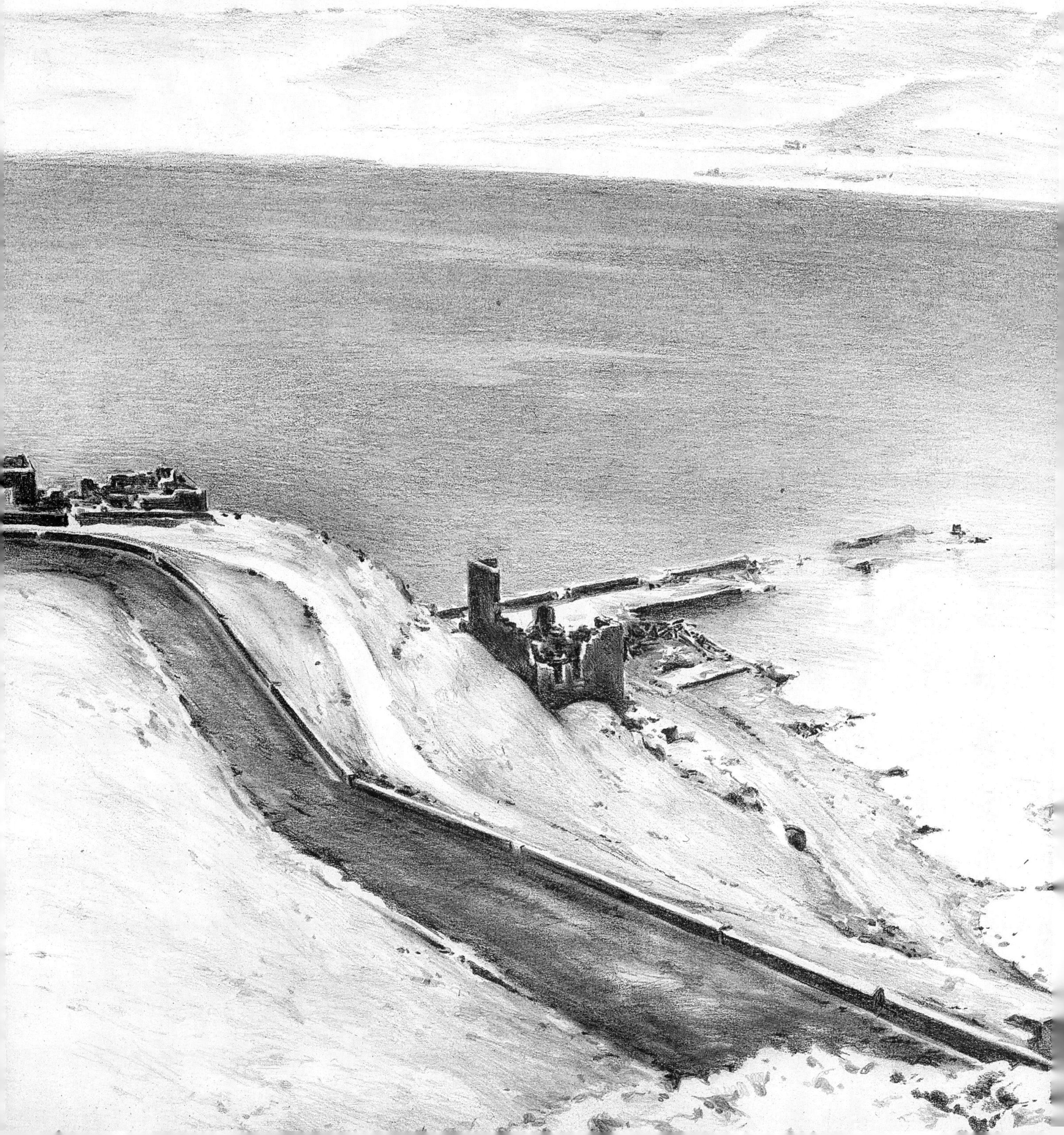

Army's front and to follow the Brandenburg detachments in their task of seizing the vital bridges. With the Axis forces on the defensive when Ramcke's Brigade arrived at the front, the military situation did not permit the employment of the paratroops in the planned spearhead role and they were instead put into the battle line, where they served as assault infantry.

The five other German divisions which served in Africa arrived in late-1942 or early-1943 and are not, therefore, relevant to this book.

On 15 August 1941, the German units in Africa were incorporated into the North Africa Command under General Bastico, with Rommel promoted to lead the Panzer Group Africa. The heart of this Group remained the German Afrika Korps (15th and 21st Panzer Divisions, with 90th Light Division in support). Also forming part of Panzer Group Africa were two Italian corps: XX Corps, comprising the 'Ariete' Armoured Division and 'Trieste' Infantry Division, and XXI Corps, consisting of the 'Pavia', 'Bologna' and 'Brescia' Infantry Divisions. In addition there was the 'Savona' Infantry Division, which did not form part of either Italian corps but acted in support of the German garrison of the Halfaya Pass; it vanished from the order of battle after 1941.

A further expansion in the early months of 1942 gave the Panzer Group the name of Panzer Army Africa when the 164th Infantry Division and Ramcke's Paratroop Brigade came onto the German order of battle. The Italian contingent was also increased by the addition of X Corps. On 1 November 1941 the Panzer Army was retitled the German–Italian Panzer Army, thus acknowledging the fact that the bulk of Rommel's troops were Italian. The Panzer Army's order of battle was five corps, four of which were Italian and one – the Afrika Korps – German. New units which came onto Italian strength included the 'Littorio' Armoured Division, the 'Folgore' Parachute Division and the 'Trento' Infantry Division.

Axis strength later increased following the retreat into Tunisia after the Allied invasion of French North Africa in November 1942, but these events fall outside the time-frame of the present volume.

# Rommel and the other German Commanders in Africa

It is altogether fitting that any account of Afrika Korps commanders should begin with Erwin Rommel, for the Afrika Korps and Rommel are inseparably linked. Rommel was its first commander, and although he held the post for only some six months before going on to lead higher formations, when one considers German involvement in the desert war it is his name which comes to mind.

Rommel's military background was as an infantry soldier, specifically an officer of a mountain unit. During the Great War he had commanded a battle group of the Württemberg Alpine Battalion, distinguishing himself in an action during the battles of the Isonzo in 1917. His outstanding success in capturing a number of strongly defended mountain peaks, during which he took prisoner thousands of Italian soldiers and hundreds of artillery pieces, gained for him Germany's highest award for bravery, the *Pour le Mérite.*

In the post-war German army he served in a succession of regimental appointments in infantry units, and wrote his book *Infantry Attacks* recalling the battles in which he had taken part. Adolf Hitler, the German Chancellor, was deeply impressed by this work and, wishing to have around him soldiers who had fought with distinction, he had Rommel posted to his staff. Guarding Hitler was a task shared by both Army and SS units, and Rommel was given command of the Army's guard detachment, in which capacity he served during the campaign in Poland. When the Führer subsequently asked him which type of formation he would like to command the immediate reply was 'A panzer division.' Despite the opposition of the Army's personnel department, which proposed that command of a mountain division might be more appropriate, Hitler insisted that Rommel be given command of the 7th Panzer Division.

Though Rommel was an infantry soldier he seemed to have an instinctive grasp of armoured warfare, and during the 1940 Blitzkrieg in the West led his division with such flair that at one time it formed one point of the German Army's panzer spearhead scything through France. The unconventional methods he adopted in that campaign produced results, and he was almost certainly the first commander of a panzer division to fight his units at night or to march them without rest for more than a hundred kilometres. Certainly his deployment of the 88 mm guns of the divisional artillery regiment into an anti-tank gun line to fight off Allied armour was unconventional in those days, but very effective. With his successes in the West to recommend him, Rommel was Hitler's first choice when the time came to select a commander for the German contingent to fight in Africa. With the new appointment came promotion.

When Rommel assumed command in February 1941 there was no Afrika Korps as such, but merely individual units of the 5th Light (*ie* motorised) Division. The first elements of this formation disembarked at Tripoli soon after and the build up of troops continued throughout the following weeks and months. It has been said that when the armoured detachments came ashore and were formed up ready to march past the German and Italian commanders, Rommel gave instructions that they were to act like a stage army: each unit was to drive several times past the saluting base, with frequent changes of position within the panzer columns. Rommel suspected that among the Arabs watching the parade there would be men ready to send word to the British authorities in Egypt on the strength and appearance of the German force, and he wanted to give the impression that he had arrived with a particularly powerful force.

Like most German soldiers who arrived in Libya, Rommel had no experience of Africa. In fact, it was not a continent in which he had any particular interest. It was surprising, therefore, that just as he had intuitively grasped the principles of armoured warfare in 1940, he swiftly mastered the peculiarities of desert fighting.

Despite the fact that Rommel had commanded the Army element of the Führer's guard detachment, and although he had had contact with Hitler since the mid-1930s, he was not himself a National Socialist. He was the

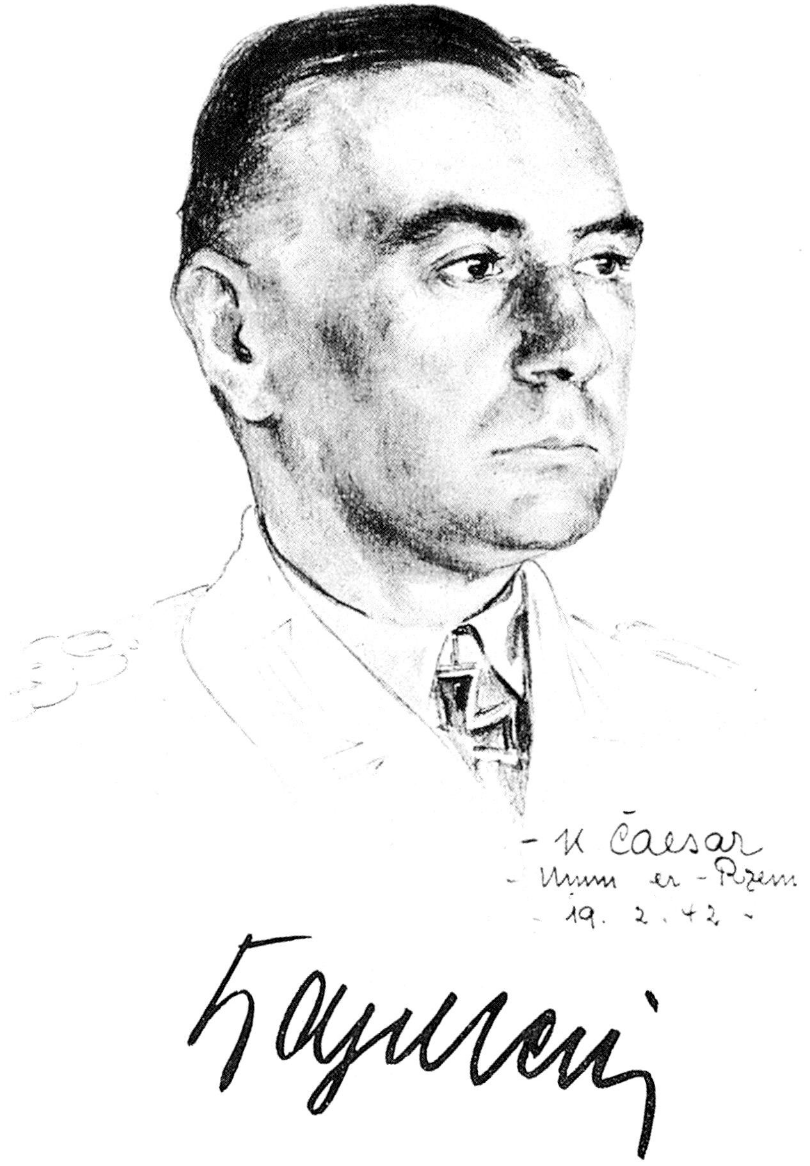


Colonel Bayerlein of the General Staff, Chief
of the General Staff of the Afrika Korps.

type of officer demanded by von Seeckt, the Army's commander-in-chief during the Weimar period. Seeckt demanded men totally dedicated to their work and completely a-political. Even though he was not politically minded, Rommel remained loyal to Hitler, despite all the evidence that the Führerhauptquartier (FHQ) was lying to him. It has even been claimed by Rommel's friends that if Hitler had supported him in the matter of supplies and reinforcements, as strongly as Rommel supported him, then the desert war might have had a different outcome.

Hitler always saw Africa as a minor theatre of operations, one which lay within the Italian sphere of influence, just as western, central and eastern Europe were within the German domain. Rommel and the Afrika Korps therefore nominally came under Italian command, though Hitler's operational directive laid down that if orders received from the Italians jeopardised the German formations, then his corps commander had the right, indeed the duty, to obtain a ruling from the Führer. Rommel was often to utilise this clause, though the answers he received and the support he was given were often not what he expected.

The command structure in Africa was clumsy. Immediately superior to Rommel was the Italian High Command in Libya, and above that layer there was the High Command in Rome, and then the Duce himself, Benito Mussolini. Later in the war another intermediate, German hierarchical level was inserted in the person of Albert Kesselring, German Supreme Commander South. In Germany there was yet another command structure –OKH, the Oberkommando der Heeres (Army High Command), and OKW, the Oberkommando der Wehrmacht (Armed Forces High Command), and then the final arbiter, the Supreme Commander, Hitler. Not all of these hierarchical layers were sympathetic to Rommel or understood the problems he faced.

Very early in his career Rommel had learned that disobedience of orders in battle is nearly always accepted if it results in victory. Acting upon that knowledge, during his years in the desert he presented both the German and the Italian high commands with a succession of *faits accomplis.* That Rommel demanded the impossible from his subordinates, and was brusque to the point of arrogant rudeness, were just two of the

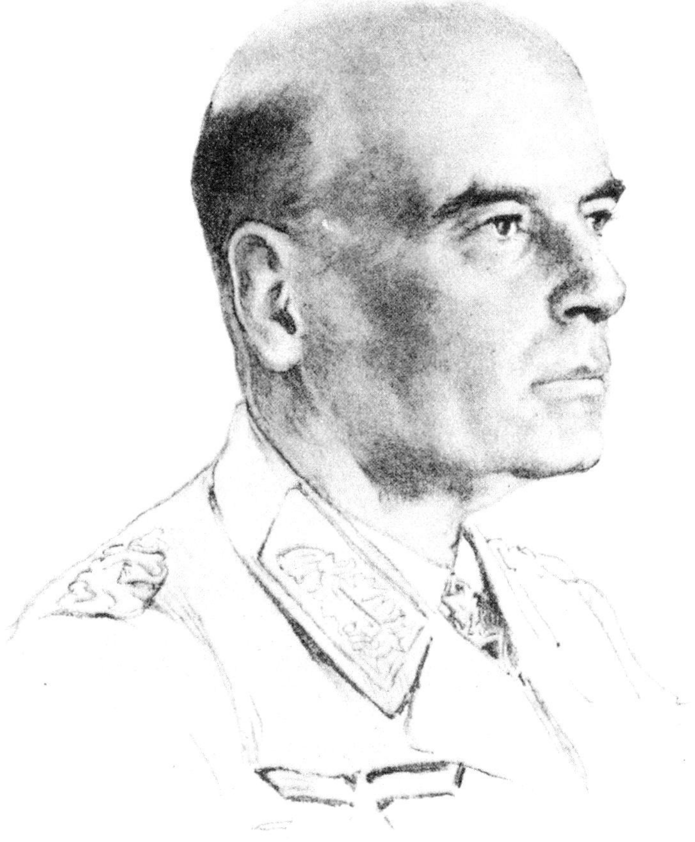

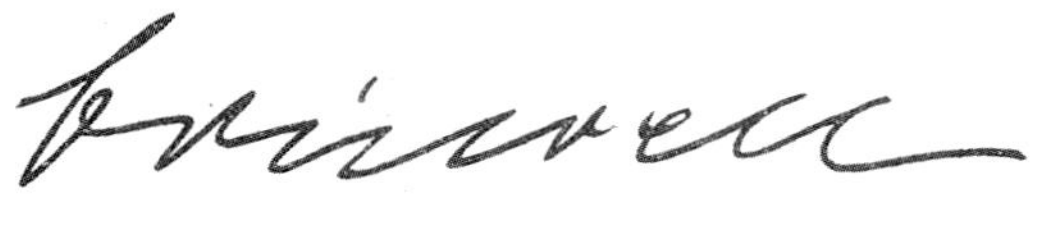

Lieutenant-General Crüwell. He was taken prisoner 27 May 1942.

charges made against him by his detractors.

Another criticism levelled at him was that during a battle he was quite often absent from his corps headquarters, preferring to accompany the spearhead units. When he was a young officer he had been told that a divisional commander should stay at his headquarters, with his maps and a telephone. He should not venture into the battle zone; his presence there was not needed. However, that was not the way that Rommel worked. In the 1940 French campaign, as commander of the 7th Panzer Division, he had hauled baulks of timber with the pioneers who were building a bridge across the River Maas, and often rode in the lead vehicle during his division's rapid advances. He led from the front, not only because seeing him inspired his men, but because tactical decisions could be acted upon more quickly if he went forward with the fighting spearhead.

The basic principle of war in the desert, which Rommel quickly grasped, was that it was akin to war at sea, comprising vast distances of emptiness in which armadas of vehicles, moving like fleets of ships, cruised about seeking to do battle with and destroy the enemy. Terrain and climate are among the factors which shape tactics in any campaign, and before the invention of railways or the internal combustion engine, war in Libya, on the scale in which it was fought between 1940 and 1943, would have been impossible. No significant military force would have been able to force its way through the barren wastes, but would have been confined to slow movement along the coast. The tank and the lorry freed armies to cross the sand seas and, in effect, fight naval battles on land. Perhaps the only tactic which Rommel created specifically for his desert offensives was the adoption of a convoy-type disposition for his columns, which were formed up into 'boxes' with the fighting echelons – the panzers – forming the outer wall, thereby protecting the soft-skin vehicles and lorry-borne infantry in the centre.

Although Rommel is the best remembered of the officers who led the Afrika Korps, he was not its only commander. When, on 15 August 1941, he was promoted and given command of Panzer Group Africa, he was succeeded in the corps post first by Ludwig Crüwell and then by other

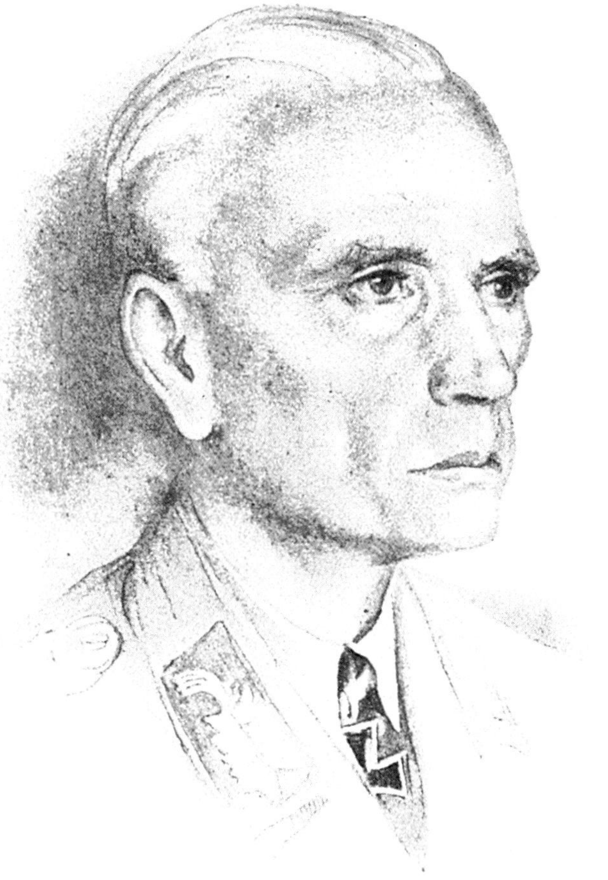

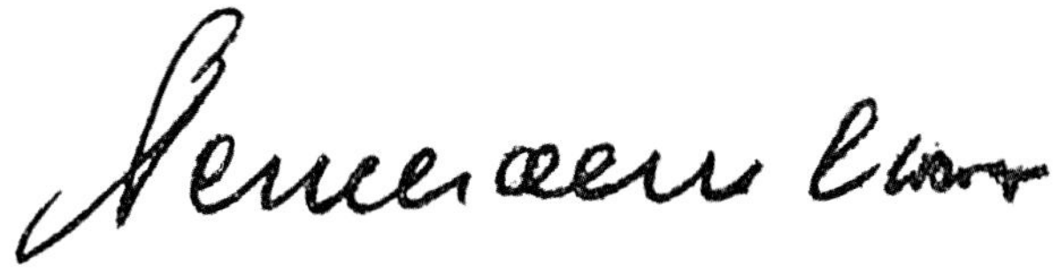

Major-General Neumann-Silkow. Died in hospital in Derna, of wounds received on 6 December 1941.

Generals. The brief biographical accounts which follow are those of men who held various senior positions during the campaign, not necessarily as commanders of Afrika Korps.

### Lieutenant-General Fritz Bayerlein

Bayerlein was born in Würzburg on 14 January 1899, and during the Great War he served with the 2nd Jäger Battalion on the Western Front. At the end of hostilities he was retained in the post-war German Army – the Reichswehr – and served in the 21st Infantry Regiment. In the 1930s he held several staff appointments, and was employed principally in this capacity during the Second World War. In Poland he served as Ia to the 10th Panzer Division, and then, in France during 1940, as Ia to XIX Corps. Promoted to the rank of Lieutenant-Colonel in 1940, he was on the Eastern Front until being posted to Libya as Chief of Staff of the Afrika Korps on 5 October 1941. During the Gazala battles of May/June 1942, Bayerlein temporarily took over the post of Chief of Staff of the Panzer Army. He was then posted away from Africa, and went on to serve in North-West Europe, first as commander of the Panzer Lehr Division and then as Commander of LIII Corps. He was awarded the Knight's Cross of the Iron Cross on 26 December 1941, the Oak Leaf on 6 July 1943, and the Swords on 20 July 1944, as well as the German Cross in Gold.

### Panzer General Hans Cramer

Hans Cramer was born on 13 July 1896, in Minden. He served as a lieutenant with the 115th Infantry Regiment during the Great War, and stayed on in the post-war Reichswehr, rising to command the Cavalry Training School. At the outbreak of the Second World War he was commanding the Panzer Training Depot, and took over 8th Panzer Regiment before returning to a staff appointment in OKH as Commander of Mobile Troops. He was temporarily commander of XXXXVIII Panzer Corps before taking up his post as General Officer commanding Afrika Korps on 1 March 1943, which he held until the war in Africa ended. He was awarded the Knight's Cross of the Iron Cross.

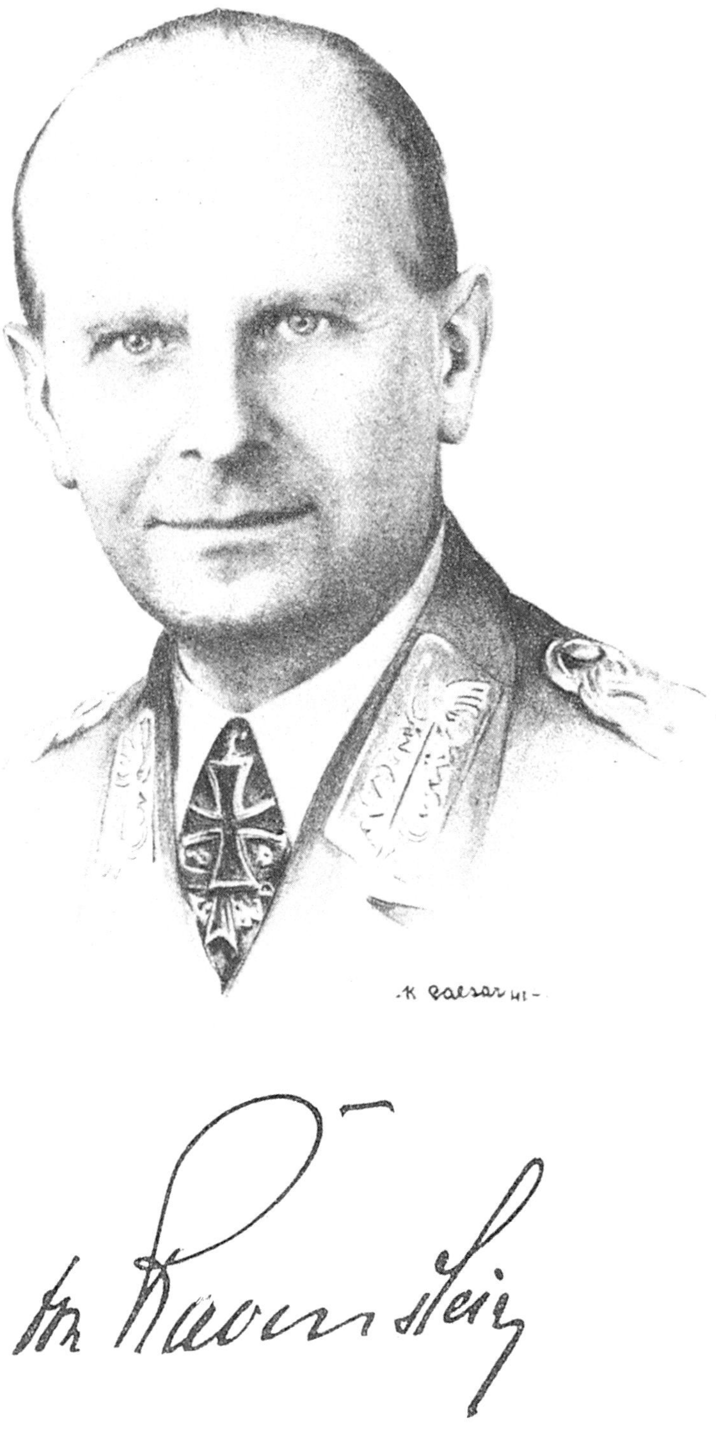

Major-General von Ravenstein. Taken prisoner outside Tobruk on 29 November 1941.

### Panzer General Ludwig Crüwell

Born in Dortmund on 26 March 1892, Crüwell enlisted into the 9th Dragoons in 1911 and served with that regiment during the First World War, on the Western Front and then in Poland. He was retained in the Reichswehr, and held chiefly staff appointments, alternating these posts with regimental commands. Crüwell worked in the General Staff and was active during the campaign against the Western Allies in 1940. During August 1940 he raised the 11th Panzer Division, and led it during the Balkan campaign of 1941, capturing Belgrade. The 11th then formed part of Kleist's Panzer Group 1, and took part in the war against Russia. Crüwell was posted to Africa to take over command of Afrika Korps when Rommel was promoted to lead Panzer Group Africa. He led the corps until he was shot down while on a recce flight in a Fieseler Storch on 27 May 1942. His awards included the Knight's Cross of the Iron Cross on 14 May 1941, and the Oak Leaf to the Knight's Cross on 1 September 1941.

### Panzer General Walther Nehring

Walter Nehring was born in Stretzin on 15 August 1892, and entered the Army on 16 August 1911. He served with the 152nd Infantry Regiment and at the end of the First World War stayed on in the Reichswehr. He rose to command the 5th Panzer Regiment in 1937, and was Chief of the General Staff of XIX Corps from July 1938. He then became General Guderian's Chief of Staff, was posted to the 18th Panzer Division in 1940, and was transferred to Africa in March 1942. He was sent home sick but returned to Tunisia as commander of XC Corps. After he left Tunisia in December 1942 he went on to serve in other posts. For his services Nehring received the Knight's Cross of the Iron Cross, then the Oak Leaf, and finally the Swords.

### General Walther Neumann-Silkow

Walther Neumann-Silkow was born in Pomerania on 10 April 1894 and served in the 10th Dragoon Regiment from 1913 until the end of the Great War. Retained in the Reischwehr, he rose to command the 8th

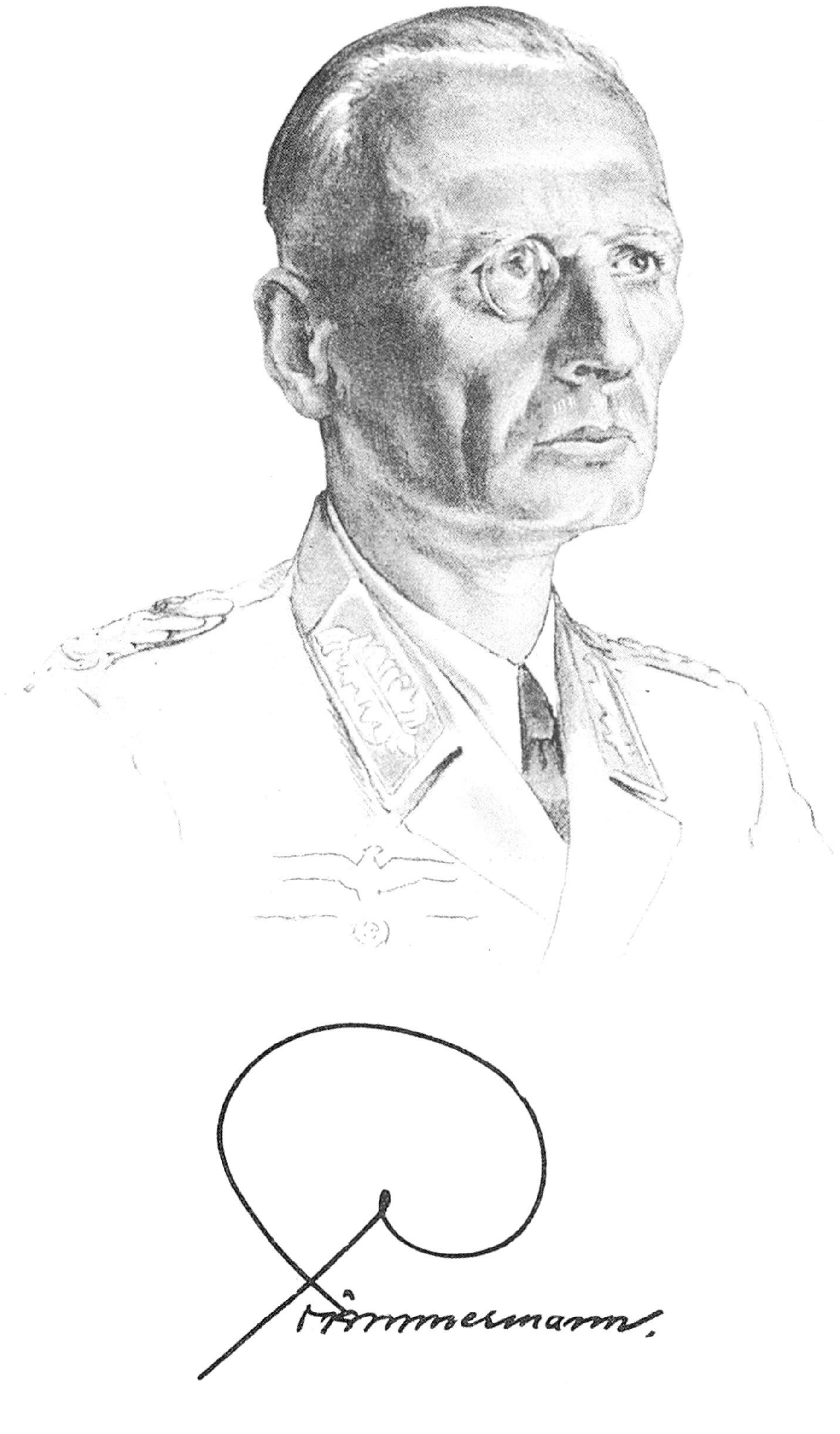

Major-General Sümmermann. Taken prisoner during
the December battles of 1941.

Reconnaissance Regiment in November 1938. During the Blitzkrieg in the West in 1940 he led the 8th Motorised Infantry Brigade, and subsequently the 8th Panzer Division. He was posted to Africa on 26 May 1941, and took over command of the 15th Panzer Division. He was badly wounded in the fighting of 6 December 1941, when the tank in which he was riding received a direct hit. Neumann-Silkow was evacuated to a military hospital in Derna, where he died of his wounds. His decorations included the Knight's Cross of the Iron Cross.

### Major-General Johann von Ravenstein

Johann von Ravenstein was born in Silesia on 1 January 1889. He enlisted into the Army in 1909 and served in the 7th Grenadier Regiment. At the end of the Great War he served in the Reichswehr, but left in May 1934 with the rank of major. He subsequently rejoined and went on to command the 4th Rifle Regiment during the Polish campaign, and then the 4th Rifle Brigade on 15 July 1940. Posted to Africa in spring 1941, he took command of the 21 Panzer Division and led it until the aircraft in which he was flying was shot down near Tobruk in November 1941, when he was taken prisoner. For his services during the Great War, Ravenstein had been awarded the *Pour le Mérite* and during the Second World War he received the Knight's Cross of the Iron Cross.

### Lieutenant-General Johannes Streich

Born in Holstein on 16 April 1891, Streich entered the Army in October 1911 and transferred to the Railway Troops in 1913. After service in the Great War he was retained in the Reichswehr, and by 1935 had risen to the command of the 15th Panzer Regiment, going on to command the 5th Panzer Brigade in January 1941. Transferred to Africa, he was given command of 5th Light (Africa) Division on 7 February, and Battle Group Streich three months later. He was then posted away from Africa, taking over the 16th Panzer Division until he was promoted to Inspector of Mobile Troops in June 1942. He was awarded the Knight's Cross of the Iron Cross.

### Major-General Max Sümmermann

Max Sümmermann was born in Westphalia on 9 June 1890, and entered the Army in 1910. He served throughout the Great War with the 117th Infantry Regiment. Retained in the Reichswehr, he rose to command of the 105th Infantry Regiment in 1937 and stayed with it until December 1940. He then took over the 213th Infantry Regiment before going on to command the 90th Light Division in Africa on 1 September 1941. He was killed in action during the December battles of 1941.

### Cavalry General Siegfried Westphal

Siegfried Westphal was born on 18 March 1902, in Leipzig. Like all staff officers in the German Army, his career alternated between regimental duties and staff appointments. In the army of the Weimar Republic, Westphal served in the 11th and 16th Cavalry Regiments and was then posted to the War Academy. He served as Ia of the 58th Division in Holland, Belgium and France throughout the campaign on the Western Front in 1940. He was then posted as Ia to Panzer Group Africa and Panzer Army Africa, in which appointments he acted for Rommel when the commander was absent from his headquarters with the front-line units. On one celebrated occasion he actually countermanded Rommel's battle orders. The commander-in-chief was furious at this interference but subsequently admitted that Westphal's decision had been the correct one to take.

At the beginning of December 1942, Westphal was given a field command and led the 164th Light Africa Division for a month before being posted away from Africa. He was eventually given a senior post on the staff of Field Marshal Kesselring in Italy and later in the West. He was awarded the German Cross in Gold on 19 December 1941, and the Knight's Cross to the Iron Cross on 30 November 1942.

# The First Campaign–March to April 1941

*Rommel ignores the orders of his superiors and opens an assault which takes the Afrika Korps from El Agheila to Tobruk.*

It was on 12 February 1941, during discussions with senior Italian officers in Sicily, that Rommel issued the first order of his African career. General Geissler, the commander of the Luftwaffe's X Air Corps, had reported that the British Western Desert Force, having captured Benghazi, stood ready to advance out of Cyrenaica, Libya's eastern province, and to invade the western province of Tripolitania. Rommel ordered the Luftwaffe to bomb Benghazi that night, to mine the coastal waters around the port, and on the following morning to continue the assault with low-level attacks against British columns advancing into Tripolitania. During the 13th he carried out a personal air reconnaissance of the forward area and returned to discuss future operations with General Gariboldi, his superior officer. Rommel proposed that, instead of waiting until the whole of 5th Light Division had arrived and had been concentrated, he should move the German units individually up to the front as they reached Tripoli. Rommel correctly anticipated what would be the tone of the Italian's reply, for his orders from both the German and the Italian High Commands had been clearly defined. Those from Gariboldi would merely confirm the directives from the German and Italian Supreme Commands, which were that once the whole of 5th Light Division had arrived he was to lead it into an eastwards advance into the Sirte desert where, together with the Italians, he was to block the advance of the Western Desert Force. His corps had been given a defensive role. Not until the 15th Panzer Division reached Tripoli was he to think of an offensive operation, limited to a reconnaissance probe in the Agedabia area.

Rommel rejected the timid operational plans of Rome and Berlin. His view was that, faced with an imminent British invasion, it was a waste of manpower to employ Italian troops in defensive positions around Tripoli. There they would remain inactive until the enemy moved

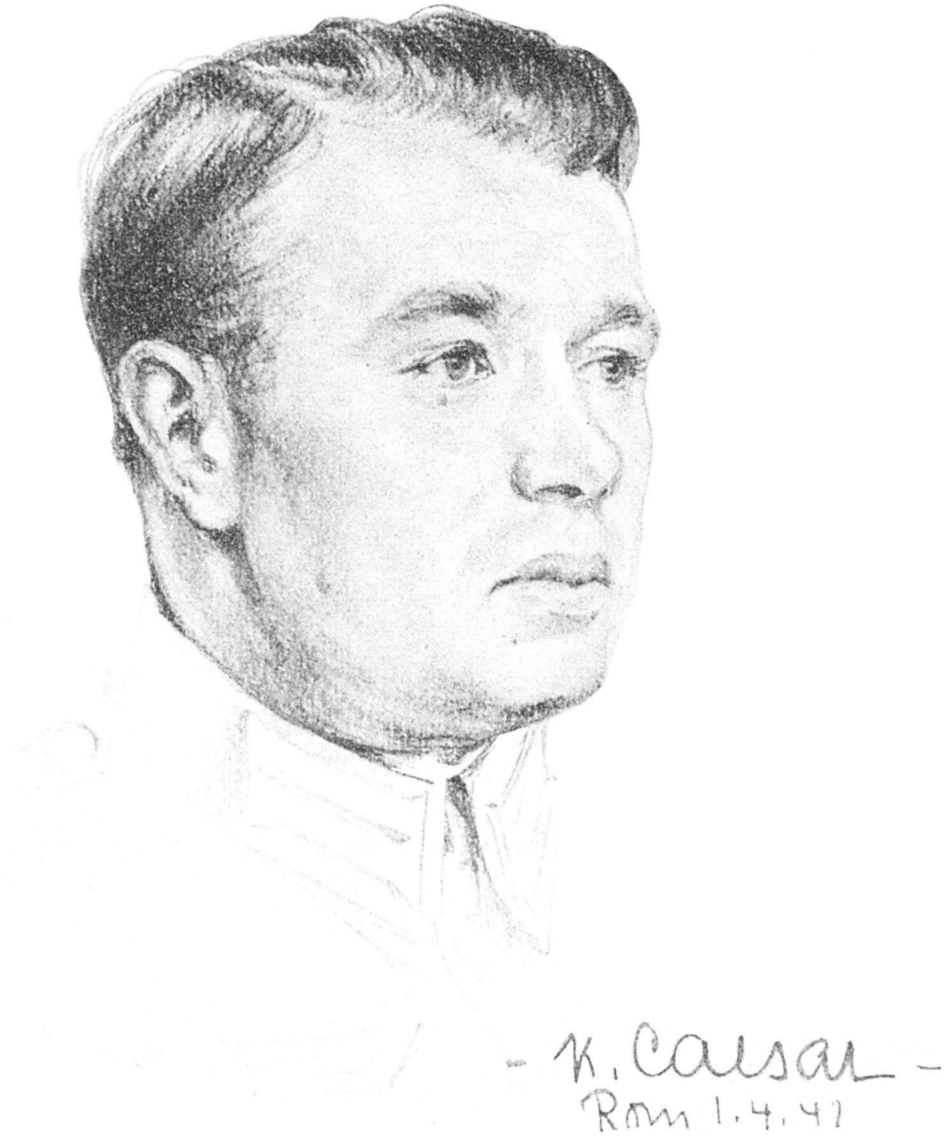


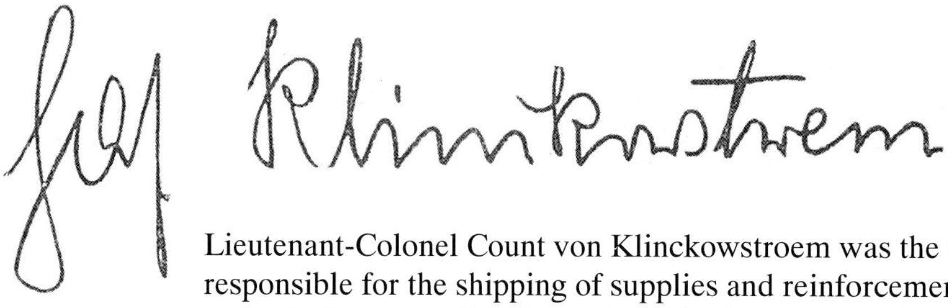

Lieutenant-Colonel Count von Klinckowstroem was the officer responsible for the shipping of supplies and reinforcements from the embarkation port of Naples to the debarkation port of Tripoli. Because of the limited space available in Libyan harbours, Klinckowstroem's planning of convoys had to be very precise and his movement orders were wirelessed by an OKH Signals detachment stationed in Naples. These signals were intercepted and decoded by the British, who then attacked the convoys as they crossed the Mediterranean or bombed the harbours in which the ships had docked.

against them and, on past performance, would defeat them. For him to wait inactive until his corps reached full strength would lose the opportunity to pre-empt the Western Desert Force's imminent offensive. He demanded that a second Italian division be moved to the Sirte area to support the one which was already defensively positioned there. In the Sirte concentration area these two divisions would eventually be joined by detachments of the 5th Light Division and, at a later date, by the first unit of 15th Panzer to be sent to Africa, the 5th Panzer regiment. Once this combined Italo-German force was concentrated Rommel intended to strike along the Via Balbia and make a probe against El Agheila. OKH (Army High Command) warned him afresh that not until all of the 15th Panzer Division had come under his command – the last week of May was now the estimated time for this – was he to consider such an operation in the Agedabia area. Rommel had other plans. In defiance of both OKH and of the Italian Commando Supremo he planned secretly to attack Agedabia earlier than OKH had instructed, and then, without High Command authority, to go on to capture Benghazi.

Despite his impatience he was nevertheless obliged to wait for his units to arrive; until they did, the Libyan front would have to stagnate. Once his units arrived, his intention was to carry out strong and aggressive patrolling around El Agheila in order to establish how deeply the British had penetrated into Tripolitania. In the matter of objectives, OKH had chosen Agedabia as a priority target because the area contained vast reserves of sweet water, which the German expeditionary force needed to survive in the desert; and Rommel selected Benghazi because it was the gateway to Tripolitania. However, he knew very well that just to capture the town would not be enough – he would have to win back the whole of Cyrenaica if he wanted to defend Tripolitania effectively, though he confided this ambition only to his memoirs. In these he wrote of his disappointment with the negative and dismissive attitude of the Army's senior commanders to the importance of the war in Africa. They could not see the strategic possibilities it offered. To them, the Libyan war was a side-show.

The first four desert operations carried out by the Germans are described in this book in some detail, in order to show the difficulties they encountered and how swiftly they adapted to the unusual circumstances of climate and terrain. The final chapter, covering the operations of 1942, is less detailed.

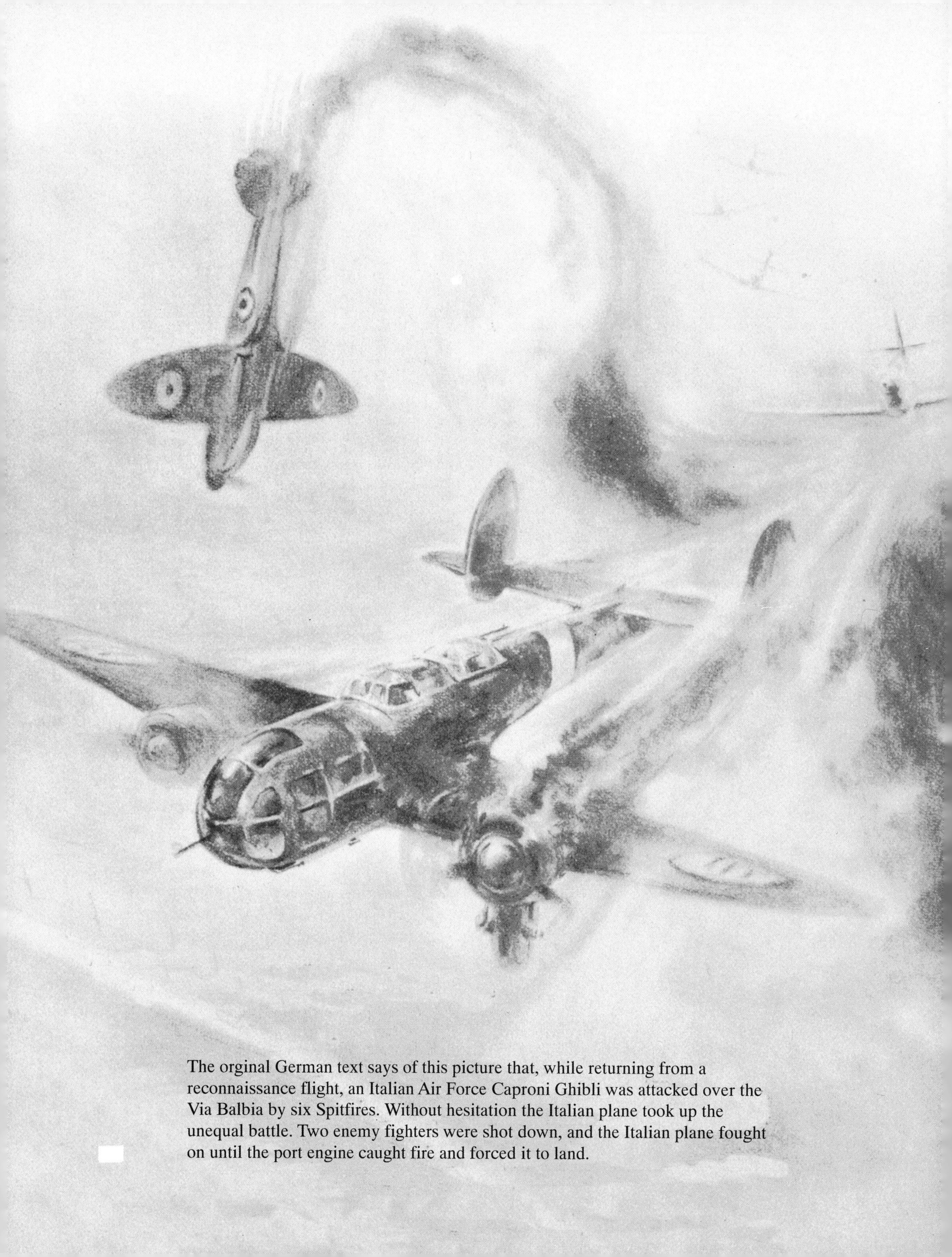

The orginal German text says of this picture that, while returning from a reconnaissance flight, an Italian Air Force Caproni Ghibli was attacked over the Via Balbia by six Spitfires. Without hesitation the Italian plane took up the unequal battle. Two enemy fighters were shot down, and the Italian plane fought on until the port engine caught fire and forced it to land.

Rommel returned to Tripoli on 14 February to greet the arrival of the first units of his command. These included a field hospital, two water purification companies, and a vehicle workshop, plus, more importantly, two battalions of combat troops, comprising the 3rd Reconnaissance and 39th Anti-Tank Battalions. No sooner had the fighting formations begun to unload their weapons than Rommel appeared and issued orders to Major Irmfried von Wechmar, commanding officer of the 3rd Reconnaissance Battalion, that he was to speed up the unloading, so that both battalions were ready to march within five hours. The men worked through the night under floodlights to complete the task, and at dawn on 15th were formed up in column of companies on the outskirts of Tripoli. Rommel came to see them drive off and took the salute as they passed him in review order. The columns picked up speed as they left the city and set off at a fast rate along the tarmacked Via Balbia. It was just as well that they had this all-weather surface as a guide, for within minutes of leaving Tripoli they were enveloped in a blinding sandstorm. For these 'green' troops it was a grim introduction to the harshness of Africa's climate.

The 600 km drive up the Via Balbia lasted for over twenty-six hours. The town of Sirte was reached in the early afternoon of the second day, and there Wechmar received fresh orders. These were that he was to report to the General commanding the 'Pavia' Division, whose temporary headquarters were in the Albergo Sirte. He was about to follow these instructions when Rommel came out of the Albergo with revised orders. The battalions were now to carry out a forced march to conduct aggressive reconnaissance in the El Agheila sector. Rommel stressed that the forced march was essential as reports had been received that the British had already captured the settlement. Wechmar was also ordered not only to establish the enemy's location, but also to estimate his strength and battle dispositions, and to conclude from his findings whether the British force was ready to resume offensive operations. It was during the ensuing forced march and vigorous reconnaissance that the first clash in Africa occurred between a German and a British patrol.

At first light three battalions – the two German units and the Italian 'Santa Maria' Reconnaissance Battalion – struck out along the road, passed through a number of Arab settlements, and pushed on until they reached the Arco dei Fileni, a huge arch which marked the boundary between Tripolitania and Cyrenaica. It was at this time, as the German

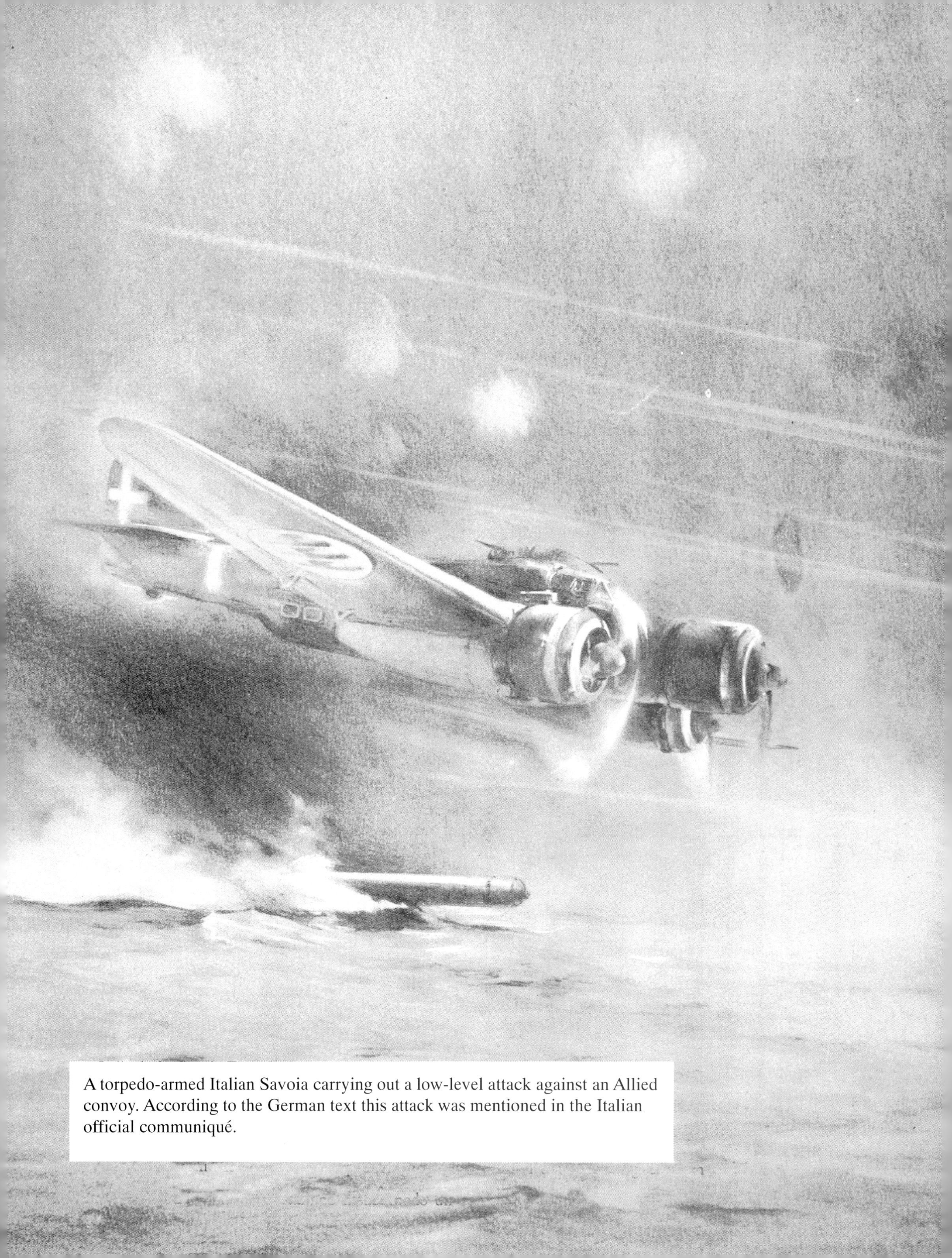

A torpedo-armed Italian Savoia carrying out a low-level attack against an Allied convoy. According to the German text this attack was mentioned in the Italian official communiqué.

and Italian patrols were making the first penetration of the Sirte desert waste, that OKW (Armed Forces High Command) announced that the name of Rommel's force was to be Deutsches Afrika Korps (the German Africa Corps.)

In the last week of February, General Streich, commanding the 5th Light Division, arrived in Tripoli and was briefed by Rommel. As soon as the 8th Machine-Gun Battalion came on strength, Streich was to assume responsibility for operations east of Sirte. A few days later the 8th debarked and was rushed up the Via Balbia. Three kilometres east of the triumphal arch, the machine-gun battalion halted and laid out the positions which would become the concentration area for the 5th Light Division. The units of the 5th then began to arrive in quick succession and German strength in the area built up. Streich, as commander of ground forces east of Sirte, worked out a battle plan to halt the British if they advanced through the Straits of Mugda. For the blocking operation he had under his command the 8th Machine-Gun Battalion, 39th Anti-Tank Battalion, a company of engineers, and both Wechmar's 3rd and the 'Santa Maria' reconnaissance battalions. He had, as yet, no panzer units, and to cover this deficiency, as well as to protect his group's open land flank against any British thrust, he ordered his engineers to lay extensive minefields on the desert side.

While this operation was being carried out, the main elements of the 5th Light Division reached the concentration area and regrouped. Rommel, convinced that his forces in the Sirte area were sufficiently strong, ordered Streich to carry out an advance through the Straits of Mugda and go on to capture El Agheila as a first objective, before pushing on to seize Marada. The spearhead of Streich's group was made up of troops from the 200th Special Services Battalion (a commando-type detachment), supported by two companies of the 8th Machine-Gun Battalion as well as a platoon of anti-tank guns. This group carried out the first deep penetration by German units in Libya, and by 17 March had captured Marada.

The operation which Rommel had planned opened at dawn on 31 March. The first objective, Marsa el Brega, 30 km south-west of El Agheila, lay between the Mediterranean and a salt marsh. General Gariboldi had given explicit instructions that the purpose of the operation was only to establish the strength of the Western Desert Force in the area, but Rommel determined to ignore these restrictive orders, just as he had already flouted the directive to concentrate the 5th Light Division in Tripoli and had instead brought up his units piecemeal into the Sirte. Now he intended to go beyond the lines laid down both by Gariboldi and his own High Command.

He planned a pincer attack. The stronger of his two columns was made up of the newly arrived 5th Panzer Regiment, supported by the 3rd Reconnaissance and 8th Machine-Gun Battalions and a few detachments of anti-tank gunners; its task was to drive up the Via Balbia under an artillery barrage. Meanwhile, the second column, with anti-tank guns mounted on lorries in the role of self-propelled artillery, supported by the 2nd Machine-Gun Battalion, would outflank the British positions. It was expected that a threat to the flank would put pressure on the British and force them to withdraw. When they did, this would allow a speedy advance by the main German column. Aware that his forthcoming attack would exceed the brief he had been given, Rommel kept the details of the operation secret, particularly the date and hour. He had good reason to do so: there were many officers in OKH who would have vetoed the operation had they known of it, as would have the Italian High Command and General Gariboldi.

It was during the Marsa el Brega operation that Rommel first used a deception trick that he was to employ time and again. Having insufficient armour to guard his open right flank, he concealed this weakness by deploying a number of worn-out Italian lorries camouflaged to look like tanks, and ordering them to throw up vast clouds of dust. This was to give British patrols the impression that a panzer armada was roaring up out of the desert.

Rommel had extraordinary good luck in this first assault. He did not know that the British garrison of Marsa el Brega was a strong one, consisting of two armoured brigades supported by the Desert Air Force. Had these armoured brigades been handled more aggressively his first offensive might have been decisively smashed, and he might not have won himself the reputation that he did. In the event the operation began badly for the Germans. The main column's initial assaults up the Via Balbia were first halted and then flung back. Undaunted by this check, Rommel insisted that further attacks be mounted. On the second day of the offensive the Italo-German column at last began to make progress, probably due to the fact that the flawless co-operation for which Rommel strove was achieved between all arms. Infantry and panzer

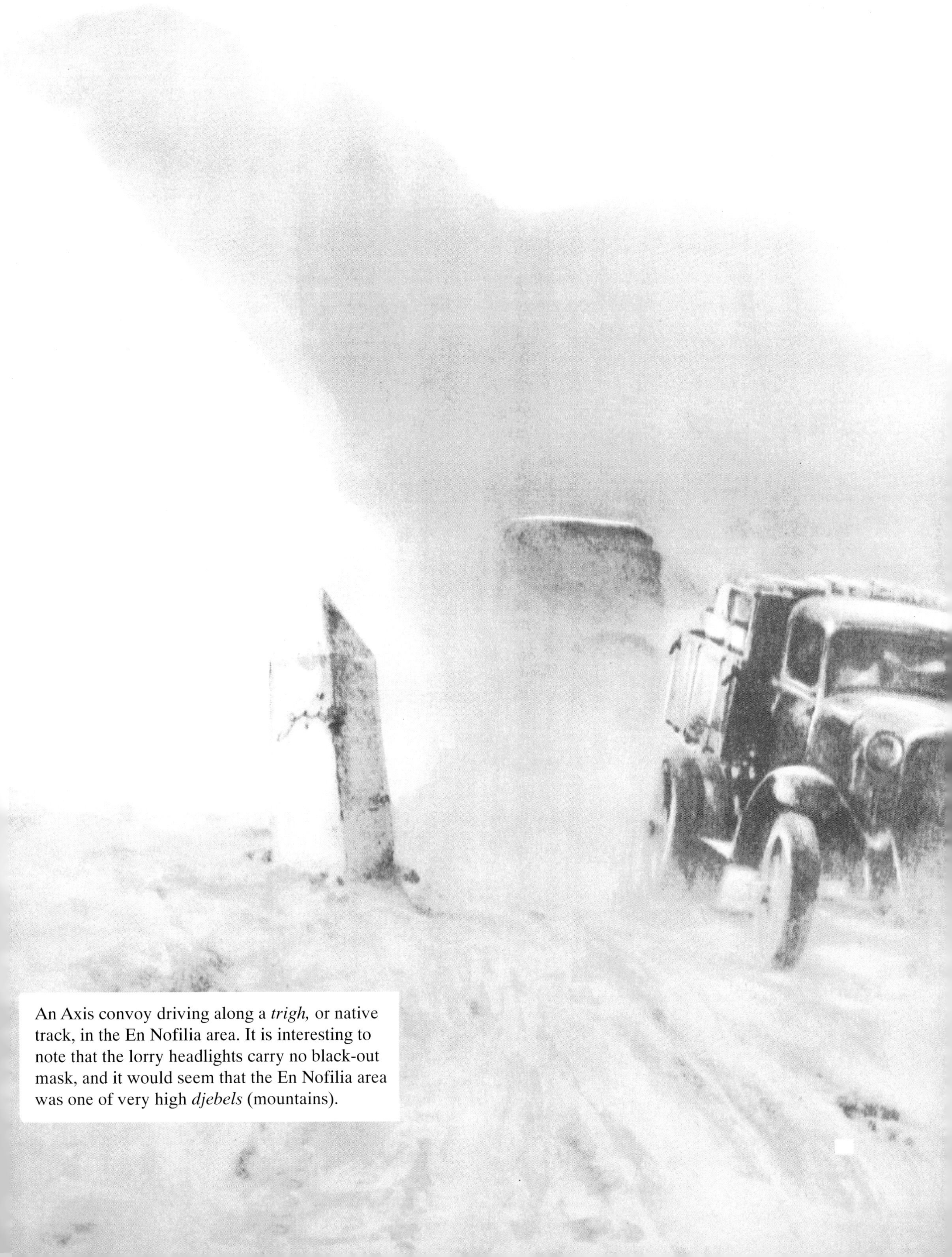

An Axis convoy driving along a *trigh,* or native track, in the En Nofilia area. It is interesting to note that the lorry headlights carry no black-out mask, and it would seem that the En Nofilia area was one of very high *djebels* (mountains).

detachments, supported by batteries of 88s and covered by a shield of Stuka dive-bombers, smashed against, into, and finally through the British defensive line. Rommel then skilfully combined and co-ordinated the pursuit stage of the battle, mounting follow-up attacks by the units of his main column until the British armour had been routed and driven from the battlefield. The main column had forced the decision even without the support of the desert column, which had been brought to a halt in a salt marsh as a result of bad navigation.

Reflecting upon the outcome of his first major operation, Rommel concluded that not only had the Marsa el Brega assault driven the British from the last good position at the south-western approach into Cyrenaica, but also that the Western Desert Force was not as strong or as aggressive as the Italians had claimed it to be. In defence of the poor showing of the British tank regiments, however, it must be remembered that Churchill had taken the bulk of the Western Desert Force from Wavell and had sent it to fight in Greece. None of Wavell's first-class fighting units had been left in North Africa, but only rear echelon and reinforcement formations, many of them new and 'unblooded'.

The Marsa el Brega offensive had also shown that German troops were able to fight in the desert. Would it be possible, Rommel must have asked himself, for his small formation to go on and achieve greater victories? He knew the difficulties of that task and was aware that it was not enough simply to drive back the Western Desert Force; the British had to be defeated in battle. He therefore resolved to act swiftly, knowing that if he were to wait for the 15th Panzer Division to reach him he would lose the initiative. Although he had only a single panzer regiment, he decided to open an all-out offensive to capture Agedabia.

The 5th Light Division was formed into a compact battle group and opened the assault on 2 April. It was the unarmoured formations which now drove along the Via Balbia, while the 5th Regiment's panzers covered the flanks of the advance – the clouds of dust which it created as it drove through the desert south of the highway must have given the impression to British reconnaissance patrols that the whole desert was covered with enemy armour. Outnumbered and outgunned, the British armoured car squadrons pulled back, but put up sufficient resistance as they did so to force the Germans to deploy into battle formation, whereupon the British armoured cars withdrew. Repetition of this delaying tactic gained time for the Western Desert Force's armoured strength to concentrate to the south-east of Agedabia, where it posed a threat to the flank of Rommel's advance. Streich ordered his battle group forward to deal with it, but the attack by the 8th Machine-Gun Battalion was halted by a firm British defence. The German situation deteriorated when Rommel took Wechmar's reconnaissance battalion for an outflanking operation and inadvertently led it into a salt marsh, where it floundered for hours. The panzer regiment deployed for battle as it moved from its positions south of the Via Balbia into the desert and there confronted 5th Royal Tank Regiment.

Rommel had already used one deception tactic to disguise the weakness of his force; now he used a second. From his experiences in France he knew that it was the practice of British tank regiments to charge into battle in line abreast, firing their main armament. This was a tactical error. Gun-fire from an unstable platform, such as a tank on the move, was of necessity inaccurate and uncoordinated. By contrast his fire would come from stable platforms – halted panzers and stationary 37 mm and 88 mm guns. This would give him the advantage of greater accuracy and better fire control. But first Rommel had to entice the British tanks to charge. The vehicles of the 5th Panzer Regiment rolled forward and opened up for battle, but as soon as they came in sight of the British armour they turned tail as if they were retreating in panic. As Rommel had anticipated, the British tanks charged the 'fleeing' enemy, racing all out to close with the panzers and 'kill' them at short range. The British commanders and gunners were blinded by the thick clouds of dust thrown up by the retreating German machines and thus did not see – until the last moment – that the enemy vehicles had passed through the intervals in a line of 88 mm guns, which suddenly loomed out of the thick sand clouds ahead, their barrels pointed directly at the oncoming tanks. Advancing at the charge, the RTR impaled itself on the shells of the 88s, losing twenty-five machines to their fire. The panzers then re-emerged through the gaps in the gun line, drove off the RTR survivors, and went on to attack a battalion of motorised infantry which was a component of the armour's support group.

The success gained by the panzer regiment had the effect of allowing the stalled attack by the machine-gunners to restart, and it was now able to resume its advance. The lorries carrying the machine-gunners bounced across a desert dotted with black 'candles', showing where the tanks of the RTR were burning. Later that day a vast, dark cloud rose

A sketch of the Albergo Sirte, which was serving as the TAC HQ of Pavia Division when von Wechmar's 3rd Recce battalion reached it on 16 February 1941. It was here that Rommel, who had arrived earlier, issued orders for Wechmar to carry out reconnaissance in force towards En Nofilia and El Agheila.

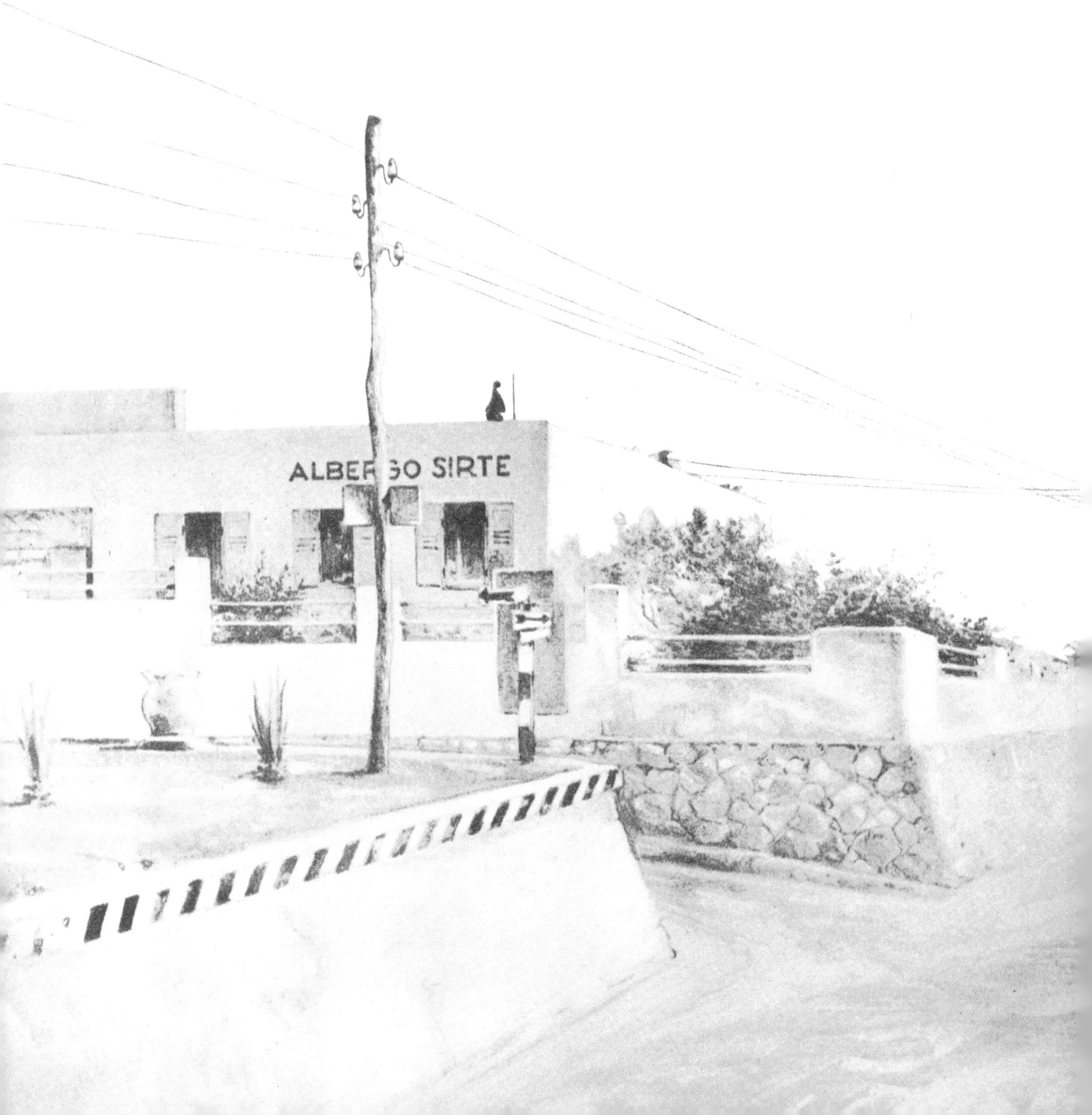

from behind the British front: the Western Desert Force was destroying its supply dumps in and around Agedabia. The town fell. It had been the expectation of both OKH and the Commando Supremo that Agedabia would be taken during May; Rommel had captured it early in April.

For the next part of his plan, Rommel intended to wheel southwards and drive the British before him, farther away from the strategically important supply route of the Via Balbia and deep into the desert. There they would encounter and be crushed against the anvil of the 5th Light Division, which he ordered to take up positions east of the recently captured town. However, his plan was not realised because the 5th had run out of fuel and lay immobile, with its units spread across the desert miles short of the form-up area from which its attack would have been launched. This situation highlighted two facts: firstly, that vast amounts of petrol – far greater than were available to Axis forces in the desert – were needed to conduct armoured operations; and secondly, that there was a vital need for Tobruk to be captured as a forward supply base, for the availability of even a couple of tankers there would have alleviated Rommel's fuel famine.

Rommel flew down on an inspection visit to the 5th Light Division and came up with a scheme to get petrol to the panzers which would not have been found in any German General Staff handbook. He gave instructions that the stores and equipment in the large soft-skin vehicles were to be unloaded and each truck was to have two drivers. The empty lorries were then to make the 2000 km round trip to Tripoli, and get back to the stranded division with fresh supplies of fuel and ammunition at best possible speed. Meanwhile, the smaller soft-skin lorries were to siphon the fuel from their own petrol tanks into those of the armoured vehicles. Transferring the petrol in this way took the whole afternoon, and then, with the suddenness that always disconcerted newcomers to the desert, darkness fell. Rommel gave orders that until the supply convoy returned from Tripoli – three days was the lowest estimate for the round trip – petrol was not to be wasted by undue movement. Nevertheless, he insisted that the advance to Mechili would be made by those panzers which had full tanks, and that the advance would be made even though the night was pitch-dark. When the column set out the AFVs had to drive almost nose-to-tail in order that the drivers could see and follow the red brake lights of the machine ahead of them. Collisions were frequent but seldom serious because of the low speed at which the column moved.

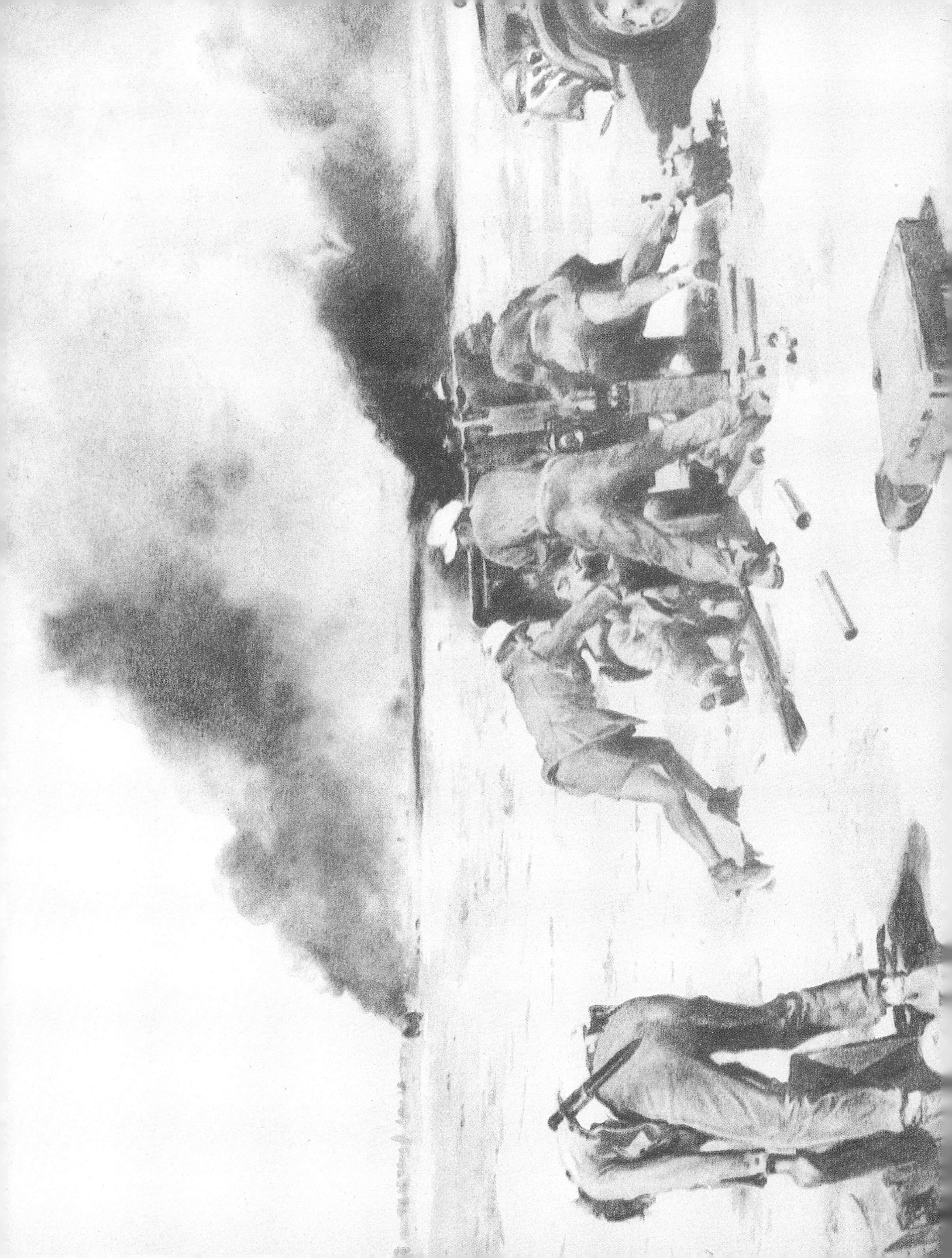

German anti-tank gunners moving their 5 cm piece into action to counter a British break-out attempt. This drawing depicts an incident typical of the battles of summer/autumn 1941. It also illustrates that front-line troops had already begun to discard elements of their full, heavy uniform; only the man at the left of the gun is still wearing a jacket.

The drive in the dark was a nightmare, not least because the *trigh* had been heavily mined by the Italians during their retreat, and a number of German vehicles were lost to their 'thermos flask' devices. Late in the night part of the column ran off the firm surface of the *trigh* and was trapped in sinking sand. Disregarding the possibility of attack from the air, Streich ordered all vehicle headlamps to be turned on so that the recovery crews could see what they were doing as they struggled to pull out the stranded vehicles. It was hard, frustrating work, and not until morning was it completed. Streich ordered the advance to continue, but the column now had far fewer machines – the effort of dragging out the trapped vehicles had used up so much petrol that a number of panzers had to be left behind with dry tanks. Streich guided his reduced command to a point some 20 km south of Mechili, where Rommel had arranged for an airlift to bring in fuel. Misfortune now struck Streich's group once again, RAF fighters attacking the two Ju 52 transports as they landed on the crusted surface of a salt marsh, and both aircraft, together with the fuel they carried, went up in flames.

Still insistent that Afrika Korps' advance be maintained, Rommel ordered Streich's small group to locate and join another force which was also advancing upon Mechili. Although this was only a small settlement, located to the south of Derna, it owed its importance to the fact that it was built around a *trigh* cross-roads. The British had set up a forward supply dump here and, following usual practice, had furnished it with a garrison, consisting of an Indian lorried brigade whose strength had been increased by the headquarters group of the 2nd Armoured Division, a battery of the Royal Horse Artillery, and an Australian anti-tank detachment.

It was essential for the further development of Rommel's battle plan

A drawing of the Arco dei Fileni, a massive stone arch built during the years of Italian colonial administration. It straddled the Via Balbia, and was located some 680 km from the capital city of Tripoli. It marked the frontier between Tripoli and Cyrenaica, and commemorated the self-sacrifice of the Fileni brothers. In ancient times there had been a border dispute between Carthage and the Cyrenians, and it was agreed to resolve it by holding a race. Two runners from each country would leave at the same time from pre-determined points in Carthage and Cyrenaica. The point at which the runners encountered each other would mark the frontier.

Though the race was won by the Carthaginians the Cyrenians disputed the result, declaring that they would only accept the decision if the Fileni brothers allowed themselves to be buried alive at the point they had reached during the race. The Fileni agreed and sacrificed themselves. To commemorate their patriotism unto death, Marshal Balbo had the arch erected in 1937 to mark the frontier between the two principal parts of the Italian colony of Libya.

The British Army knew the Arco dei Fileni as 'Marble Arch'.

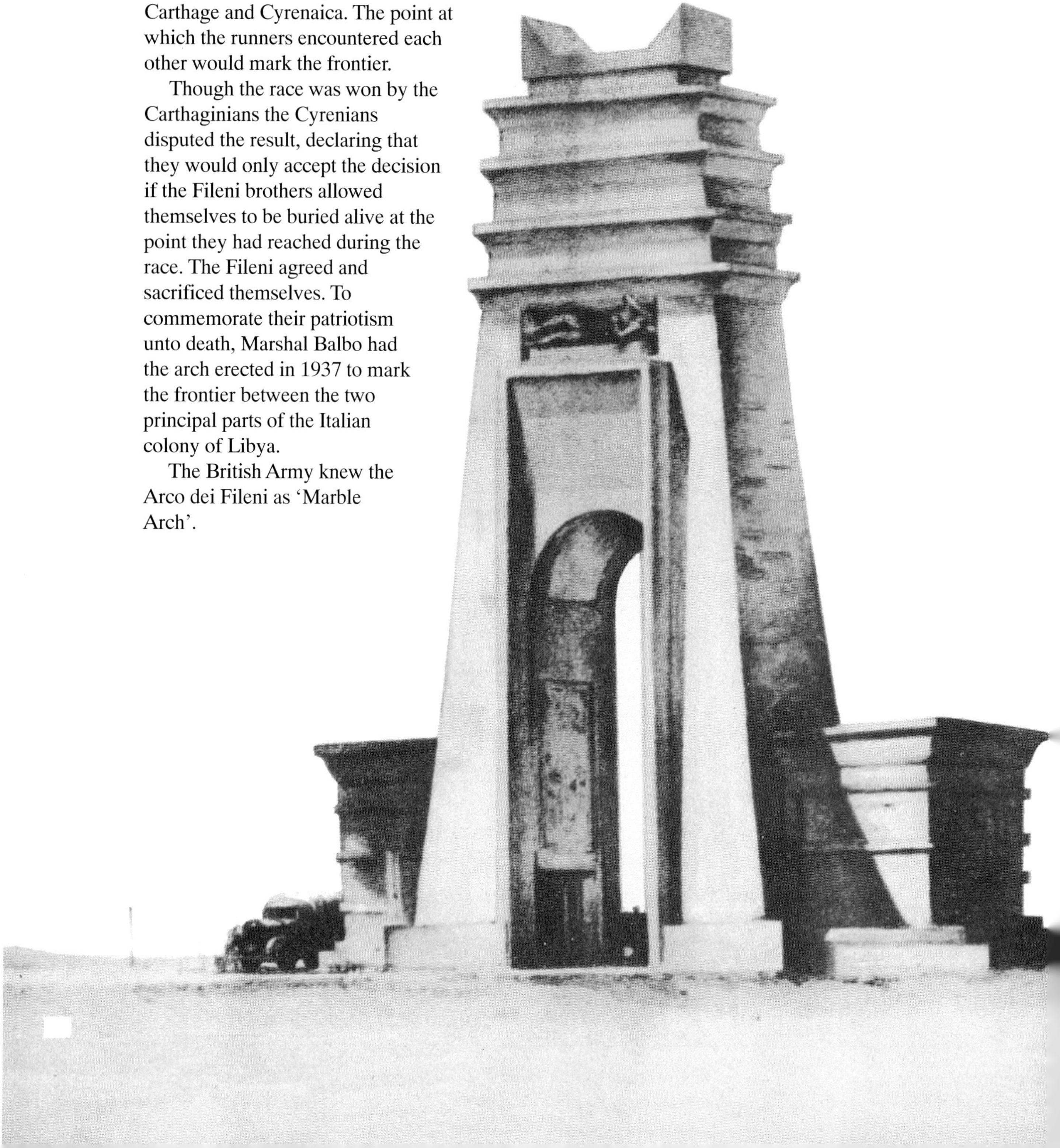

that Mechili be captured quickly. Until it was in German hands he could not wheel his forces northwards and advance upon Derna and thereby cut off the British forces retreating along the Via Balbia. During the evening of 5 April, the Quartermaster-General in Africa, Lieutenant-Colonel von Klinckowstroem, reached the stranded 5th Light Division with over 300 tons of petrol and 200 tons of supplies. The refuelled division then advanced on Mechili, where the British garrison rejected several demands to surrender and prepared to hold out. Back in the Western Desert Force headquarters in Cairo, the Staff was deeply conscious of the dangerous situation in which the Mechili garrison was placed. Warnings were sent to its commander that the whole German force in Africa was moving against him and he was ordered to begin a withdrawal eastwards during the early morning of 8 April. The soft-skins were to leave first and the armour was to form a rearguard. By a tragic mischance, as the column of lorries drove out it was struck by a platoon of panzers which was rolling forward to strengthen Streich's attack. The British supply columns were cruelly exposed by the bright sunlight, while the panzers were almost invisible to the Australian anti-tank gunners, who were dazzled by the low-lying early morning sun.

Having the sun in one's eyes or at one's back greatly influenced the outcome of a battle, and, aware of this, both sides used it as an auxiliary, natural weapon, either attacking with the sun behind them in the morning or being attacked by an enemy advancing with the setting sun behind him. The heat of midday and early afternoon distorted images so badly that estimates of distance could seldom be made with total accuracy. At Mechili, half-blinded by the glare of the low morning sun, the gunners opened fire at the shimmering shapes of the German vehicles but had incorrectly calculated the distance and caused them no damage. The German vehicles did not need to come close to the Australian gun line. Their superior armament allowed them to stay out of range and to destroy the guns at distances which the Australians could not match. The panzers used high-explosive shells to knock-out the guns and then attacked the soft-skin columns and 'brewed them up'. It was a short-lived engagement which ended with 2000 British, Indian and Australian soldiers being taken prisoner. Included among them were General officers, two battalions of the Indian Brigade, and the rear echelon of the 2nd Armoured Division. Mechili had been captured by the Germans, but its stores and, in particular, its precious fuel supplies, had been put to the torch and thus denied to the German victors.

Streich then ordered the panzers on up the Via Balbia and himself went to the 'White House' in Acroma to confer with Rommel. But Rommel was not there. He had rushed off to lead the 8th Machine-Gun Battalion in its attack from the south against Tobruk.

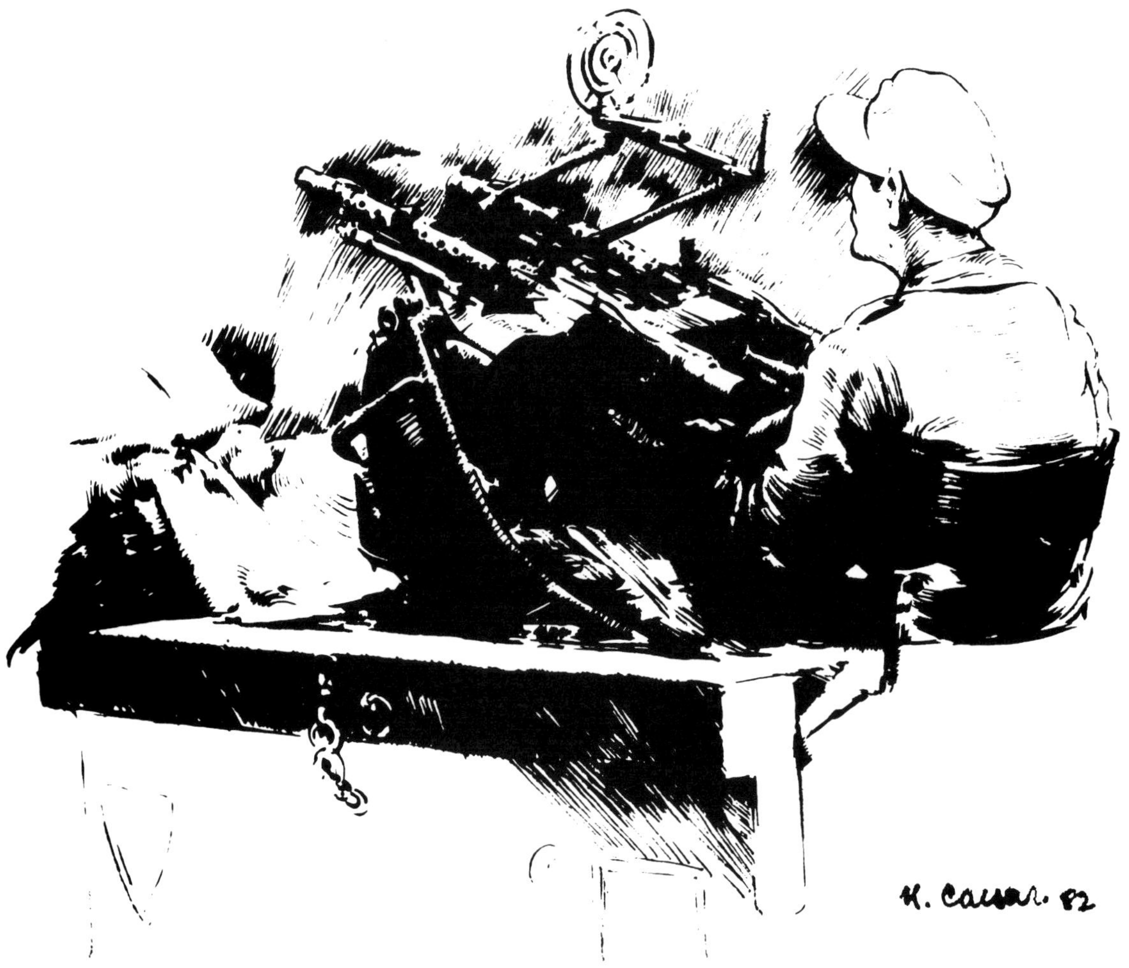

Twin MG 34s mounted for anti-aircraft defence.

# The Second Campaign – April to May 1941

*Rommel fails to take Tobruk but besieges the town and sends out battle groups to capture the Halfaya Pass, the gateway to Egypt.*

It may be claimed, with a high degree of accuracy, that Tobruk was the key to the war in North Africa. There were three major ports along the North African coast – Tripoli in the west, Tobruk in the centre, and Alexandria in the east. Of course, there were also other harbours, but these were either too small to handle more than a couple of vessels at a time or else lacked the cranes needed to unload heavy military vehicles. Tobruk had adequate harbour facilities as well as unloading equipment, and just a few ships arriving in its harbour could bring more supplies or weapons than could be transported by a convoy of lorries, whose vehicles consumed – or perhaps burned up is a better description – substantial amounts of precious fuel.

Aware of its importance, the Italians had created a 54 km perimeter to protect the city and harbour. This consisted of a double-line of fortifications with a 500 m gap between the lines. At 500 m intervals along both perimeters were cement-roofed strong points, all of which were mutually supporting. Each held either a mortar or an anti-tank gun as well as a machine-gun, and was garrisoned by about forty men. The flanks of the perimeter were protected by deep and impassable wadis – the Wadi es Sahal to the west and Wadi es Zeitun in the east. There was also another natural defence: the rising ground on which the town was set contributed to making the fortress well-nigh impregnable. For added protection the Italians had dug and concreted an anti-tank ditch 3.5 m wide and 6 m deep. The above-mentioned strong points lay behind this. There were also belts of barbed wire and extensive minefields. Outside Tobruk a concrete road ran 25 km to a small airfield at El Adem, and within the fortress area there was another small aerodrome.

Although the garrison of Tobruk had consisted of an entire division, morale which was already low had sunk still further when the Italians learned of the speed with which the Western Desert Force was closing in on them. When the British attacked Tobruk in January 1941 it fell quickly, and it was now the

German panzers driving
into El Agheila

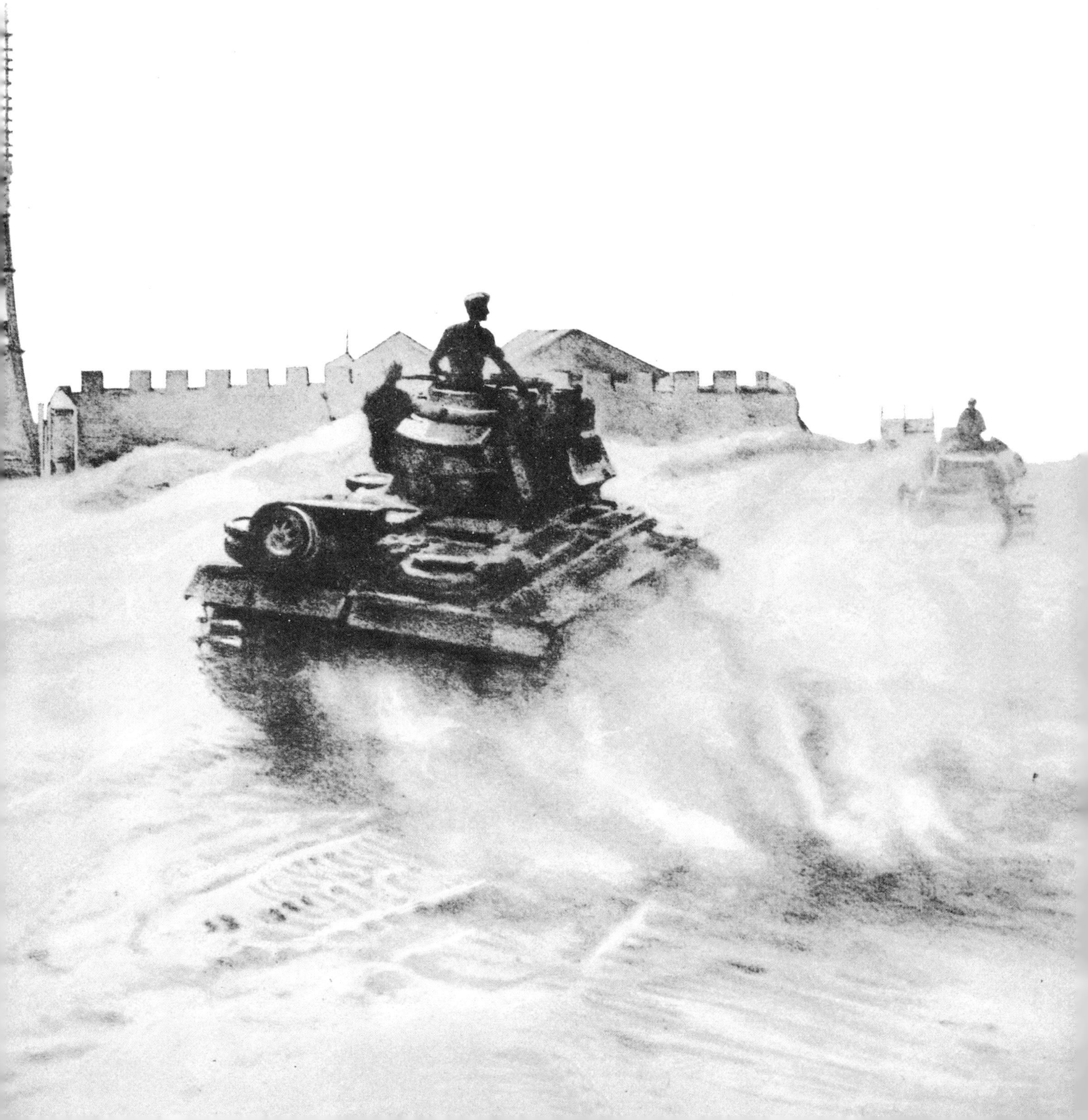

Western Desert Force's turn to hold it against the Axis forces advancing rapidly up the desert road. Well aware of the weakness of the forces under his command, General Wavell, the British commander-in-chief, was given permission to transfer three divisions into the Western Desert which had been fighting in other parts of Africa. The 9th Australian Division reached Tobruk on 7 April and took post in the fortress, where it was subsequently joined by other British and, later, Polish formations. The Western Desert Force garrisoned the outer perimeter with three infantry brigades, holding a fourth infantry brigade and an armoured unit in reserve. Wavell now had a strong force within Tobruk, and deep down in the desert, far to the south of the Via Balbia, he assembled a number of armoured units and some battalions of an Indian infantry brigade. It was the task of this so-called 'mobile force' to confront an enemy which was advancing through the desert with the aim of bypassing Tobruk and to defeat him in open battle. The British were now positioned and ready.

The entry in the War Diary of the Afrika Korps for 9 April recorded that Rommel's intention was to use those of his forces which were driving up the Via Balbia to hold the British frontally, *ie* west of the town. While the attention of the Western Desert Force was thus concentrated upon attacks coming from that sector, he proposed to swing the 5th Light Division in a wheeling movement and attack the fortress from the south. Under those two blows, delivered in quick succession, he considered that the fortress must fall. On 10 April, Rommel issued an order of the day to his soldiers and later that morning briefed his senior commanders. The Axis forces were to advance at their fastest speed up the Via Balbia in line of column, headed by a German advance guard. Behind that screen would come the 'Brescia' Division and then the main elements of the 5th Light Division. The 'Ariete' Armoured Division would follow behind the 5th Light, and the end of the column would comprise as much of the 15th Panzer Division as was ready to join the advance.

The offensive opened with the advance guard driving eastwards until, during the evening of the 10th, the 'White House' was reached, some 40 km west of Tobruk. During the same night the British made their final preparations to meet the onslaught which they knew was coming. Rommel, whose forces were now racing toward the town without a well and properly thought-out battle plan, urged his men on. He was confident that a swift thrust would carry them through Tobruk's defences, and that in the confusion of the assault the town and harbour could be seized.

Chronologically, the first operations around Tobruk fall into three distinct phases. On 11 and 12 April there were probes from the west, followed during the 13th and 14th by attacks from the south and assaults from the south-west which went in on the 16th and 17th. All of those attacks failed. Thereafter, although there were probes, reconnaissances and operations all around the Tobruk perimeter, the focus of attention switched to an eastern outpost around Sollum which Rommel ordered to be set up.

Rommel's orders for the assault on Tobruk had been drawn up in a spirit of unfounded and wild optimism. The Axis situation was not as favourable as he saw it or imagined it to be. The mass of the 5th Light Division was still south-west of Mechili and would not be able to follow the 'Brescia' Division in the pell-mell charge along the Via Balbia towards Tobruk. Both Italian divisions were, in any case, a long way behind the advance guard, and the 15th Panzer Division was still being unloaded in Tripoli. Only two units from the latter could be despatched – the divisional anti-tank battalion and the 15th Motor Cycle Battalion. Forced to adapt his plan to the changed circumstances, Rommel acted pragmatically and gave revised briefings to his senior officers. The commander of the 15th Panzer Division was directed to select positions from which the corps' heavy artillery could shell any ships attempting to leave or enter the harbour. Wechmar's 3rd Reconnaissance Battalion was to advance upon El Adem and seize the town and airfield. The 'Brescia' Division was to set up a concentration area and to lay out a start line from which the main Axis attack would open. General Kircheim, who had chivvied forward the tardy 'Brescia' Division, was sent to find a suitable area from which it could open its attack, but was wounded in a fighter-bomber attack en route to the front line. As he waited for an ambulance the staff car of General Prittwitz, 15th Panzer Division's commander, came racing down the Via Balbia towards him, the shaken driver reporting that Prittwitz had been killed by a direct hit from an anti-tank shell. The British, the driver said, were holding the road in force. It was clear that without support no further advance towards Tobruk could be made. Another concentration area would have to be found. Even before the battle for Tobruk began, the Afrika Korps had sustained serious losses; one General had been killed and another wounded. The degree of opposition which his forces had encountered brought the realisation home to Rommel that he had seriously underestimated the strength and determination of the British garrison.

Worse was to come. At a point about 24 km west of the town the German spearhead detachments crashed into British units holding the road. Their first impetuous rush was slowed and then halted. Annoyed at this check but determined to maintain the momentum of the attack, Rommel, who was up with the leading troops, ordered two battalions of the 'Brescia' Division to sweep the

British from the road so that the advance could be resumed. The Italian units deployed, shook out into assault formations and advanced. They were immediately blanketed by a barrage of artillery and machine-gun fire, and broke. Orders which were issued for the shattered battalions to renew the attack were subsequently cancelled, for it was clear that the British defenders were strong and resolute. Rommel now accepted the bitter truth that the Western Desert Force garrison in Tobruk could not be taken by a coup de main, and that his own forces might well be destroyed if he persisted in launching weak, piecemeal assaults. He halted operations in order to regroup, his units having become spread out along the coast road and strewn across the desert.

However, the orders cancelling the opening attack by the 8th Machine-Gun Battalion had arrived too late. Its first assault had gone in at dawn on 11 April and the unit was out of wireless contact. The machine-gunners came under a rain of fire which halted them. They dug in on the open desert and waited for the barrage to die down. Runners to divisional headquarters, together with walking wounded making their painful way back to the regimental aid post, brought news of the setback. Other runners sent out from divisional headquarters braved the fury of the shellfire to carry orders stopping all further attacks by the battalion until the 5th Panzer Regiment had come forward in support. However, that support was minimal: the number of armoured fighting vehicles which reached the machine-gunners' forward line was just twenty, about the strength of a company. Petrol shortages and navigational errors had prevented the others from arriving. The machine-gunners' lorry-borne companies nevertheless resumed their attack. Driving into action with the panzer company protecting their right flank, they were struck, once again, by a hurricane of British shellfire. The machine-gunners were ordered to debus and continued the attack on foot, marching steadily through the explosions as they rose to a howling crescendo. Amidst the fury of the barrage the machine-gunners' advance faltered and stopped.

The remnant of the battalion began to dig shallow slit trenches once again, but could do little more than gouge out scrape holes in the rocky soil, crouching in these for shelter against the lethal shrapnel flying across the battlefield. Huge clouds of dust churned up by exploding shells and panzer tracks blanketed the whole area. It was truly the fog of war. The panzer commanders, unable to locate or identify enemy targets accurately through the driving sand, could only order their gunners to fire at the muzzle flashes of the British artillery. A number of panzers were knocked out by 25-pdr shells while others, running short of fuel or ammunition, withdrew from the battlefield to refuel and refill their

A view of the battlefield around kilometre 18.2 stone, at Agedabia.

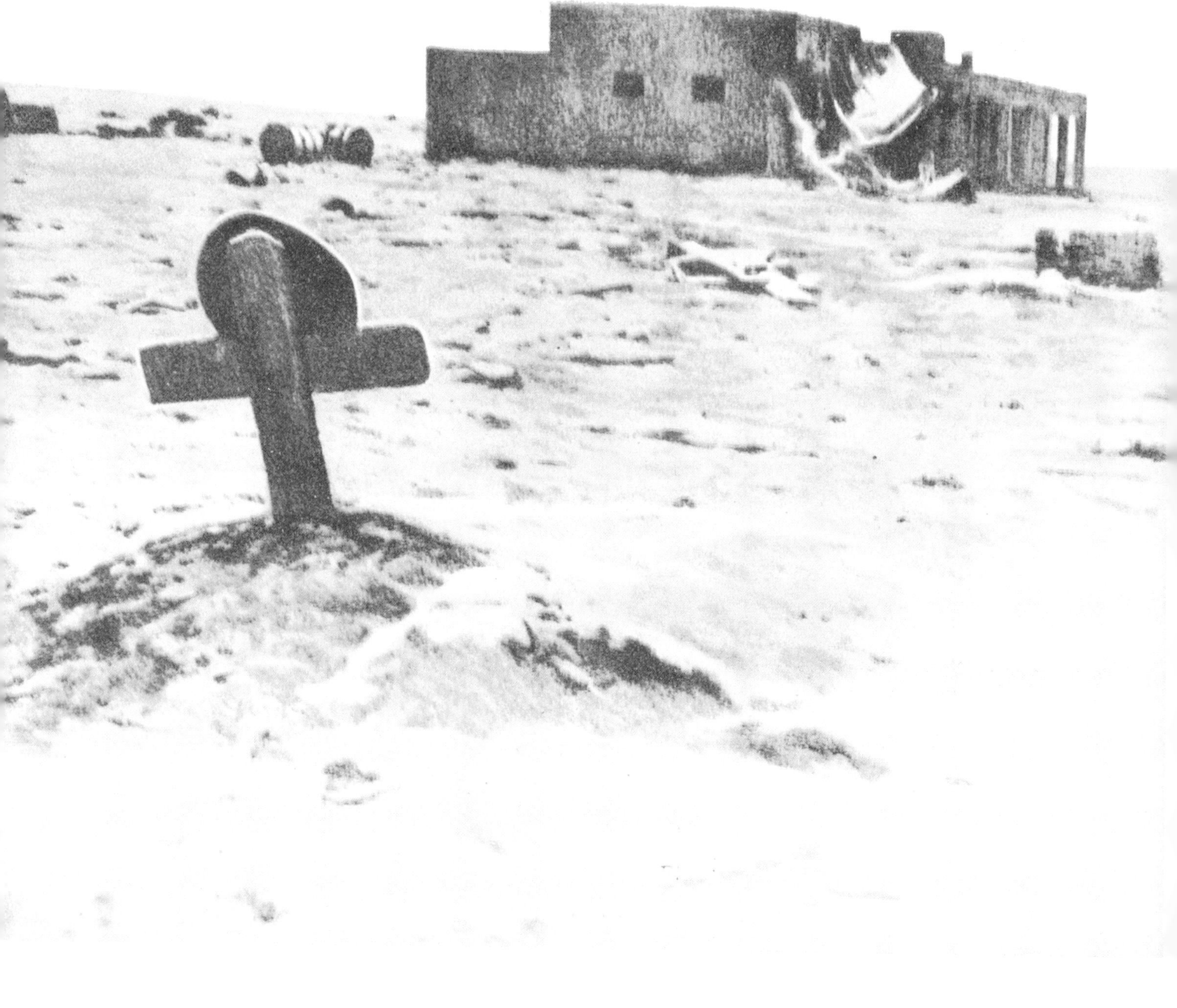

ammunition lockers. The attack could make no further progress, but Rommel insisted that the battalion should make a fresh attempt the following day.

By this time Rommel had flung a cordon of infantry around Tobruk, but it was a very thin cordon which needed to be strengthened with artillery units. Unhappily, there were no spare weapons or vehicles – every gun and truck was already in action. Moreover, the guns of the artillery which had supported the machine-gunners now stood silent: they had fired off all their ammunition and no trucks carrying fresh supplies had come forward. In the absence of conventional artillery, Rommel therefore ordered the panzers to act in the role of self-propelled guns, using their fire to support the 8th Battalion's new assault. The panzers rolled into action at 11.00 hrs, and as the vehicles clattered across the line of infantry scrape holes the machine-gunners climbed out to take advantage of their support. But there had been too little time spent on reconnaissance and liaison, and the panzer commanders, who either had not seen the machine-gunners, or else had miscalculated the speed at which infantry could advance on foot, roared off at speed and soon left them behind. However, the panzers were not gone for long. Within minutes they roared back out of the dust clouds and reported that an anti-tank ditch lay only a few hundred metres ahead. They then drove off, leaving the infantry unsupported. As the dust clouds thinned, the machine-gunners saw that barbed wire fences and the British infantry positions were immediately before them. They were in full view of the enemy, who poured down a destructive fire along their whole front.

For a second time the machine-gunners' attack had to be aborted, but Rommel, still convinced that a new assault would succeed, ordered a fresh one to go in on the 13th. The ammunition situation having been rectified, he intended to smother the ground ahead of the weary 8th with so great a concentration of shell fire that the belts of barbed wire and the infantry positions beyond would be obliterated. Alas for Rommel's intentions, the promised massive artillery barrage did not materialise. Just a single battery of 2 cm light flak guns, whose task it should have been to beat down the last flickers of British resistance, came up to act as the 8th's fire support. These weapons, mounted on light trucks or *Schwimmwagen,* charged forward into the concentrated fire. Not one came back.

Even with no artillery barrage to support them, the men of the 8th Machine-Gun Battalion fought their way forward as far as the anti-tank ditch. There the advance was halted by a hurricane of artillery and machine-gun fire. The battalion commander, Ponath, still determined to carry out Rommel's orders, decided that he would lead his shattered companies in an attempt to infiltrate

A column of Pz IIIs passing the wreck of a British 15 cwt truck mounted with a portee anti-tank gun.

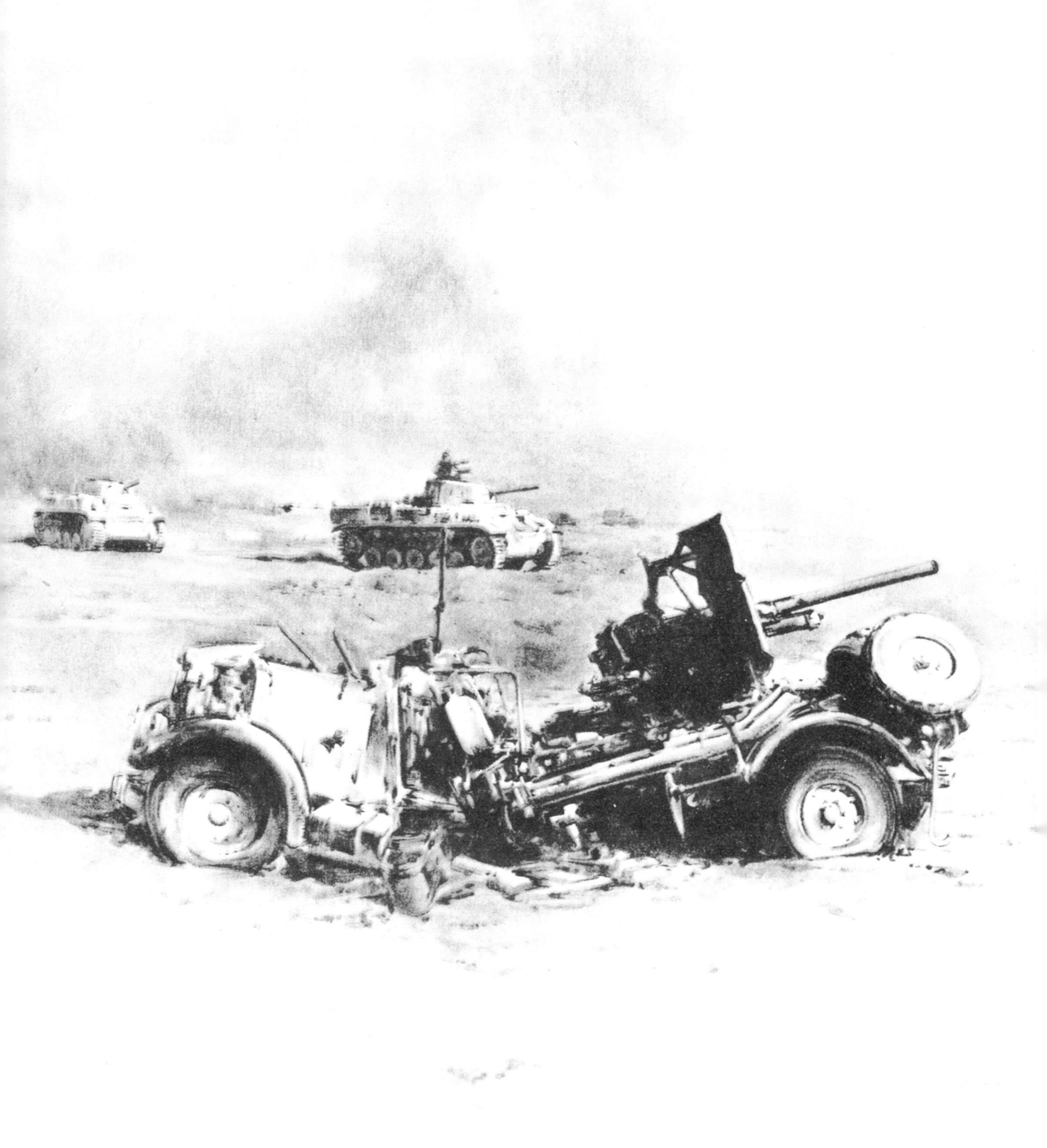

the British positions under cover of darkness. Several attempts were made, but each was driven back by Australian counter-attacks. Nevertheless, German persistence eventually prevailed, a small bridgehead being created in the early hours of the morning. News of this was brought to Rommel, who ordered the panzers in to exploit the gap. Twenty-four machines were all that could be spared, and these reached the gapped area at 03.00 hrs. The British artillery, which had meantime fallen silent, resumed firing as the first vehicles approached the bridgehead. Aware that the panzers would need infantry back-up as they advanced into the British positions, Ponath ordered his men to ride on their backs.

The battle to expand the bridgehead was fought at close quarters, with the Australians either beating off German assaults or else having their own thrusts driven back. Before the sun rose eleven of the twenty-four panzers had been destroyed. The scale of his losses persuaded their commander to order his vehicles to retreat. He expected the machine-gunners to withdraw with him, but they refused to pull back from the positions they had won. Only a succession of hard assaults by the Australians forced them to leave their scrape holes and begin a withdrawal towards their original start line. As they fell back the survivors were caught in a withering fire, and on that day, 14 February, the 8th Machine-Gun Battalion died. It had been in Libya for only fourteen days and in that short time had lost 700 men and all its weapons. The first attempt to break into Tobruk from the south, using a single machine-gun battalion, had failed. With hindsight we know that the fortress could not fall to piecemeal assault, but Rommel had not immediately recognised this, and until he did he continued to mount wasteful attacks.

While the assaults of the machine-gun battalion were being bloodily repulsed on the southern side of the perimeter, Rommel had launched another series of assaults from a new direction. A battalion of tanks from the 'Ariete' Division was ordered to attack on 16 April, but its assaults met with as little success as those of the machine-gunners, and were crushed under the weight of British gunfire. After that the fighting around Tobruk slowly diminished in intensity, and eventually there was a brief lull.

Rommel had been advised that units of the 15th Panzer Division were en route, and was waiting for them to complete the long road journey from Tripoli. They reached him on the 19th, and, impatient to resume the battle for Tobruk, he allowed them only one day to regroup. His orders were that they were to mount an attack on the 20th. Given no time to familiarise themselves with the new and strange conditions of the African theatre of operations, these units were put into action from a point close to the 'White House' outside Tobruk. The first assault went in with great elan but was blown away by the weight of British gunfire. Rommel ordered fresh attacks to be mounted but they too made no gain. By 4 May even he had to concede that the task was beyond the power of the forces under his command. Reluctantly, he broke off the battle; but the exhausted units of the 15th Panzer Division were given no time to rest. Instead he hurried them eastwards, to the enclave round Bardia and the Halfaya Pass.

Let us now consider that outpost. While the main elements of the Afrika Korps had been battling for Tobruk, Rommel had seen beyond the mere encirclement of the fortress, and as early as 14 April had sent a battle group, commanded by Colonel Herff, deep into the desert to protect Afrika Korps' open eastern flank. Herff took his men up to the barbed wire fence which marked the Egyptian frontier and, together with the 3rd Reconnaissance Battalion and a motor cycle battalion, captured Bardia, Fort Capuzzo, and Sollum. Only the Halfaya Pass remained in British hands. He then received supplementary orders: 'The defence of the Egyptian frontier is to be conducted aggressively. There must be constant patrolling to the south and to the south-east to locate the enemy who is then to be attacked and destroyed.' So far as Rommel was concerned, if Tobruk would not fall to direct assault then he would strangle it. The shortest overland supply route of the Western Desert Force from Egypt was through the Halfaya Pass, and if he could capture that objective he could prevent the flow of supplies and units on which the British depended to raise the siege of Tobruk. His forces on the eastern flank were small but they were aggressive, and he would add to their numbers as reinforcements became available.

The strategic importance of the Halfaya Pass cannot be too strongly emphasised. It was the major pass through a high escarpment which ran 80 km or more on a south-easterly line into the interior of Egypt. This long, high escarpment was impassable to vehicles other than by means of the steep, serpentine road which ran through Halfaya to Sollum. Were Halfaya to be captured and held by the Germans and Italians, then the only means by which the British could supply their units in the field was a long haul across the southern desert. The capture of the pass was, therefore, essential for Rommel's future plans. The German attack to seize the Halfaya Pass went in on 26 April – a day later than planned. The assault had had to be postponed after the Luftwaffe had accidentally bombed the German and Italian forces forming up for the assault. Within a day 15th Panzer, using Rommel's battle tactics and supported by other Axis units, had captured the whole defile. Now the Western

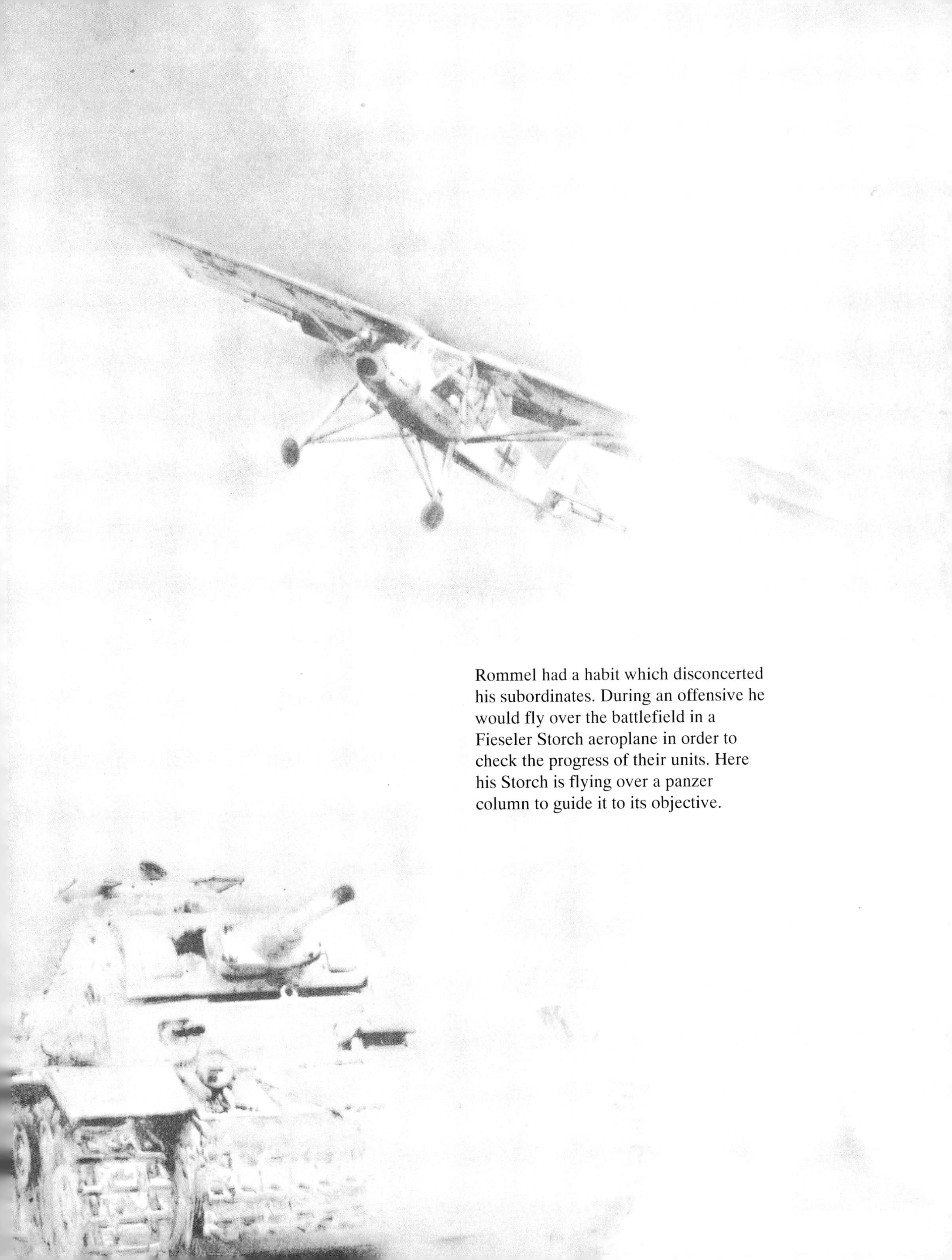

Rommel had a habit which disconcerted his subordinates. During an offensive he would fly over the battlefield in a Fieseler Storch aeroplane in order to check the progress of their units. Here his Storch is flying over a panzer column to guide it to its objective.

Ramcke's paratroops in action against British tanks. The standing man, who is wearing paratroop overalls, has just flung a stick grenade, and the left-hand man is firing a machine pistol.

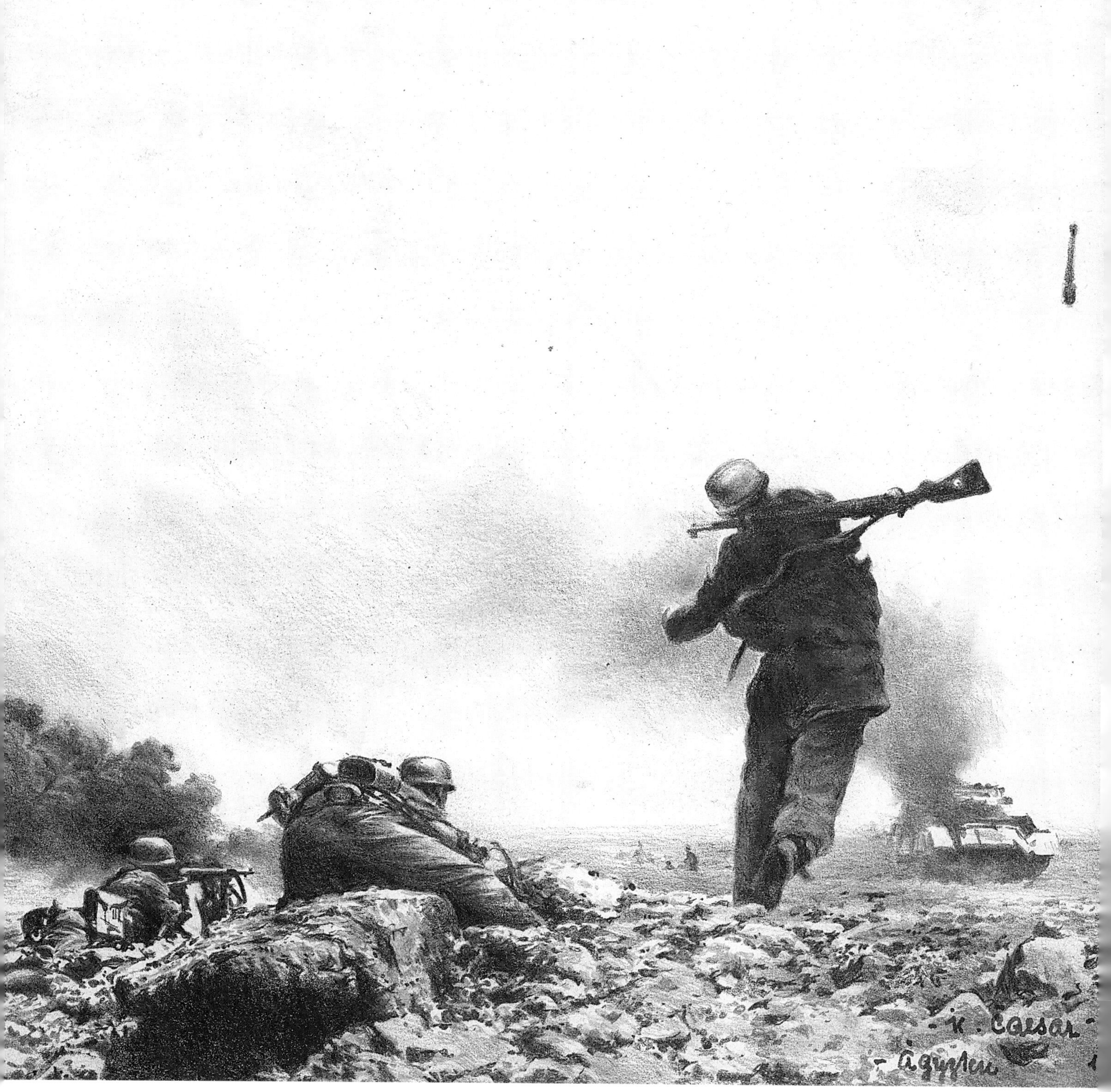

Desert Force would have to undertake the long desert drive via Sidi Omar, and when they did they would be observed by German patrols, giving Rommel the time to take appropriate action. Now that 15th Panzer had gained the victory around Halfaya, it was no longer needed in the eastern enclave and Rommel ordered it to return to the cordon around Tobruk.

Rommel's concern for the situation on his eastern flank was now, albeit temporarily, eased. Reconnaissance forays, wireless intercepts, and other intelligence sources made it clear the British were not yet in a position to mount a new offensive. There was now little that Rommel could do until further reinforcements and supplies arrived, and he was forced to remain impatiently inactive. On the other side of the frontier wire, the British remained aggressive and launched 'Operation Brevity', a series of small-scale counter-attacks to recapture the Halfaya Pass. They supported these assaults with fire from a Royal Navy monitor, a target too tempting for the Luftwaffe to ignore. The monitor was dive-bombed and sunk. But for all his speed of decision and pragmatism, Rommel could do nothing to stop the 'Jock columns' – patrols which ranged across the desert seeking out and destroying German supply convoys. So effective were the 'Jock columns' that they caused the Axis garrison in the eastern enclave to suffer a cut in rations.

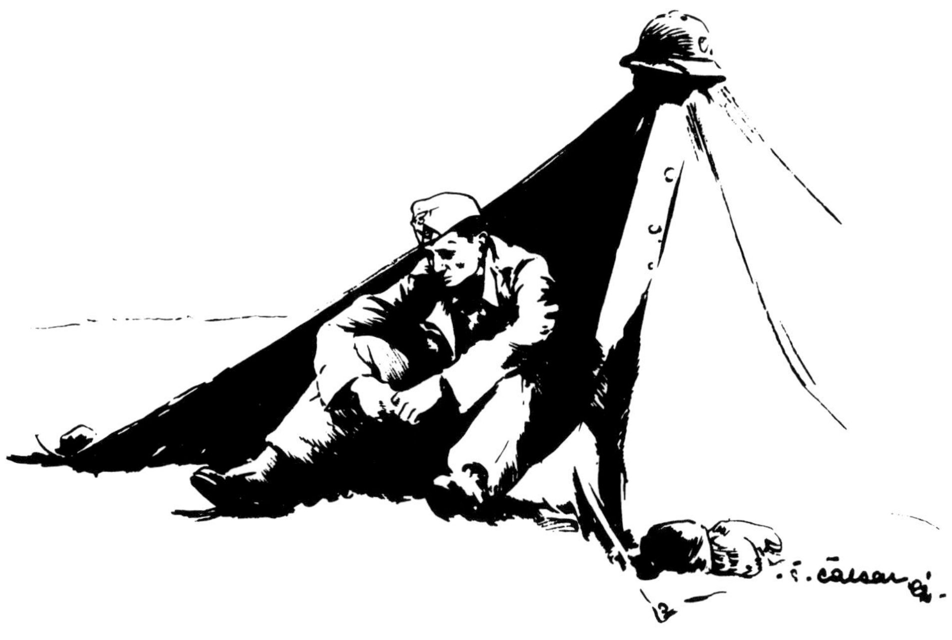

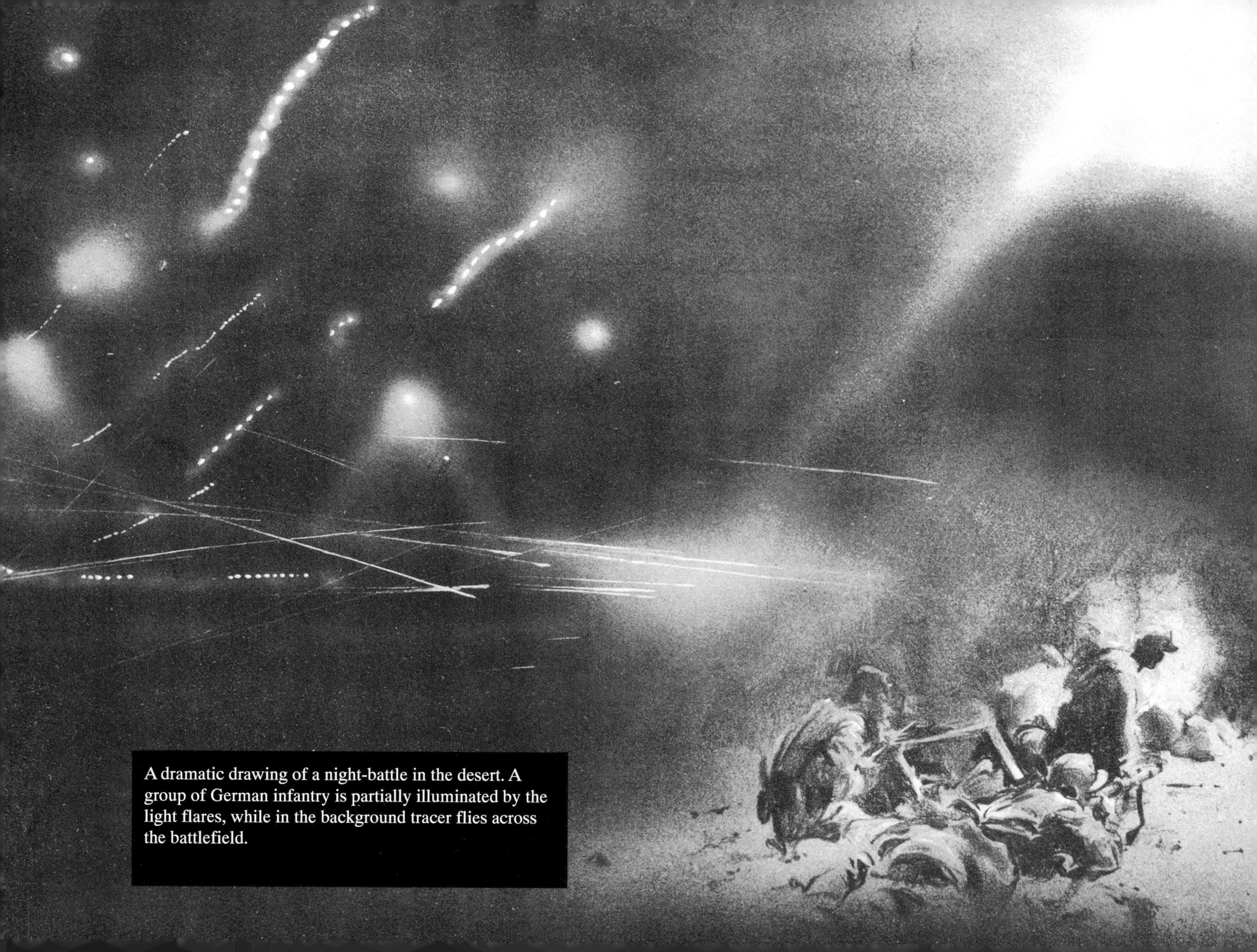

A dramatic drawing of a night-battle in the desert. A group of German infantry is partially illuminated by the light flares, while in the background tracer flies across the battlefield.

# The Third Campaign – June 1941

*Bardia, Sollum and the Halfaya Pass fall to the Axis forces, who set up an eastern enclave. A British offensive between 15 and 17 June fails to raise the siege of Tobruk and is broken off.*

The preceding pages have shown that as early as the beginning of May 1941 Rommel was conducting a battle on two widely separated fronts. Tobruk was still the main one, but temporarily less active, and increasingly it was the Sollum – Capuzzo – Halfaya triangle, the eastern enclave, which caused him more concern. It was worry about this sector of his battle line that prompted him to consider whether or not he should take the newly arrived 8th Panzer Regiment of the 15th Panzer Division from its place in the fortress perimeter and send it to strengthen the eastern flank. In the event he moved it to a deep defence position at El Duda and then, in order to create an even stronger defence arrangement in the desert around Tobruk, ordered the 'Ariete' Division to seize and to hold El Adem.

The arrival of the 8th Panzer Regiment in Tripoli prompted Rommel to believe that he would soon have sufficient troops to undertake the major offensive which would capture Tobruk. Anxious for a more speedy build up of his forces around the perimeter, he sent OKH a signal requesting that the infantry component of 15th Panzer be airlifted in. When the unit arrived, the way in which he handled it during the opening phase of his offensive was to show how ruthlessly he was prepared to sacrifice his soldiers in order to achieve the aim of his battle plan. OKH having agreed to his request, a battalion of the 115th Regiment was flown in to Tripoli. As soon as it had disembarked it was hurried up to the battle zone in such haste that it had to take all its arms and equipment with it instead of these being brought along at a later date as was normal. Still without any rest, the battalion was then

Anti-tank gun in a trench system
in Cyrenaica, 1942.

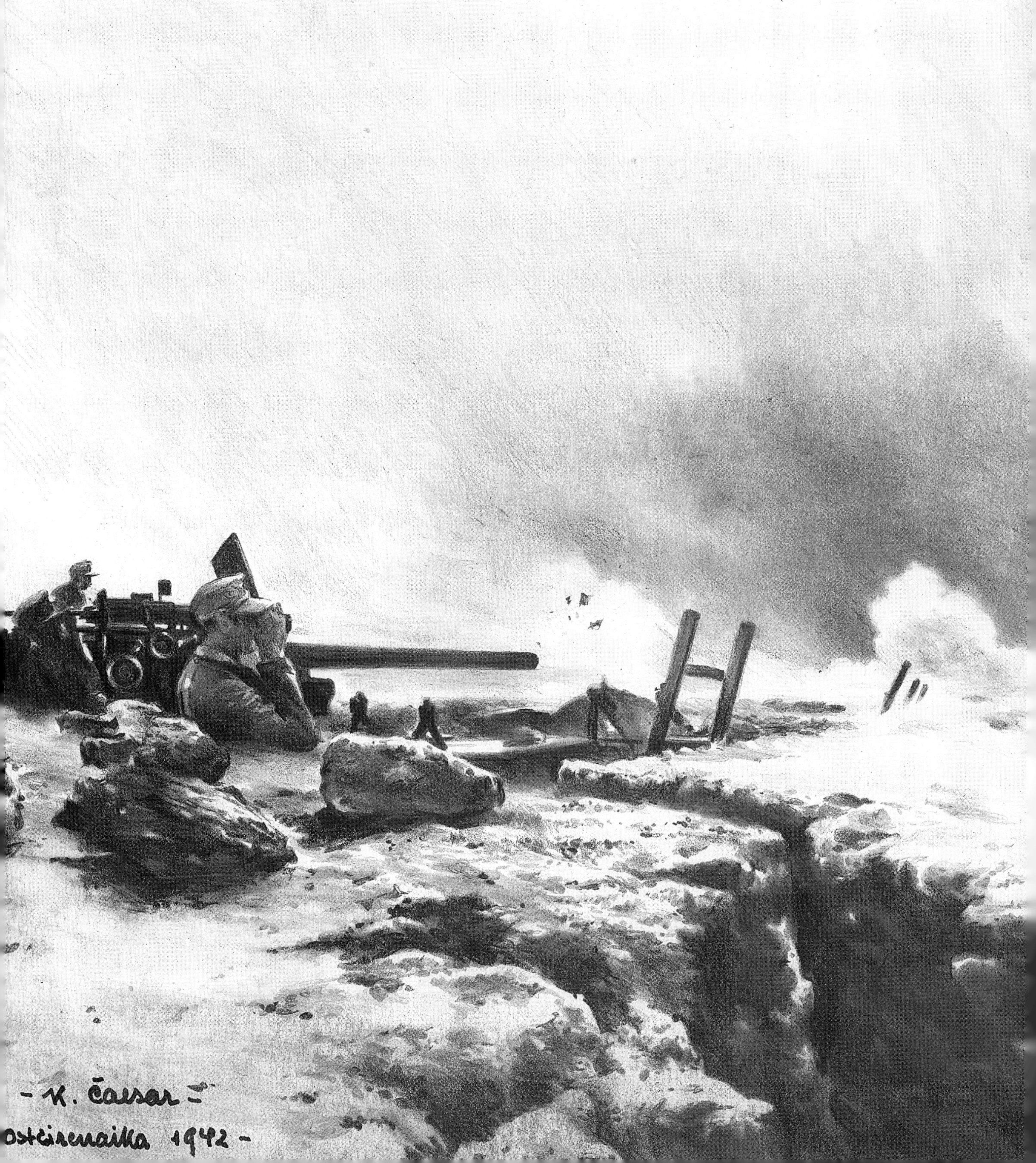

ordered to carry out a night attack aimed at taking out a number of strong points in the fortress perimeter and thereby making a breach in the British defences. In vain did the 15th Panzer Division's commander and the battalion commander protest that their men were being expected to carry out a storm-troop assault, at night and over unreconnoitred ground, while still exhausted from their long journey. Rommel was adamant; the attack would go in as ordered.

It opened at 02.00 hrs on 1 May, and initial reports indicated that the attack was going well. But these reports were inaccurate, for they had been based on false assumptions. The attacking troops had not been told that Tobruk's field defences were sangar-like constructions set at ground level. They had expected to find European-style pill-boxes standing on the desert surface. They had indeed found a few positions built on that principle as they advanced and had captured them. But finding no others they had assumed that all of the strong points had been captured, and it was the reports of these early successes which had given the impression that the attack was making good progress. Most of the ground-level sangars, however, had gone undetected, and had therefore not been taken. From the cover of these positions the Australian defenders fired into the rear of the advancing German infantry. Struck by fire from this unexpected direction the assault began to collapse in confusion. To compound the chaotic situation, the panzer detachment which had been advancing with the battalion suddenly changed the direction of its thrust and moved away from the infantry. This was because orders from corps headquarters, which had not been passed down to the battalion, had directed the armour to go to the assistance of the 'Ariete' Division, whose own assault had been halted by British artillery and anti-tank fire.

The commander of the 15th Panzer Division, realising that firm control was essential, set out for the front line, reaching it in the early hours. He promptly stopped all further infantry attacks. The assault battalion, now on the defensive, had to endure an unceasing, day-long British barrage. Nevertheless, it held the small breach it had won in the Tobruk defences and maintained the tiny bridgehead against a number of Australian counter-attacks. The battalion's efforts are all the more remarkable for the fact that, due to battle conditions and administrative incompetence, it had neither been issued with rations nor

Knocked-out British Bren-gun carriers near Solluch.

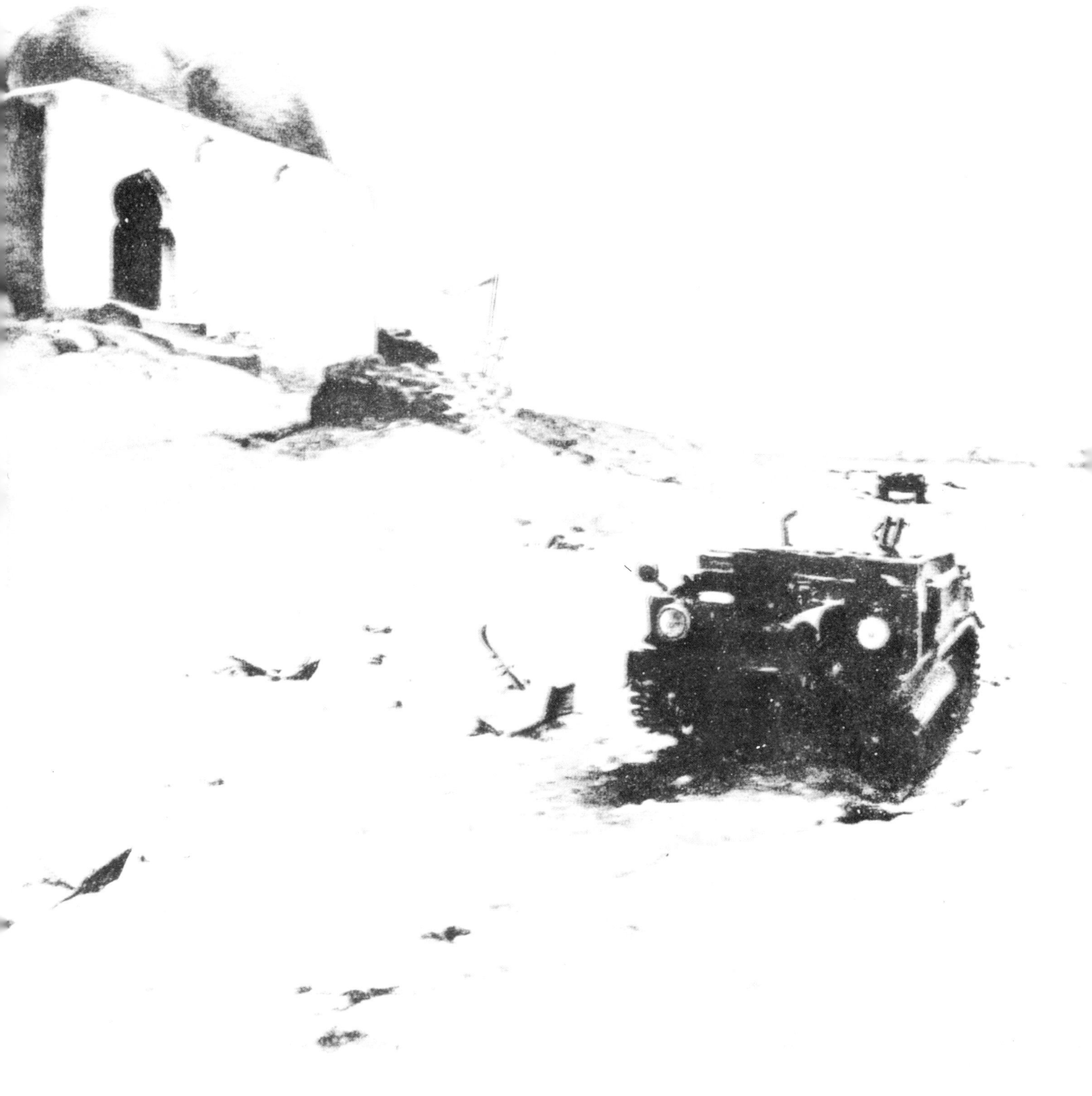

supplied with water. In addition most of the unit's officers had been killed in the attack. But despite being leaderless, hungry, thirsty and exhausted, the battalion's rank and file still continued to mount one attack after another.

Some days previous to that on which the 115th's battalion had made its first disastrous assault, part of a motor cycle battalion and one of the battalions of 104th Regiment were put into an attack on another sector of the fortress' perimeter. The start line for this operation was the 'White House' outside Tobruk, and the attack moved off with as much elan as could be mustered by tired men in the dead of night. The forward companies of the 1st Battalion immediately came under fire from British machine-guns positioned in the sangars, and within minutes the whole battalion had been almost cut to pieces. This attack, as well as others which went in on 3 and 4 May, also failed, proving once again that Tobruk would not fall to assaults of such limited size and power as those which Rommel had thus far mounted – or had been able to mount.

Fighting around the fortress then diminished in intensity and began to die down. By 4 May a sort of calm had descended upon the Tobruk area as both sides reflected on the past period of conflict and considered what the pattern of future operations might be. Some units which had suffered heavily during the first days of May were withdrawn from the perimeter and sent eastwards. Included amongst these was Lieutenant-Colonel Knabe's 15th Motor Cycle Battalion which, together with a number of minor units, was formed into 'Advanced Guard Knabe' and was hurried off towards Sollum, while Wechmar's 3rd Reconnaissance Battalion was ordered to reach Bardia. All these moves were defensive operations designed to strengthen the eastern outpost. The only positive activity around Tobruk during these weeks of inactivity was the construction by Italian engineers of an asphalt road, 75 km long and 8 m wide. This Tobruk relief road, sited beyond the range of British artillery, carried convoys of Axis supply trucks swiftly and in safety.

It will be recalled that in mid-April, Rommel had ordered Battle Group Herff to carry out vigorous reconnaissances along the Egyptian frontier, where it was to confront any advance by the Western Desert Force towards Tobruk. The British, whose military policy has always been to dominate No Man's Land, sent out 'Jock columns' to attack German soft-skin supply convoys. In addition the Western Desert Force had assembled a large, mobile force under Brigadier 'Strafer' Gott, which not only carried out aggressive sweeps across the desert but also sent out reconnaissance detachments to establish the strength, combat readiness and fighting ability of the Afrika Korps units it encountered.

Communications had always played a prominent part in German battle plans. Every major formation had an intercept service which listened in to enemy wireless traffic and transmitted the details back to headquarters for evaluation and action. Rommel was fortunate that the commander of one particular intercept group within Afrika Korps was a master in this type of military intelligence. Wireless traffic between armoured units of the Western Desert Force was the chief source of all German information about British military intentions. The signals which these units sent showed an alarming lack of discretion, and Rommel soon learned from intercepted signals that a British offensive was being prepared to go in against his eastern outpost. Almost concurrently, he also received a post-operational report from Battle Group Herff. This force based in the eastern enclave had carried out a penetration patrol on 12 May, which had probed more than 50 km deep into Egypt. Herff's report made no mention of a build-up of British forces but did contain the confident observation that Halfaya was strongly held by a company of the 15th Motor Cycle Battalion and an Italian artillery battery. Rommel had to compare the reports of his intercept service against that of Herff's reconnaissance. He was not to remain in doubt for long that Herff's report had been misleading.

How quickly the military situation could change is shown by the fact that within a very short time of Rommel receiving Herff's report, which had made no mention of a British build-up, Gott's Mobile Force had launched a major operation. His three-column assault opened during the morning of 15 May. The intention was that while attacks by an Indian infantry battalion held the Germans frontally in the Sollum and Halfaya sectors, a second column, consisting of infantry with armoured support, would position itself near the other end of the Pass and attack Capuzzo. To the west of those groups the tanks of the 7th Armoured Brigade were to drive through the desert and seize Sidi Azeiz. Gott's men went in with a rush and captured the Pass as well as

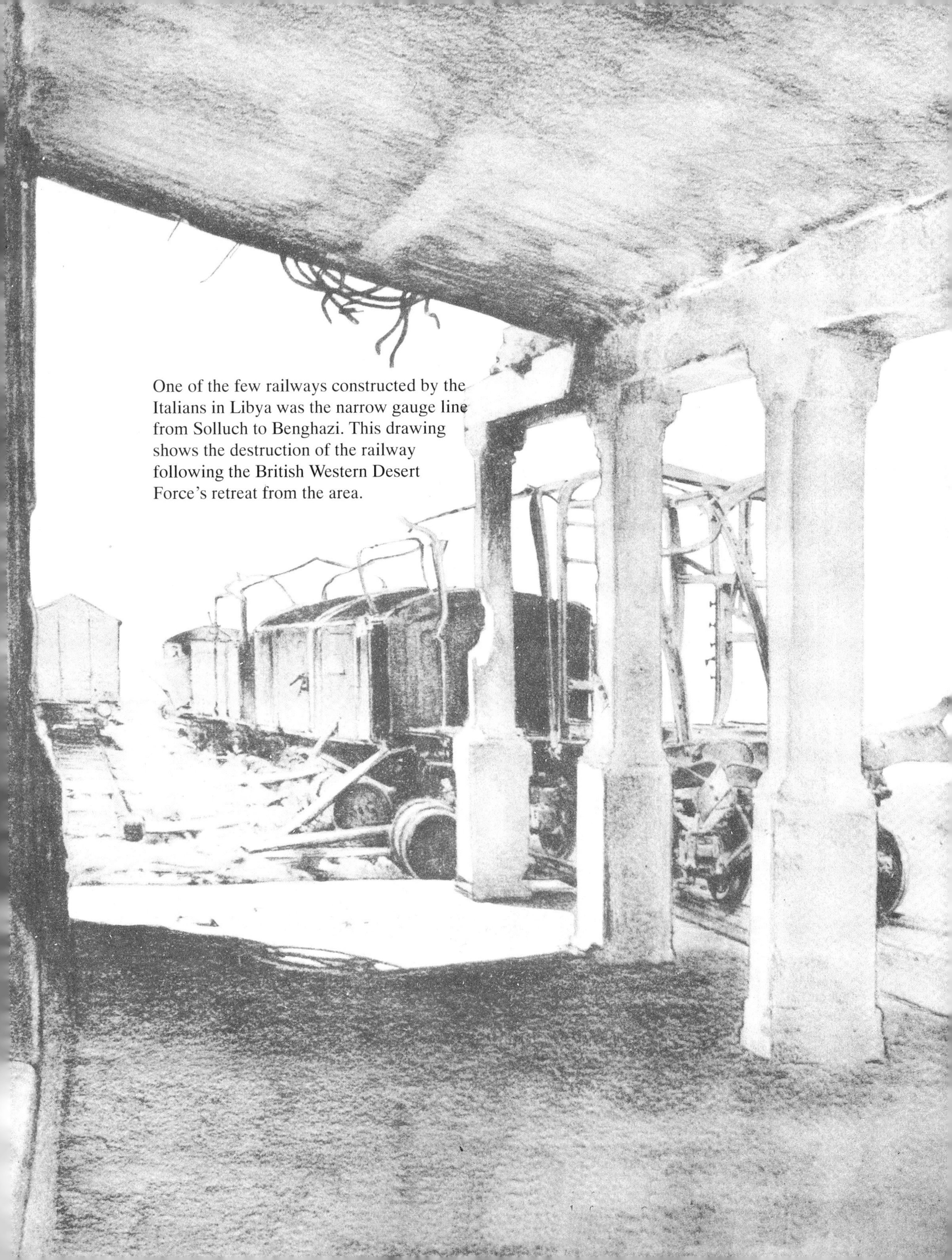

One of the few railways constructed by the Italians in Libya was the narrow gauge line from Solluch to Benghazi. This drawing shows the destruction of the railway following the British Western Desert Force's retreat from the area.

both Sollum and Capuzzo. By the afternoon of 15 May, Herff's group was being forced back northwards. However, not only did it manage to evade direct confrontation with Gott's force but it was also able to march on and recapture Bardia, before going on to seize Fort Capuzzo and Sollum. Though these were valuable successes, the really vital area in the eastern enclave was Halfaya, and Herff signalled Afrika Korps HQ to ask whether his battle group should attack and regain it, to which Rommel agreed in principle.

To provide additional reinforcement to the eastern sector Rommel moved the 8th Panzer Regiment from El Duda, ordering Cramer, its commander, to join forces with Herff's group in preparation for the attack to recapture the Pass. Cramer, whose panzer regiment had been reinforced for this operation with a light and a heavy flak battery, met up with Herff and they planned the combined attack. Both officers were acting in the spirit of the German Army's standard response to any loss of ground, which was to launch an immediate and strong counter-attack to regain it. Rommel's agreement to their signal asking for permission emphasised its importance and stressed that the fate of the Tobruk encirclement rested upon its success. The attack went in on 16 May and the opening moves were encouraging. The combined battle groups quickly took most of their given objectives, but the Halfaya Pass was so strongly defended that it could not be wrested from British hands. Rommel ordered another attack to go in during the early hours of 26 May. This fresh offensive opened with what had now become the classic Afrika Korps attack tactic: the panzers of Cramer's 1st Battalion were positioned in the centre of the battle front and formed up in line abreast, their extended line being protected on the open right flank by the 3rd and 33rd Reconnaissance Battalions.

For the infantry attack – the main blow with which Rommel intended to seize the Pass – he selected the 1st Battalion of the 104th Infantry Regiment, commanded by Captain Bach. This unit was to be supported by a motor cycle battalion, which would act in the role of a mobile reserve. Bach, who had been a pastor in civil life, led his men with such spirit that Halfaya was captured in a single day. Without pause or let up he set about improving its defences and ordered the laying of extensive and intricate minefields. As far as Bach could make it so, Halfaya was rendered impregnable. Rommel, deeply conscious of the dangerous weakness which still existed among his units in the eastern triangle, set about improving the defences which Bach had created and ordered the construction and garrisoning of a number of field fortifications, which were to extend along the tops of djebels and other pieces of high ground from Point 208, deep in the desert, all the way to the Mediterranean. Following the inconclusive and worrying battles of the past weeks, Rommel was determined to ensure that the units on the eastern flank would be strong enough to hold onto the gains which had been made.

As a further example of the confused nature of the struggle and of the speed with which the military situation could change, during the fighting for Fort Capuzzo the Italian 'Montemurro' Battalion was overrun but was then liberated by a panzer counter-attack, which not only released the Italians but went on to retake the fort. The German garrison in Halfaya which had been overrun had no such luck, only twelve of its men managing to escape.

Gott's operation may be seen as a reconnaissance in force, for he soon pulled back his forces to the frontier wire, allowing the Germans to re-occupy the important triangle. It may also be true that Gott's probe was the curtain-raiser for another British offensive which had its background in the directive sent from London to Wavell ordering him to carry out an offensive and relieve Tobruk. Wavell protested that his forces were insufficient to fulfil such an ambition, faced as they were with the might of the German–Italian force. However, London overruled him, and the Western Desert Force began to move across the wire and into Libya.

The preliminary moves of an offensive as complex as Wavell's 'Operation Battleaxe' could not be concealed from the patrols of the 15th Panzer Division, which reported the British advance to Afrika Korps HQ. On 16 June Wavell's units drove up to the Halfaya Pass, where the German ground commander, Captain Bach, ordered his flak gunners to wait until the range had come down sufficiently to ensure that every shot fired was a 'killing' one. When that time came, 88s sited on the floor of the Pass and anti-tank guns holding enfilade positions engaged the British armour. Forcing their way through the hail of German fire, the tank regiments thrust towards the 88s; but then a battery of well-camouflaged Italian guns opened up on them at point-blank range. Within minutes a number of tanks lay smashed or burning. Those which sought to evade the storm of gunfire ran into Bach's minefields and were blown up.

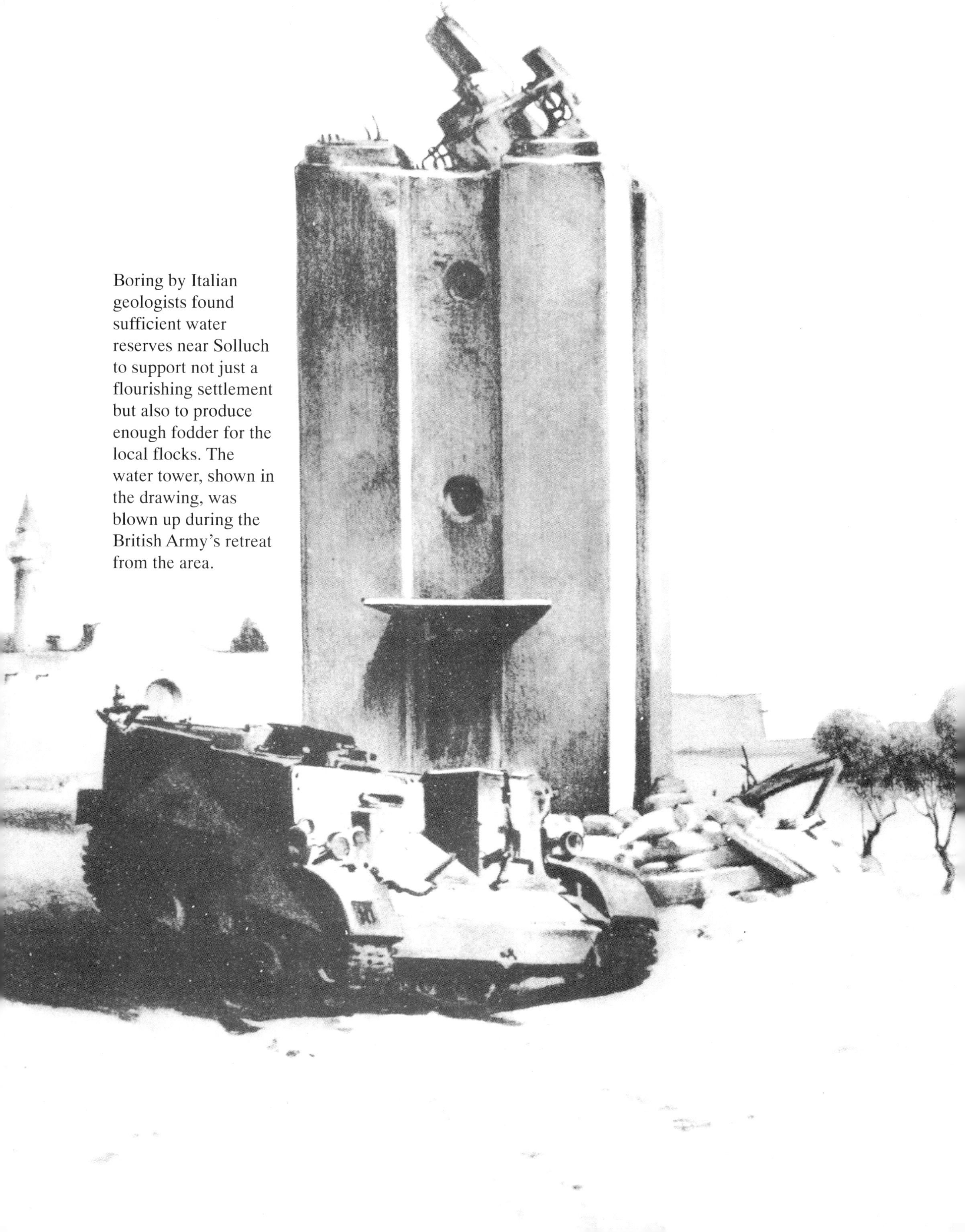

Boring by Italian geologists found sufficient water reserves near Solluch to support not just a flourishing settlement but also to produce enough fodder for the local flocks. The water tower, shown in the drawing, was blown up during the British Army's retreat from the area.

An attack was launched on the Capuzzo sector the same day, when Wavell, dismayed by the poor results of his opening moves but determined to maintain the assault, brought forward more Indian battalions and set them the task of capturing Capuzzo. The British enjoyed one successful action when, further south in the desert, 7th Armoured clashed with the outpost line of 15th Panzer, brushed it aside, and advanced towards Point 208. The initial success of this operation brought hope that Wavell's strategic intention, to thrust into the back of the Afrika Korps, might yet succeed. But it was not to be; that minor victory was followed by a disaster when a detachment of British tanks rolling into the assault was taken under fire by a battery of 88s, which exercised excellent fire control. The German artillery commander allowed the British machines to come close in before ordering his guns to open fire.

In an armour versus gun scenario there was a simple equation known as 'gun density'. In this, if a gun line was attacked by more tanks than it could 'kill' before the enemy machines opened their own destructive fire, then the gun line would be destroyed. The same equation applied in reverse, if too few tanks faced a larger number of guns. In the guns versus too many tanks scenario, the imbalance could be reduced if the gun line commander and his crews had strong nerves. The artillerymen would have to wait, watching the armoured fighting vehicles coming closer and closer, until their commander was certain that every shot fired would be a 'killing hit'. In the case of the four-gun battery involved on this occasion, the commander took the calculated gamble that his men could fire so rapidly that the British sevenfold superiority would be cancelled out. In the event they could and did. The British armoured regiment turned away leaving eleven of its tanks destroyed.

At 11.00 hrs the survivors of the original thirty vehicles, now reinforced to a strength of seventy tanks, returned. At a distance of 1000 m the German guns spoke again. The battery commander was confident. He knew that his 88s outranged the main armament on the British machines, and that even if the tank guns had been able to reach the German artillery line, their shells would have little penetrative effect. Also, British vehicles carried only solid shot in their lockers – armour piercing shells. (Panzers carried, in addition to solid shot, high-explosive shells for use against infantry or artillery ground targets. The explosion of a HE shell flung off steel fragments which could kill

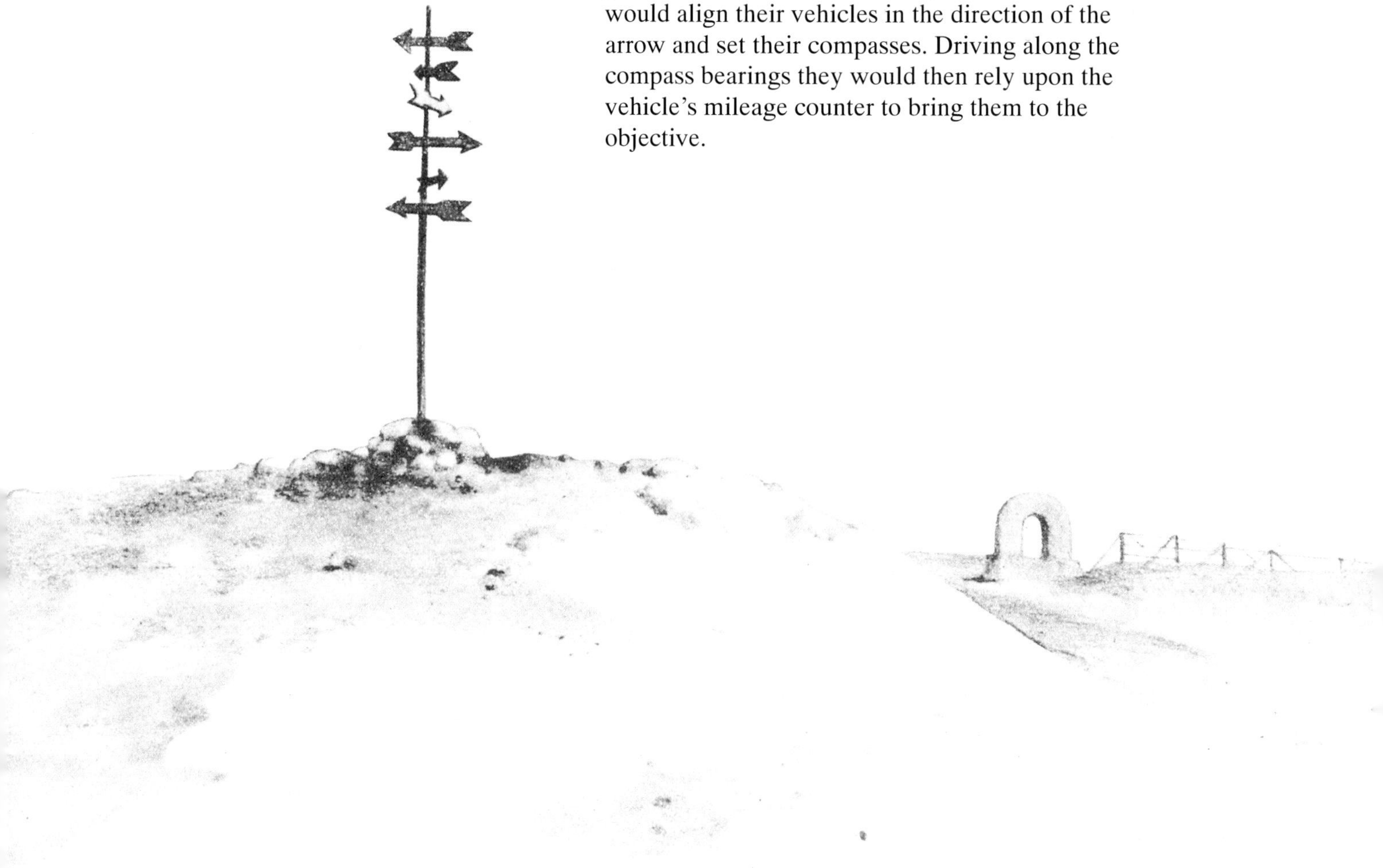

The signpost at Mechili was famous throughout 1941. Wooden arrows nailed to an upright post pointed to a number of distant places. Drivers would align their vehicles in the direction of the arrow and set their compasses. Driving along the compass bearings they would then rely upon the vehicle's mileage counter to bring them to the objective.

infantrymen or a gun crew. Solid shot did not.) The British regiments advanced again in the heat of the early afternoon, the vehicles this time forming two waves. As before, the attack broke up under the fire of the 88s. Only one tank fought its way through the shellfire, getting close enough to ram and overturn an 88 before escaping undamaged, pursued by a flurry of shots from the battery's remaining guns.

A fourth tank assault, a forlorn hope made by only ten machines, was destroyed at long range. After a short pause a fifth attempt was made. This one was heavier in weight, involving eighty-five machines according to the Germans. The vehicles thrust forward, aiming to take the tactically important Point 208, but just as it seemed that this assault would overwhelm the battery's guns some panzers of the 5th Regiment emerged from a shallow wadi and took the British tanks in flank, momentarily averting the danger to the flak battery. This episode illustrates the speed and confusion which characterised armoured conflict in the desert.

The fighting in the eastern enclave had been more than usually confusing, with both sides seeking to attack from a flank or from the rear. The blindingly hot midsummer days were filled with a great many minor engagements in which Axis and British units advanced or retreated, only to find themselves confronted and under fire from new enemy formations attacking from an unexpected direction. The pace of the battles was exhausting, and the need to find supply and fuel columns was always a difficult problem. It was a time of small unit operations with little control from divisional or corps headquarters. Speed of decision and immediate action were the factors which decided life or death.

It was during the final stages of Wavell's offensive that British wireless traffic from the tank regiments reported they were low on ammunition. These messages to Western Desert Force HQ were overheard by the German intercept service and passed to Afrika Korps headquarters, where the atmosphere immediately changed from one of concern about the outcome of the fighting to realisation that a complete victory was about to be won. The constant and enduring worry for the corps was whether the Axis garrison in the Halfaya Pass could hold out. If it could, then the British supply route was long, slow and difficult. If the Axis units were overrun, then Wavell could reinforce and supply his formations in the field swiftly and surely. The outcome of 'Operation Battleaxe' depended upon who held the Halfaya Pass. The German garrison was still fighting hard and confident in the belief that victory was in sight. The soldiers of the Afrika Korps went into battle with heightened elan. In the haste to be first into the field the gunners of the 88 mm flak batteries drove ahead of the panzers of the amalgamated, but depleted, forces of the 5th Light and 15th Panzer Divisions as these poured across the desert to deal the death blow to the British. In the first clash of 16 June, the 7th Armoured Division lost fourteen tanks, but at Sidi Suleiman its units put up strong resistance to the assault by the 5th Light. The German division's advance was halted, and remained so until Stuka dive-bombers scattered the British armoured units and allowed the panzer advance to resume.

Despite being low on ammunition, the 7th Armoured Division–still controlling some 300 vehicles–fought on, and took out both Capuzzo and Musaid. Units constituting the main body then wheeled southwards, aiming to capture Point 208, and struck through the 15th Panzer Division's outposts, while a smaller group of tanks retook Sollum and Bardia. The advance of this smaller group threatened the German hold on the eastern outpost until a lieutenant of the 33rd Pak (anti-tank) Battalion commandeered a single 88 mm gun and brought it into action against the British vehicles rolling down towards him. He destroyed three in quick succession, forcing the remainder to seek escape under the cover of smoke shells. It was then that support and relief came to the officer and his gun crew, as the 1st Battalion of Cramer's 8th Panzer Regiment arrived and engaged the tank group. The panzer commander, Captain Kummel, who for his actions that day was to become known as the 'Lion of Capuzzo', destroyed eight tanks. When the 8th Regiment's 2nd Battalion also joined the fray the British regiments pulled back. It had been a hard-fought struggle: the 8th Panzer Regiment had lost fifty of its eighty machines, although some were later repaired.

At 11.00 hrs on 17 June, 7th Armoured Division's commander gave the order for his regiments to withdraw. The reason which forced this decision was that, as German wireless intercepts had indicated, the British tanks had fired off all their ammunition: they had neither the means to attack targets nor to defend themselves, and no supply or fuel columns had been able to reach

A military cemetery near Derna, with the graves of fallen Italian and German soldiers.

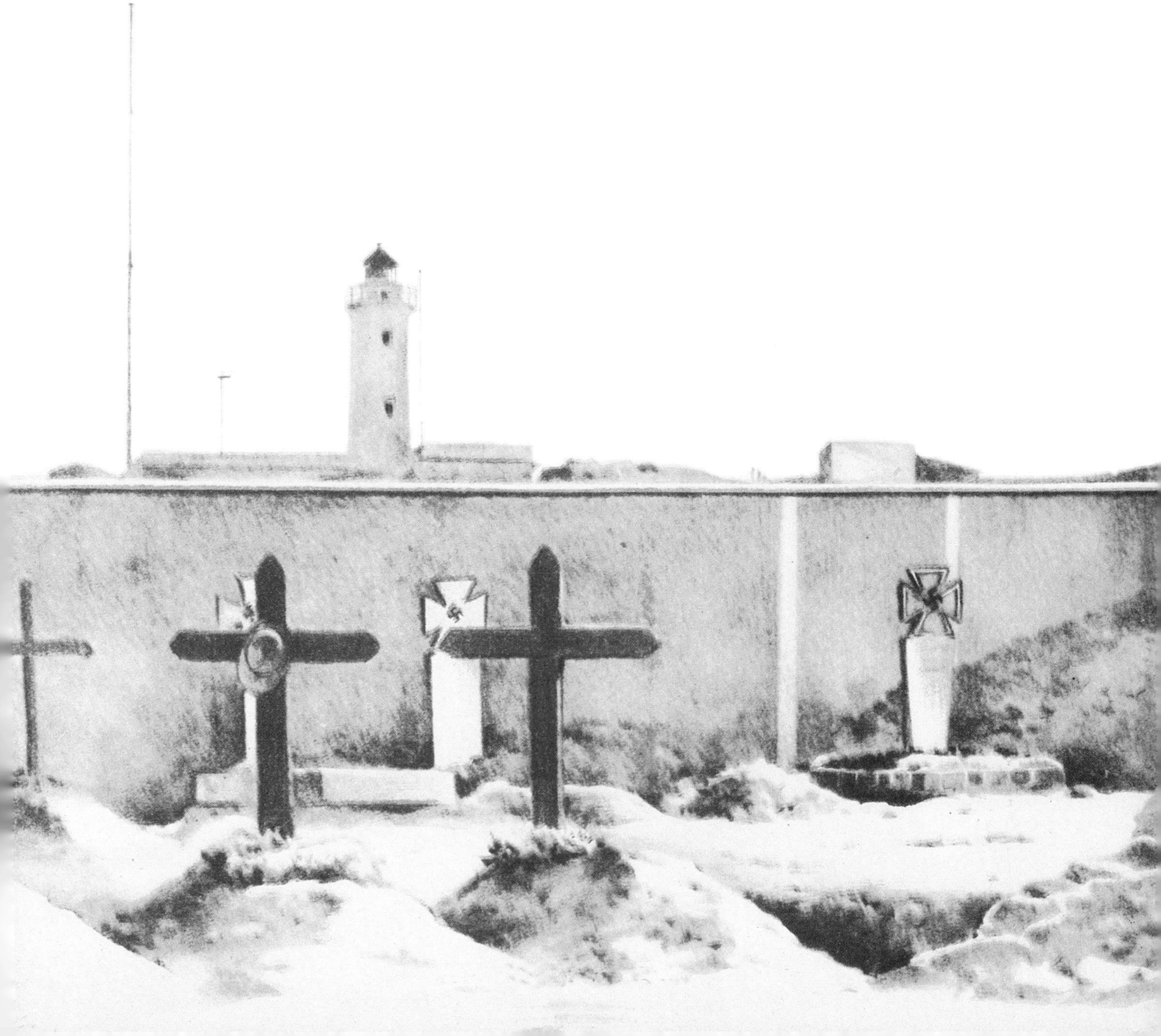

German troops to the south-east of Mersah Matruh. In the right foreground is a Panzer IV with a short-barrelled 7.5 cm gun. To the left a half-track is towing a field-gun, while in the centre and the far distance are various soft-skin vehicles.

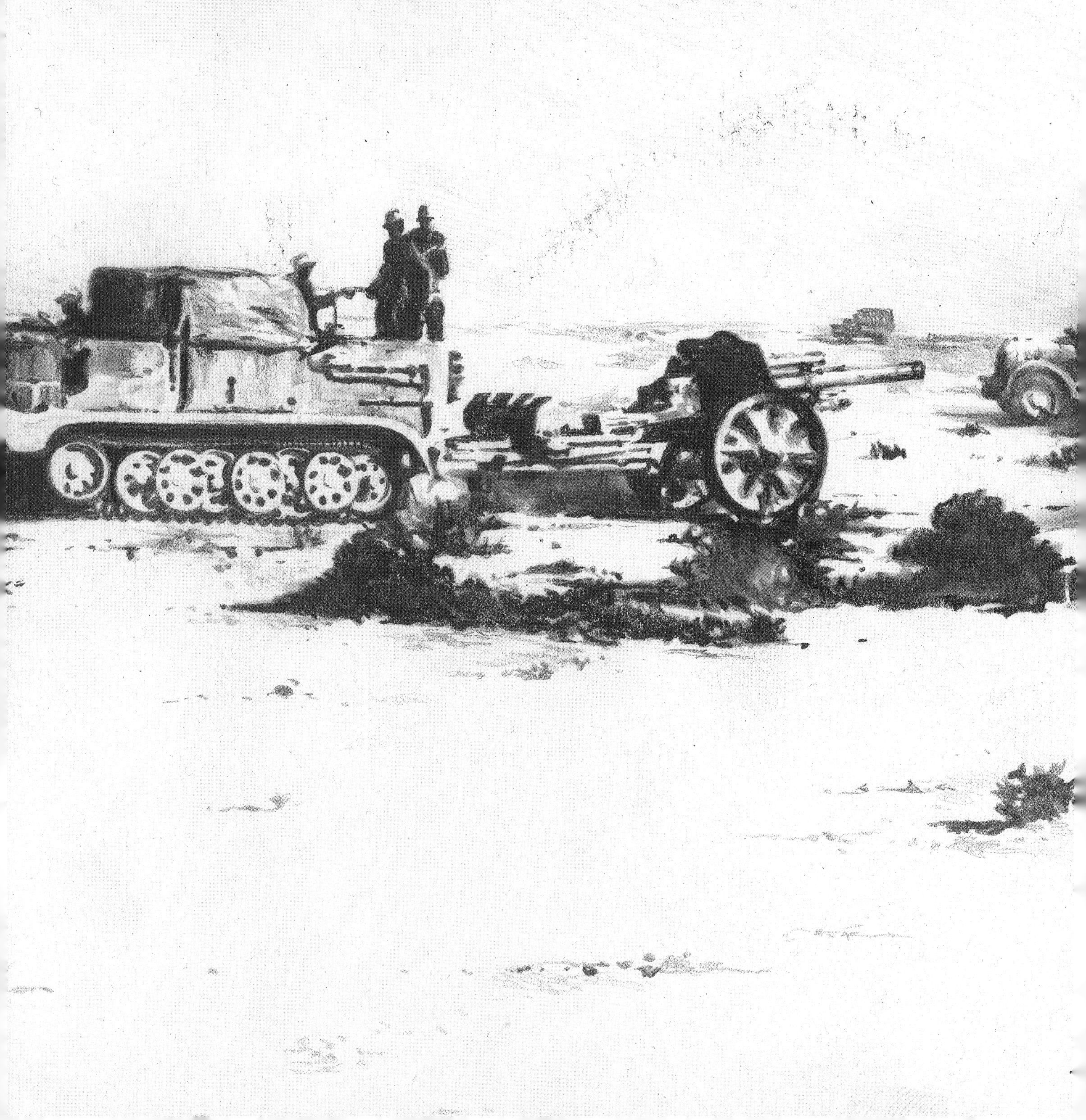

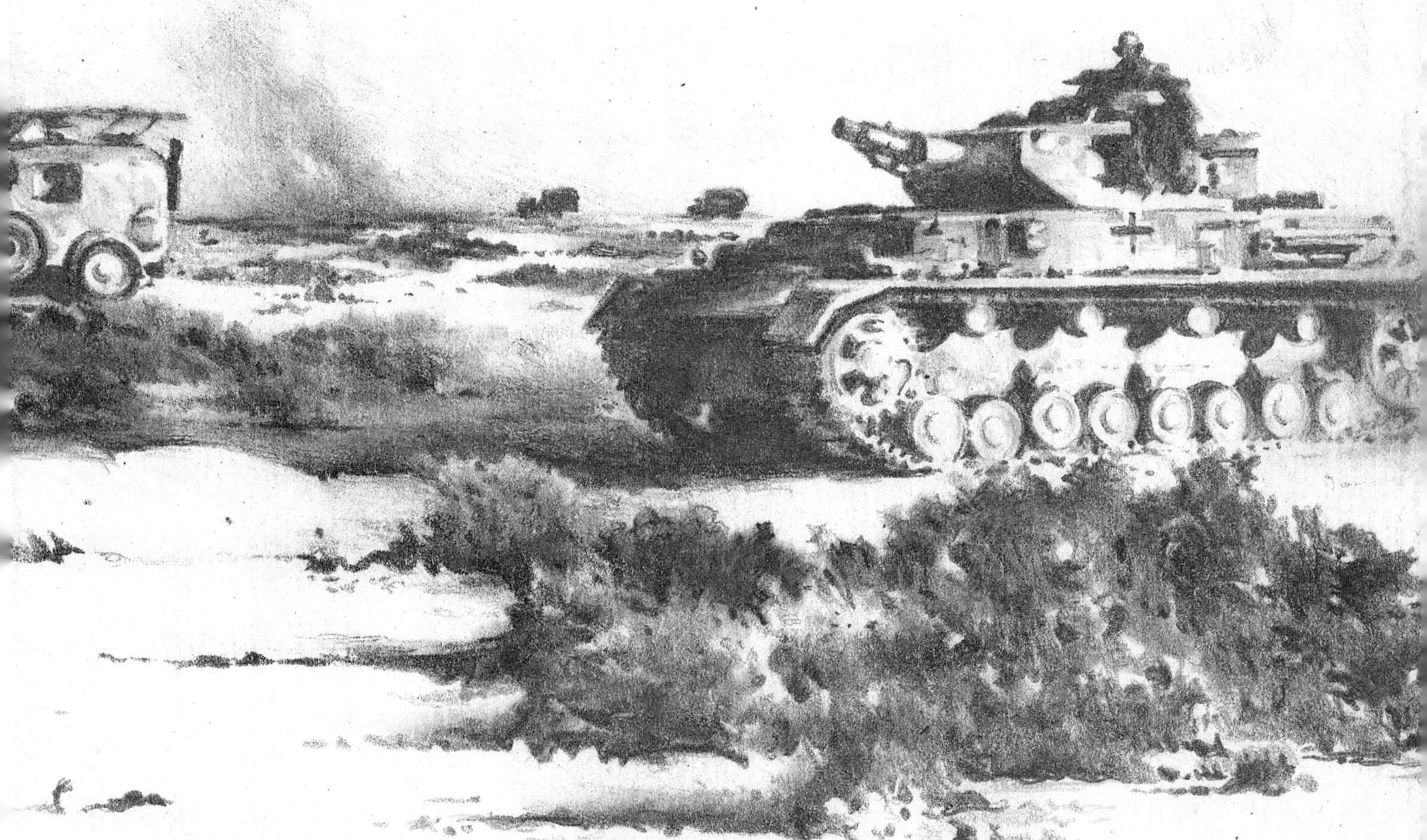

The 'White House' on the Via Balbia outside Tobruk. This house was referred to in many accounts of the fighting of 1941, particularly in the first attacks on Tobruk.

them. Flight was their only salvation, and they withdrew from the battlefield. Late in the afternoon of the 17th the two German divisions closed front and advanced towards Halfaya, forcing back the 4th Indian Infantry Division units which had been attacking the Pass. The greatest part of the Western Desert Force then began to stream back across the frontier wire into Egypt. Afrika Korps was master of the eastern enclave again. All that remained to be done was for its units to round up British prisoners and bring in undamaged weapons, rations, and usable equipment.

The three day tank battle of Sollum was at an end. It had been a confused action. As regards gains and losses, the British had lost 200 tanks, so that the armoured strength of the Western Desert Force was reduced to just twenty-four machines. On the German side, the 15th Panzer Division lost fifteen and the 5th Light Division ten of their establishments. Three days later Afrika Korps' first-class workshop repair organisation had brought the strength of these formations back up to a total of 136 'runners.' A British book published in 1956 stated: 'Operation Battleaxe, which had begun so full of promise, failed because we failed to take the important Halfaya position and to bypass the strong point on (Point) 208. The bravery and firepower of the enemy was too much. The German 88 proved itself to be a deadly weapon against all types of British tank. Rommel's victory was a victory of his leadership, of the superiority of his fighting troops and his better weapons.'

It was clear to Rommel that only with a strong reinforcement of men and massive amounts of equipment could his aim of destroying the British Army in Libya be realised. Although priority had to be given to the war on the Eastern Front, both OKW and OKH accepted Rommel's requests for weapons, men and supplies, but their good intentions were frustrated by the inability of the Italians to convoy the men and machines from the European mainland to the Libyan theatre of operations. The Afrika Korps needed an absolute daily minimum of 1500 tons of supplies, but this amount seldom arrived because the Royal Navy and the RAF were sinking so many vessels in the Italian convoys. In addition, Italian merchant marine skippers were afraid to bring their ships to the small ports behind the Axis front for fear of being bombed by the RAF.

They therefore tied up their vessels in Tripoli, which meant that every piece of equipment, every soldier, every piece of firewood, and every box of rations, had to be taken by road to the front line, now nearly 1500 km away.

Rommel proposed that he be allowed to re-open the battle for Tobruk during August, but both his German and his Italian superiors rejected his pleas, instead naming November as the earliest month in which the operation could open. During the period from June to November 1941 both sides regrouped and trained. Wavell was replaced by Auchinleck, and the old Western Desert Force was renamed the Eighth Army, and reinforced by a number of new divisions sent from the United Kingdom. Reorganisation on the German side saw the Italian General Gariboldi replaced as commander-in-chief by Bastico, and there was an increase in German strength in August, when the 90th Light (Africa) Division came on to establishment. During October, the 5th Light Division was renamed the 21st Panzer Division.

Aggressive, wide-ranging and deep penetration patrols sent out by Afrika Korps throughout the summer and autumn of 1941 found no evidence that the Eighth Army was preparing a major new offensive. Secure in this knowledge, Rommel drew up plans for the attack with which he intended to reduce the Tobruk fortress. He waited impatiently for the time to arrive when his superiors would allow him to initiate the new offensive. In the meantime he utilised this period of little military activity to build up his artillery arsenal to a strength of 4651 barrels of all calibres, the greatest number of guns he had ever had under his command. His soldiers were well and thoroughly trained and of high morale, his stores were adequate for the task ahead, and he was convinced that this time his offensive would not fail. Tobruk would fall, the Eighth Army would be beaten, and he would go on to seize the strategic prize of the Suez Canal.

German infantry somewhere near the Via Balbia. From their attitude it would seem that they are receiving orders from a commander in the recce half-track vehicle in the middle distance. The infantry are probably paratroops from Ramcke's Brigade.

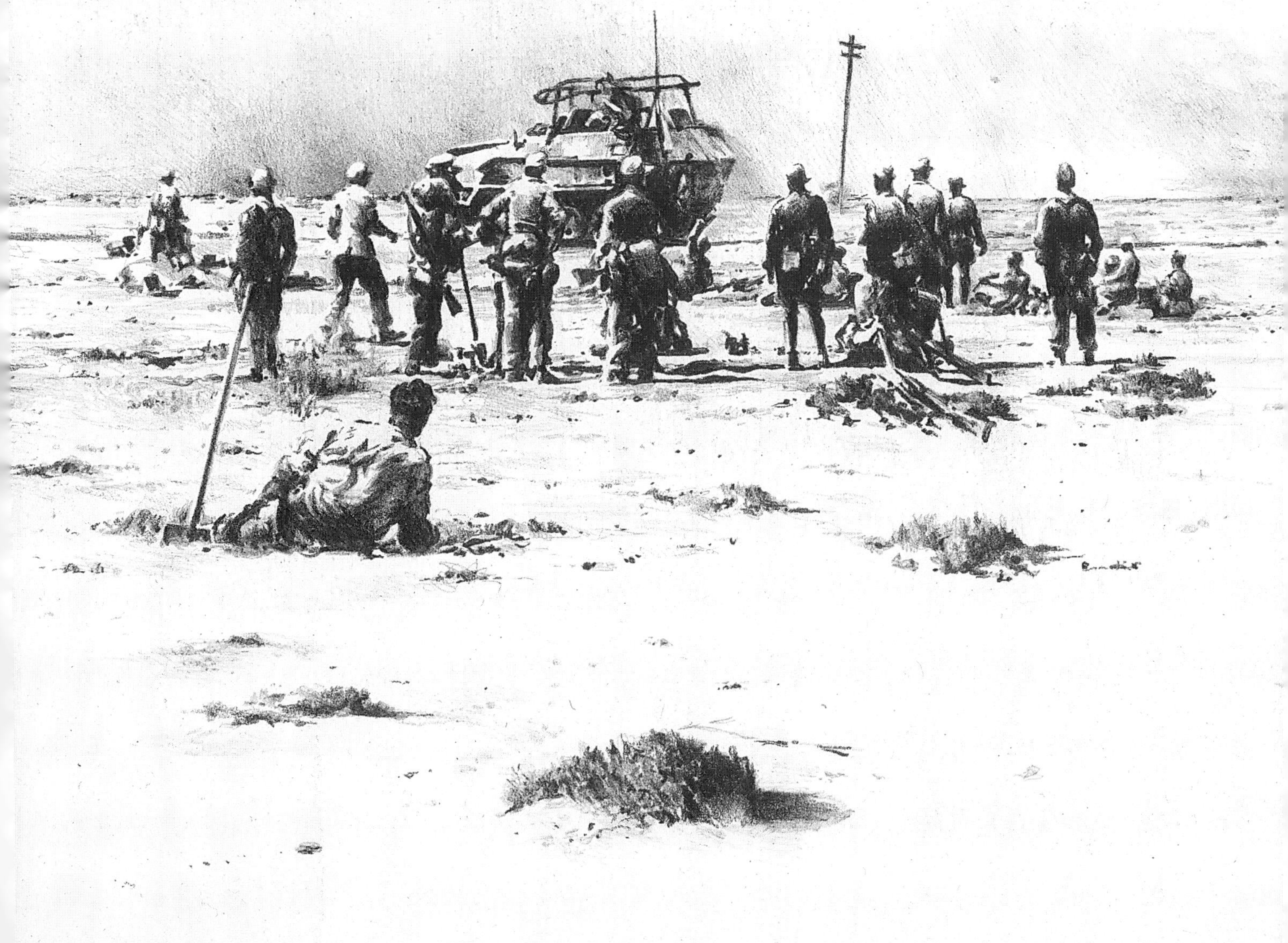

Caesar's note at the bottom of the picture says 'Bir Hachim', and the prisoners it depicts are probably soldiers of the Free French forces which had defended this fortress at the southern end of the Gazala line. Bir Hachim fell during the Gazala offensive. In the foreground are several British anti-tank mines.

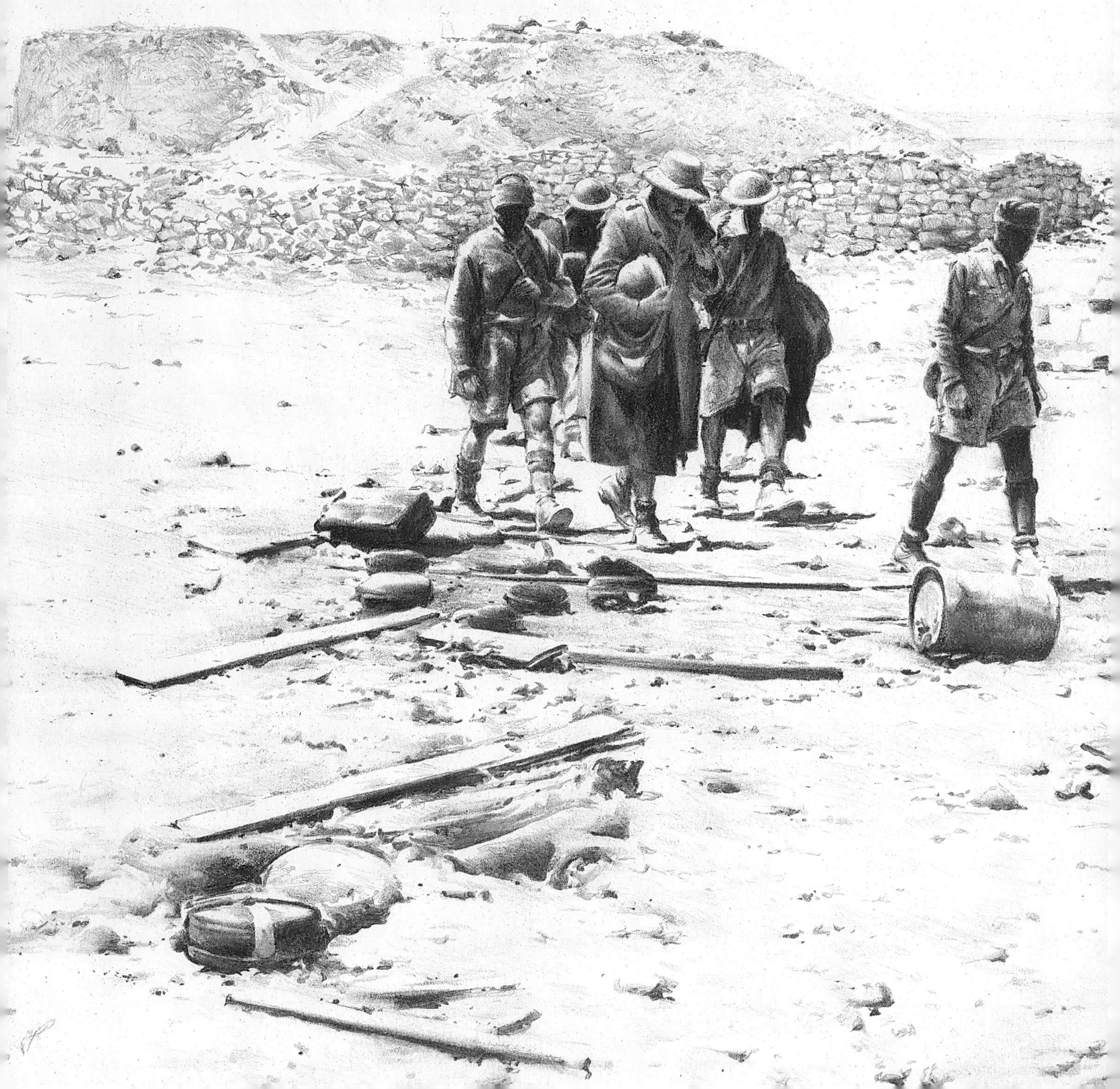

# The Fourth Campaign – November 1941 to February 1942

*The second British attempt to relieve Tobruk results in heavy and confused fighting, at the end of which Rommel is forced to retreat back to the area from which he opened his first campaign. He recovers swiftly and launches a counter-offensive, which drives back the British Eighth Army and reaches the Gazala line.*

The June battles had ended inconclusively and in their wake both sides planned for what each expected would be the final offensive. The strategic target for both sides remained what it had always been, the fortress of Tobruk, and it follows, therefore, that the port played the central role in their operational plans.

The first part of the British plan was to raise the siege using both its corps, XXX and XIII. For that first part of the offensive, XXX Corps – the armoured and therefore the more mobile force – was to thrust north-westwards between Maddalena and Sidi Omar and go on to reach Gabr Saleh, some 50 km further westward. En route it was to find and to destroy the enemy armour. It had the additional task of protecting the left flank of XIII Corps. The principal task of XIII Corps – an infantry, and thus less mobile, formation – was to pin down and cut off the enemy troops in the eastern enclave, and later to advance westwards towards Tobruk. The 4th Armoured Brigade, which had an independent role during the offensive, would form the link connecting both corps. The Tobruk garrison was to make a sortie when the Eighth Army gave the order. Oasis Force, an Indian infantry brigade with armoured car support, was to secure Jerebub and then advance to protect Landing Ground 125 and seize Jalo. The second stage of the Eighth Army's offensive foresaw a set-piece battle which

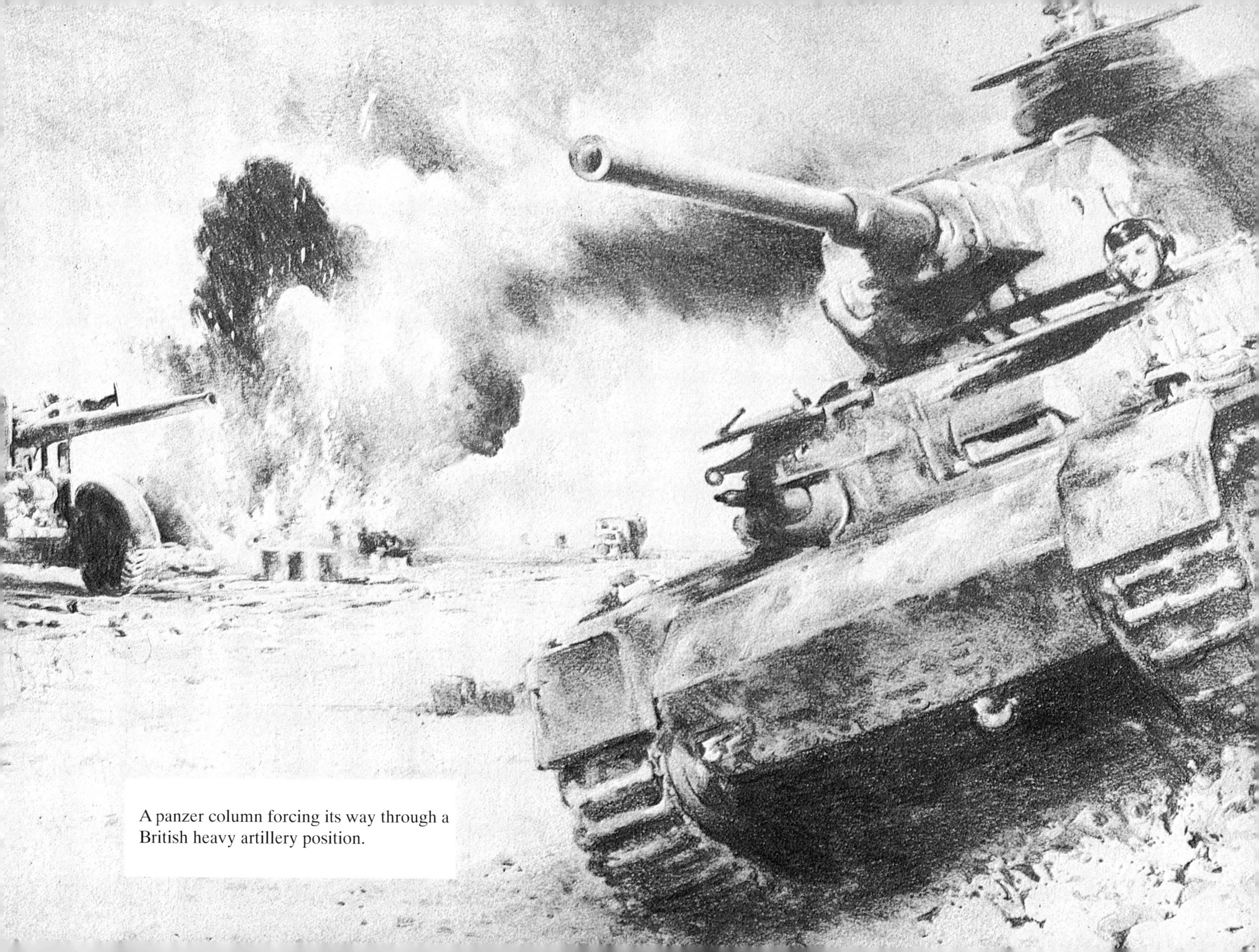

A panzer column forcing its way through a British heavy artillery position.

would smash the Axis panzer force. The Eighth Army would then go on to raise the siege of Tobruk before opening an advance upon Tripoli. For his part, Rommel planned to capture Tobruk in a meticulously prepared swift assault, and then to regroup his forces before opening a massive panzer attack which would destroy the British armour and open the way for an advance upon the Suez Canal.

This, in outline, was the way in which the course of operations was expected to run in the winter of 1941. But if we anticipate events it will be seen that the strategic outlines of both plans were changed as a result of the armoured battles which were fought out between 19 and 22 November in the area to the south of Tobruk. A series of confusing outflanking actions was fought during these clashes, which resulted in severe losses on both sides. The high commands of both the Eighth Army and Afrika Korps drew the wrong conclusions from the outcome of these battles, and changed their battle plans. The engagements fought to the south of Tobruk were then followed by a fresh series of armoured clashes in the eastern enclave between 25 November and 1 December. Rommel rushed his forces to the eastern outpost intending to cut off the Eighth Army, which in his opinion was retreating, and by cutting its supply route force it to withdraw back into Egypt. This eastern move became known as 'Rommel's dash to the wire'.

The British and German offensives in the last months of 1941 might have been assessed as fairly standard but for the bewildering speed with which Rommel acted in his attacks, as well as his swift reaction to the crises which developed when his Panzer Group came under assault. It is his pragmatism which makes the actions of those weeks so interesting.

Like Wavell before him, Auchinleck, the new Commander-in-Chief Middle East, was put under pressure by his political and military superiors in London. They gave him a direct order to undertake an offensive which would not only produce a victory to impress the neutral United States, but would also boost civilian morale at home. The London directive was passed to Cunningham, the commander of the new Eighth Army, and the result of the deliberations between him and Auchinleck was the operation which has passed into military history as 'Crusader'.

In the plan's advance to contact stage, the offensive involved the Eighth Army forming a river of armour and lorries flowing out of Egypt. This single column would separate into three once it had crossed the 'wire'. In retrospect it can be clearly seen that the dispersal of its forces was the British plan's fatal flaw. In the German Army it was a fundamental principle that though the several components of an army in the field might march separately they must strike together. German commanders were trained to fix a point where the main blow would be made – called *die Schwerpunkt* – and in each of his offensives Rommel had gained his victories by swiftly creating a *Schwerpunkt* and launching his armour in a concerted attack on that point. Now the British were intending to reverse the German principle, by preparing to march collectively but intending to strike separately. Against any modern army this would have been a risky operation. Against such a flexibly minded commander as Rommel it was the recipe for total disaster. The Eighth Army's strategy relied for its success upon engaging the panzer divisions of the Afrika Korps on a field of its own choosing – the high ground at Gabr Saleh. The British plan depended upon Rommel being so obliging as to be there when Cunningham wanted him to be.

During the fallow months which followed the end of the June offensive Rommel worked his men in the eastern enclave hard, and under the spur of his unpredictable and unannounced visits to check on progress they had soon completed the task which he had set them. This was to undertake the conversion of a few weak field fortification complexes into a strong defensive line, behind well laid out minefields, from Sollum in the north to Sidi Omar in the south. The Italian garrison of this eastern area was the 'Savona' Division, which had a reinforcement of German infantry as well as some batteries of 88 mm and 50 mm guns. Rommel knew that his eastern outpost would be attacked during the opening moves of any new British offensive, and he prepared its garrison for this testing time by provisioning it so

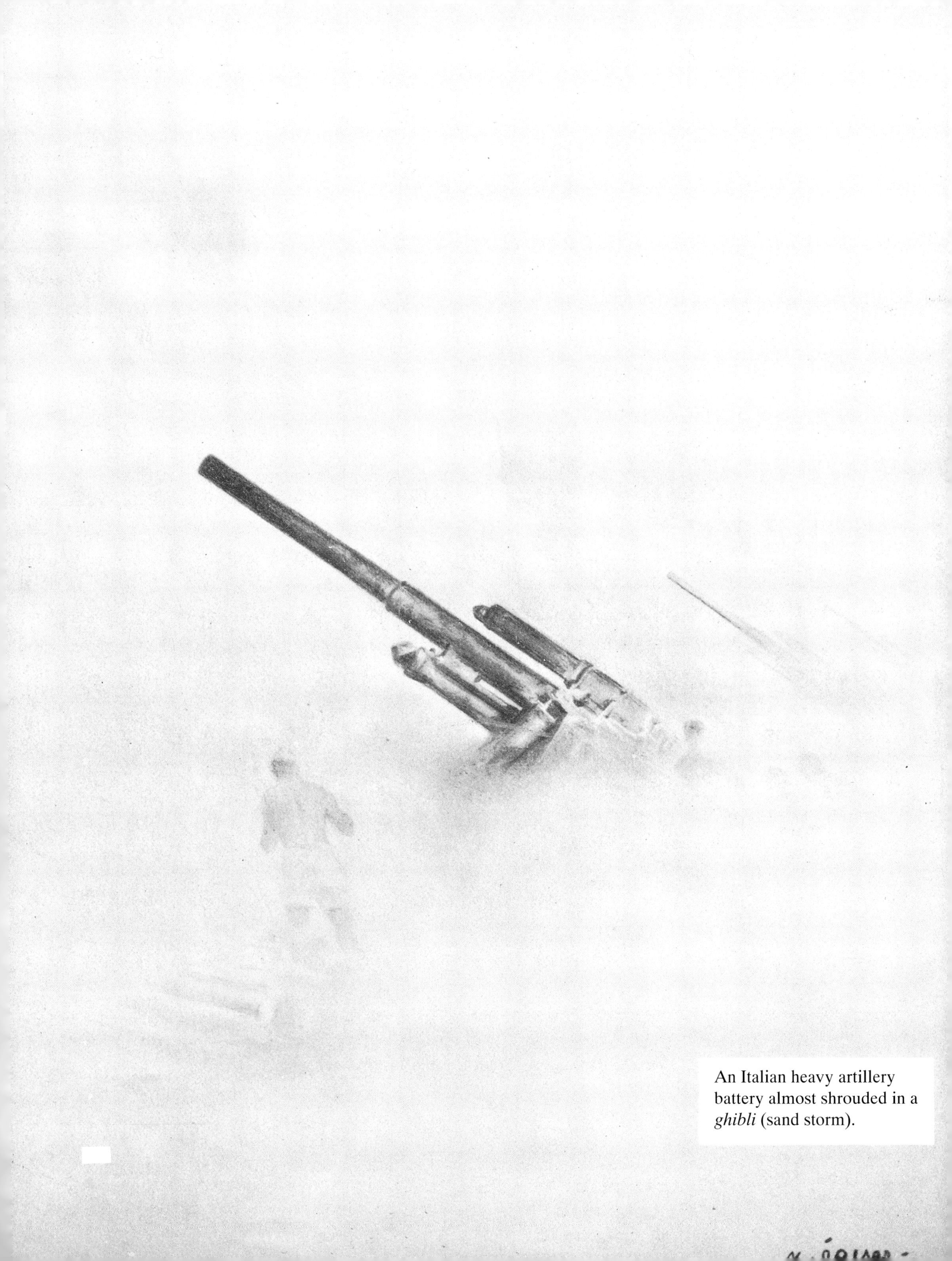

An Italian heavy artillery battery almost shrouded in a *ghibli* (sand storm).

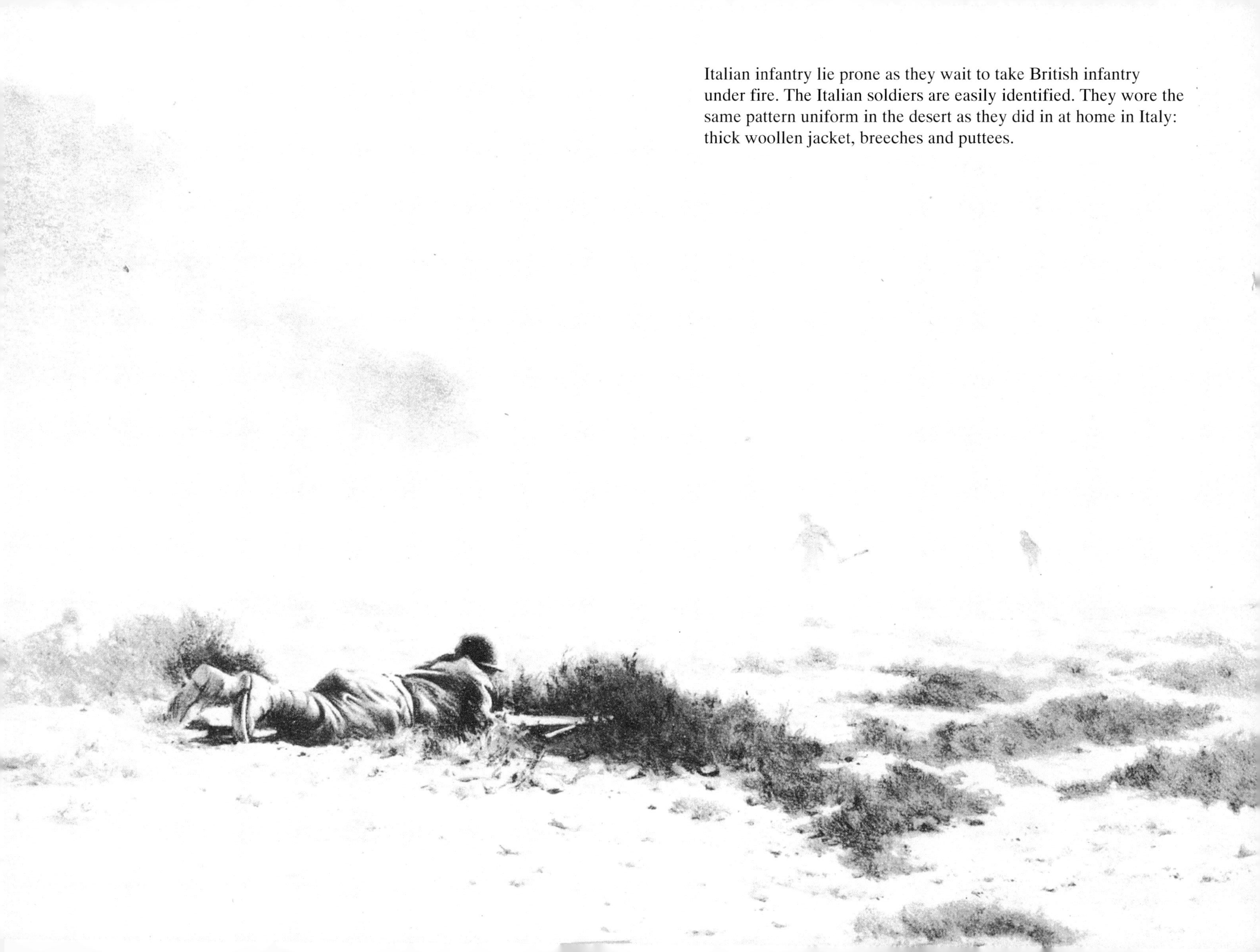

Italian infantry lie prone as they wait to take British infantry under fire. The Italian soldiers are easily identified. They wore the same pattern uniform in the desert as they did in at home in Italy: thick woollen jacket, breeches and puttees.

that it would be able to hold out for a minimum of three weeks. Within that period he expected to have won the battle for Tobruk.

Rommel was now a full General of Panzer Troops, with effect from 1 July, and commander of the newly-formed Panzer Group Africa, consisting of the Afrika Korps and the Italian XXI Corps, supported by a Corpo di Manovra, also known as the Corpo Celere, a mobile corps under the direct command of the Italian commander-in-chief. It was at about this time that the strength of the German forces was increased when the 90th Light (Africa) Division came into the battle line together with the 21st Panzer Division. Both had been in the desert from the earliest days of the conflict, but in different forms. The 21st Panzer Division was the upgraded 5th Light Division, built around a nucleus of Colonel Stephan's panzer regiment with the bulk of its non-armoured units being made up of the 104th Infantry Regiment and von Wechmar's reconnaissance battalion. The 90th Light (Africa) Division was a mobile division created around a nucleus of miscellaneous formations.

The Axis forces investing Tobruk consisted of the 90th Light Division together with the Italian 'Brescia', 'Trento' and 'Bologna' Divisions. The Corpo di Manovra was guarding the desert flank, with its 'Trieste' Division located around Bir Hachim and its 'Ariete' Division in the area of Bir el Gobi. Rommel had disposed his forces skilfully so that he not only had a strong investing force around Tobruk but could back it up and protect it with the formations in the desert, each of which could be switched swiftly to a threatened sector. In addition to the infantry and panzer formations on the perimeter and in the desert, Rommel had created a battering ram designed to smash its way into the fortress. This assault force was made up of the 15th Panzer Division and the 155th Infantry Regiment. To counter attempts that might be made by the Eighth Army to interfere during the break-in battle, the 21st Panzer Division, which was located between Bardia and Tobruk, had orders to hold back any British advance until the fortress was taken. Once that happened the 21st, spearheading the eastwards drive, would lead Panzer Group Africa – striking as a single

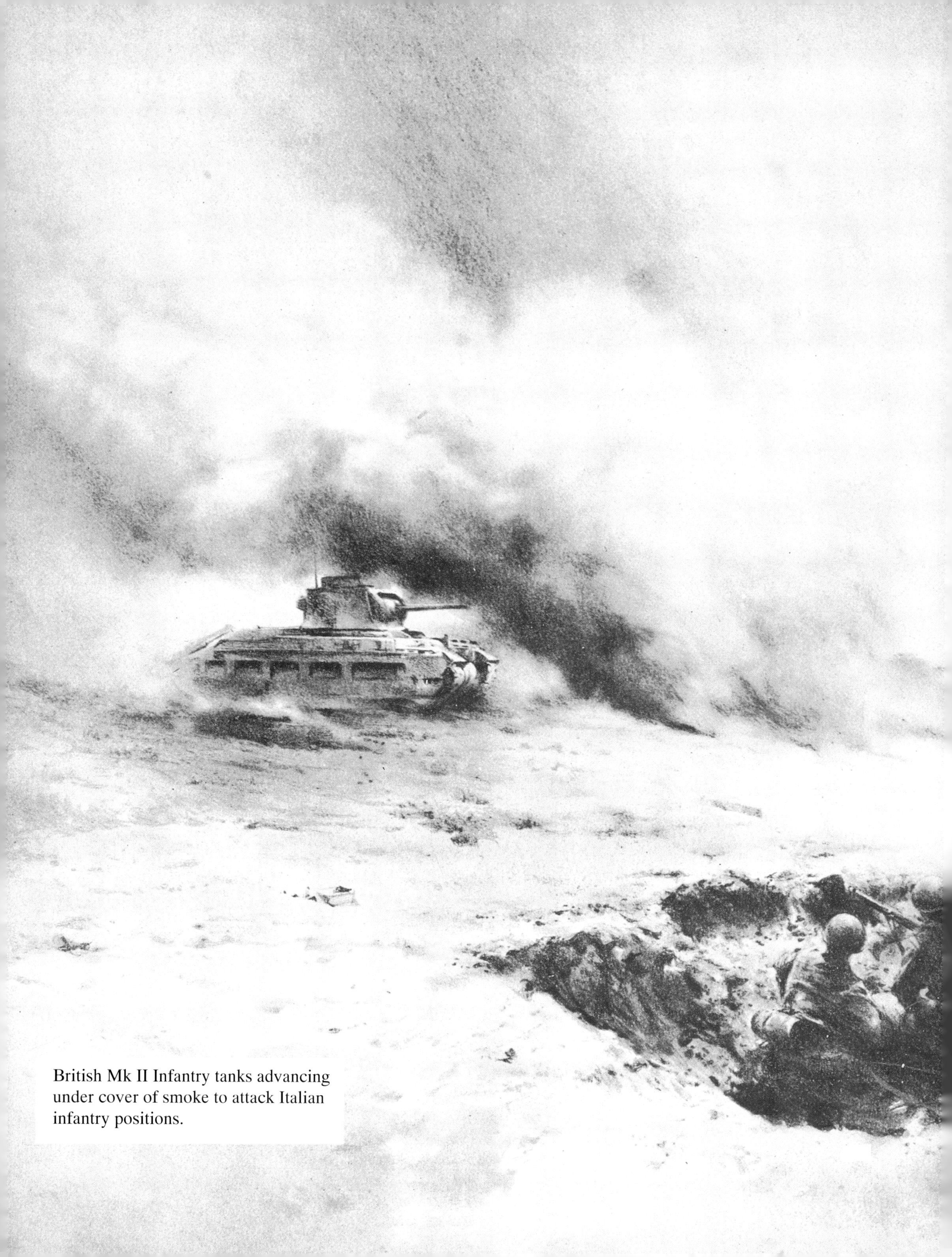

British Mk II Infantry tanks advancing under cover of smoke to attack Italian infantry positions.

fist – in the decisive armoured clash which would destroy the Eighth Army. The other objectives would then fall into German hands.

Rommel, conscious of the great strength of the Tobruk fortress and of the determination of the British garrison to hold it, was anxious not to repeat his earlier mistakes. He trained the men of his break-in Group as thoroughly as he had his units in the eastern enclave. The two panzer divisions were subjected to especially thorough training, while the 90th Light was ordered to waste no time in acclimatising its soldiers but was to give them a short, three-week course of intensive instruction. The 155th Regiment, which was to carry out the break-in assault, was trained in storm-trooper tactics. On a piece of desert simulating the sector of the Tobruk perimeter on which the assault would be made, the regiment carried out mock attacks, using live ammunition. Its battalions were trained to 'lean on the barrage', that is, to advance as close as possible behind the artillery fire and then to charge and capture the sangars and pill-boxes of Tobruk's outer defences before the defenders had recovered from the shock of the barrage. Once those positions had been overcome the men of the 155th would have to carry out a six-kilometre approach march across flat and open terrain before going on to assault and take out the principal infantry and artillery positions located behind the main perimeter. Rommel laid the greatest emphasis on inter-arms co-operation between infantry, panzers and artillery. The Luftwaffe was also tied in, and training went on until each man knew the sort of task he had to carry out. It was mentioned in the previous chapter's account of the June offensive that Rommel had built up his artillery arsenal significantly. Just how successful he had been in this endeavour is shown by the fact that to bombard the fortress he now had nine howitzers of 21 cm calibre, thirty-eight of 15 cm calibre, and twelve of 10.5 cm calibre.

By misreading the situation both sides had chosen almost the same week for the opening of their respective offensives, and each had selected the south-eastern corner of the Tobruk defences as the sector in which their main effort would be made. In the British plan the

Men of an Italian anti-tank gun team in action against British armour.

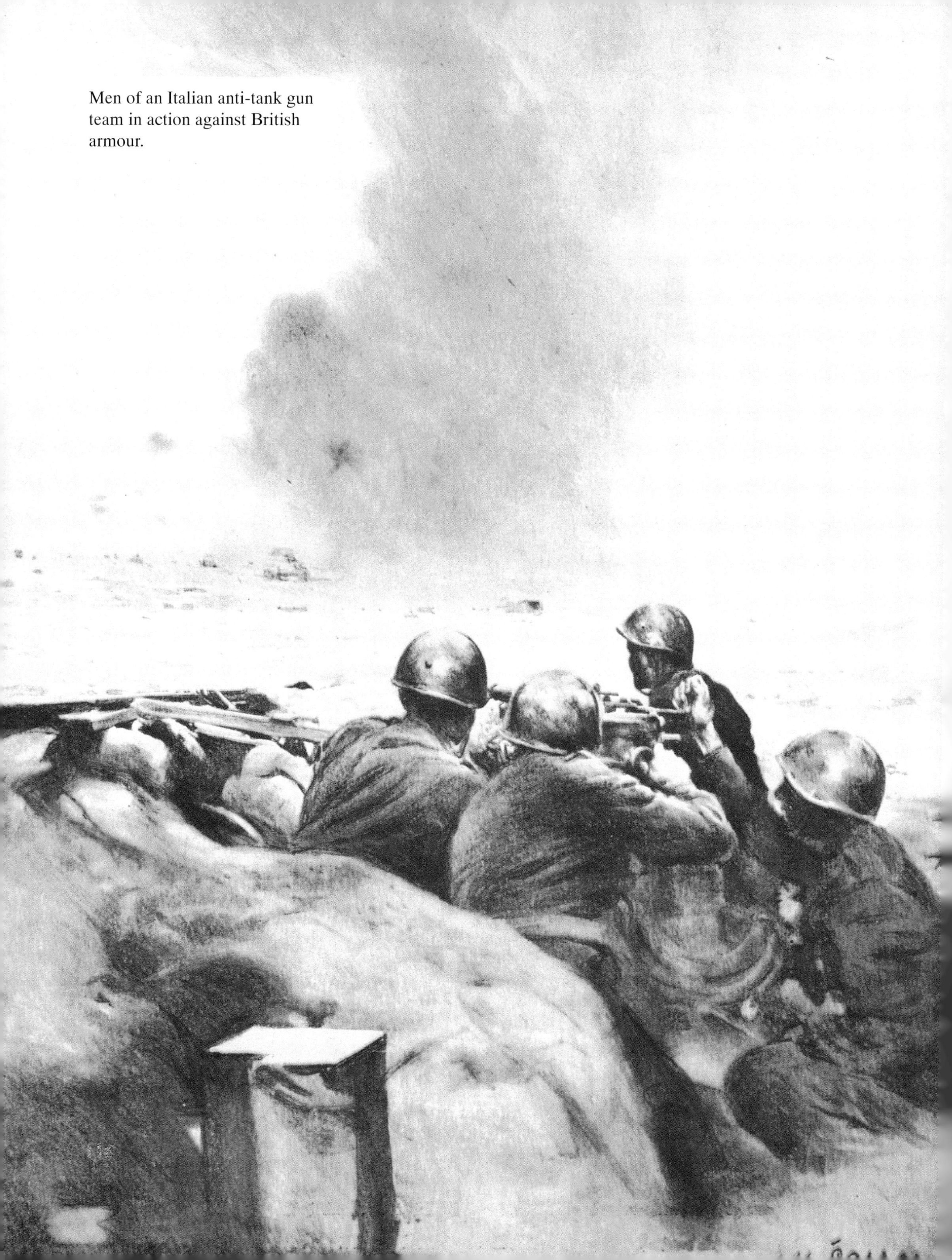

approach of the Eighth Army towards the fortress would be the signal for a break out from this sector by the garrison. The break-out force would drive south-eastwards to gain contact with the 1st South African Division, the spearhead of the relieving group. On the German side, Rommel intended to launch his break-in force against the same south-eastern corner of the perimeter. A rough sketch which he drew makes it clear that he anticipated a swift victory. He planned that his men would be on the start line at 03.30 hrs and that the attack would open at 04.00 hrs. The junction of three roads would be taken between 06.30 and 10.00 hrs, and the advance would reach the Mediterranean between 10.00 and 15.00 hrs. Tobruk harbour and town would be taken by 17.00 hrs and the attack would end with the capture of the pumping station and Wadi Sahal. It was a bold plan, simple in design, and would be executed by highly trained assault units.

Late in August Luftwaffe air reconnaissance photographs had shown that the Eighth Army had constructed four huge supply dumps forward of its lines, each sited around a *bir* or well. In a raid that was intended not only to gain supplies from the Deir el Hamra dump, some 55 km to the south-east of Sollum, but also to carry out a reconnaissance to discover British intentions, Rommel led a force of two battle groups from the 21st Panzer Division. Kampfgruppe Schutte drove along a northern escarpment towards Quaret el Ruweibit, while Kampfgruppe Stephan followed a parallel but more southerly route. Rommel and von Ravenstein, the divisional commander, both rode with the Schutte group, which sent out a smaller detachment, Kampfgruppe Panzenhagen, to protect the main battle group's open flank. During the advance all three columns brushed with the Eighth Army's armoured car patrols, and Panzenhagen's column was also attacked by British infantry. In the expectation that it would find and remove the contents of a British supply dump, Schutte's column had taken along a convoy of lorries, but on reaching it the supply dump was found to be empty except for a few cases of corned beef. The raid was thus a failure.

The two groups then moved deeper into Egypt, carrying out a

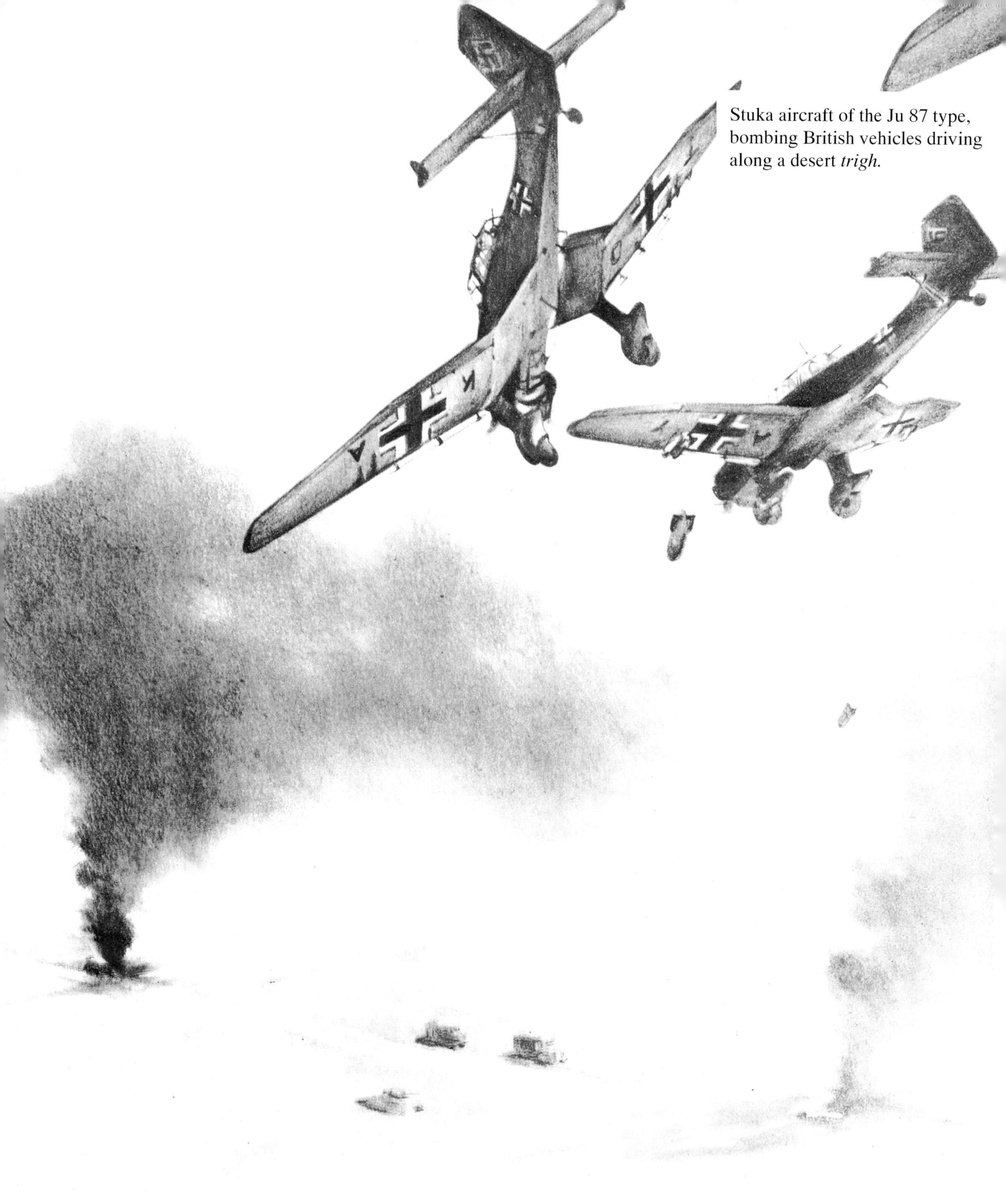

Stuka aircraft of the Ju 87 type, bombing British vehicles driving along a desert *trigh*.

reconnaissance in force, but as they drove forward they were intercepted and shot up by a 'Jock column'. A short, sharp battle was fought, and when it was broken off the group found itself to be low on petrol. Supplies were ordered up, but through an error in navigation the fuel convoy did not gain contact with the fighting echelons quickly enough, and the panzers, with their petrol tanks running dangerously low, were forced to halt and wait – a large, immobile target – until the errant supply trucks could find and refuel them. However, it was not the supply trucks which found the stranded panzers first, but an Eighth Army reconnaissance patrol. The South African patrol commander, realising that he was outgunned, called for an air strike, which not only caused a great many casualties but also destroyed thirty fuel lorries. Rommel himself had a lucky escape when a fragment of bomb casing tore the heel from one of his boots.

As if to emphasise the frustrations of the day a tyre burst on the Mammoth, a huge British vehicle which Rommel used as a command truck. Changing the tyre took so long that darkness fell, and the Mammoth, containing the senior commanders of the Panzer Group, had to spend the night isolated in the desert protected by only a small escort group. By dawn the tyre had been replaced and the Mammoth rolled back across the wire into the safety of Axis-held Libya, bringing 'Operation Midsummer Night's Dream', as it had been named, to an end. Although it had failed to loot a British food dump, the German commanders were satisfied with the results of their deep reconnaissance, which had indicated that the British were making no preparations for an offensive. This absence of British preparations meant that the Germans had no need to worry about their eastern enclave, and certainly Rommel was more concerned about the possibility of an Australian break out from Tobruk than with the inactive main body of the Eighth Army which lay on the far side of the frontier wire. In expressing that concern, however, he was clearly unaware that the 9th Australian Division, which had once formed the bulk of the Tobruk garrison, had been withdrawn in a three-stage operation and its place taken by British and other Allied units. Toward the end of October only its headquarters and some divisional troops remained.

Rommel's signal to OKW stated that he intended to start operations during the period between 15 and 20 November, and as early as 26 October he issued orders for the attack which would take out Tobruk. The conviction that the British were not about to attack was still held as late as 11 November 1941, when Rommel's intelligence officer, von Mellenthin, advised his Italian opposite number not to worry; there would be no Eighth Army offensive. Despite this confident prediction, Mellenthin must have been aware of reports to the contrary. One of these came in as early as 16 November, when Battle Group Wechmar – the amalgamated 3rd and 33rd Reconnaissance Battalions – signalled that it had observed a flow of British vehicles in the Maddalena – Sidi Omar frontier area, moving westwards towards the Trigh el Abd. Wechmar's report was confirmed by others which came in from the 21st Panzer Division. But despite the intelligence details supplied by its units on the ground, Panzer Group HQ seemed unaware that a major British offensive was about to be launched.

News that Eighth Army units had begun an advance towards the airfield at Sidi Rezegh brought an order from Rommel that a strong battle group was to be sent to Gabr Saleh. As a precaution Rommel then directed 15th Panzer to be prepared to withdraw from the Tobruk operation at 24 hours notice if an emergency arose, and this directive makes it clear that although he knew some sort of British operation had opened it did not worry him unduly. Certainly he did not consider the British move to presage a major offensive until 20 November, and thought of it rather as a reconnaissance in force. His belief that he could therefore ignore the British across the 'wire' was backed by the consensus of opinion among the Panzer Group's intelligence officers that it would take about three days for any operation by the Eighth Army to have an effect upon the German assault against Tobruk – three days during which the fortress would have been captured and the Afrika Korps regrouped ready to attack the British armour.

During the evening of 17 November, the 15th Panzer Division was

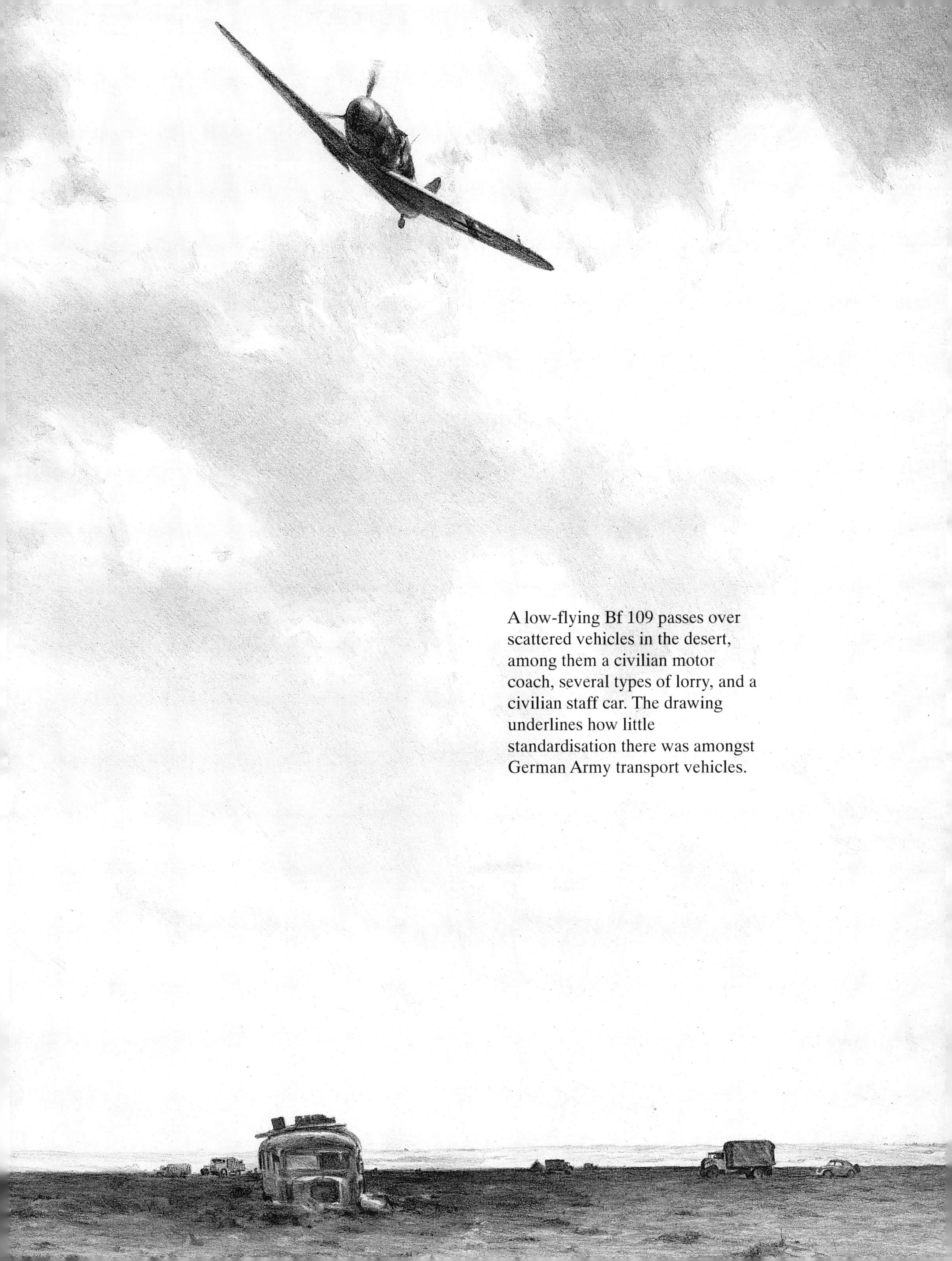

A low-flying Bf 109 passes over scattered vehicles in the desert, among them a civilian motor coach, several types of lorry, and a civilian staff car. The drawing underlines how little standardisation there was amongst German Army transport vehicles.

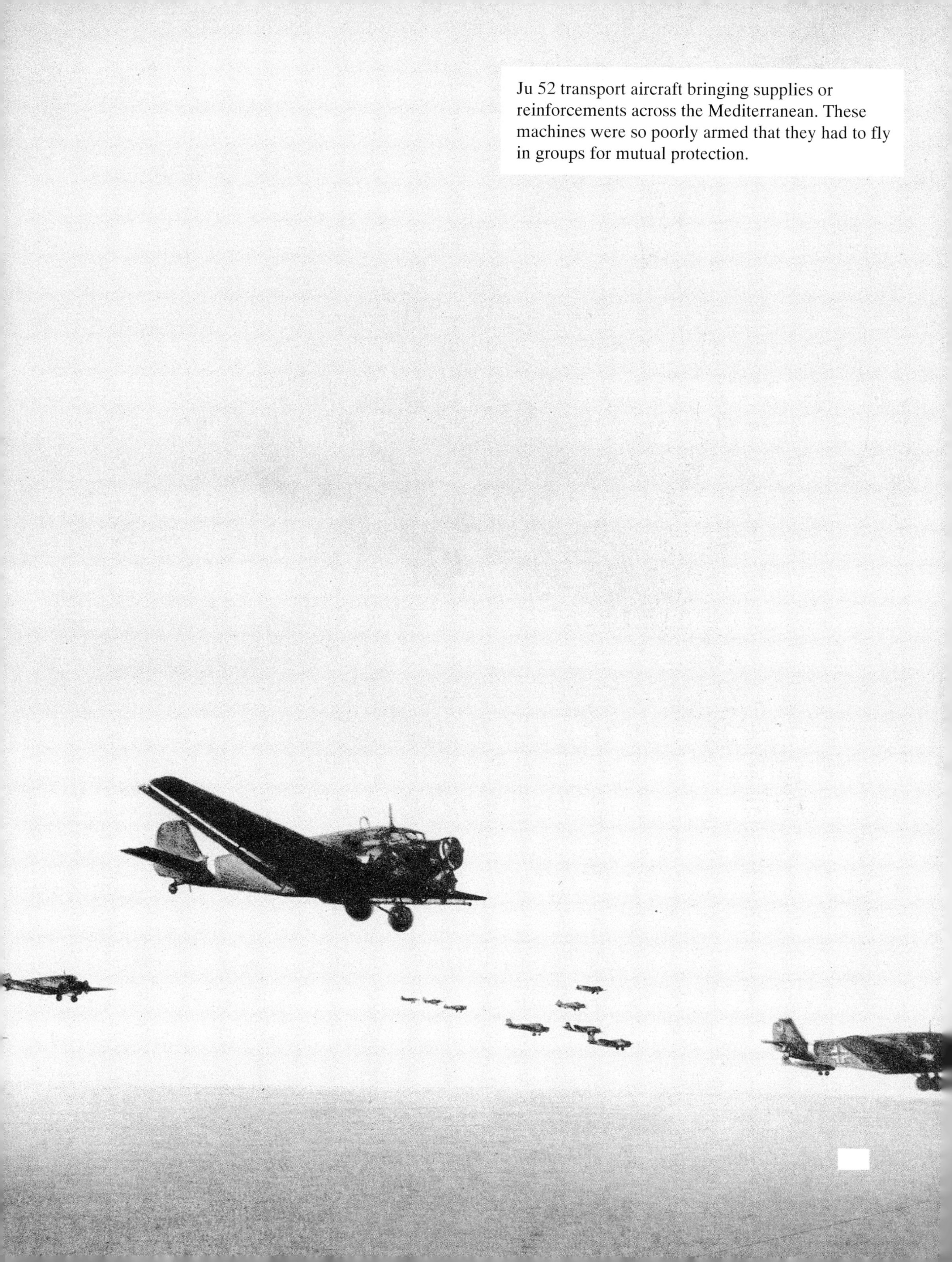

Ju 52 transport aircraft bringing supplies or reinforcements across the Mediterranean. These machines were so poorly armed that they had to fly in groups for mutual protection.

grouped to the north of Trigh Capuzzo, and Wolfgang Wahl, commander of the 8th Panzer Regiment's 2nd Battalion, was briefing his men on the forthcoming battle when it began to rain. The first few drops were followed by a downpour of monsoon intensity. To begin with the panzermen came out of their tents and dug-outs to stand in the shower bath which Nature had so generously provided, for in this part of Libya rain was so unusual that there had been none for over fifty years. But the downpour showed no sign of letting up, and news of the first tragedies which it had caused soon began coming in. Parts of the Via Balbia had been washed away, and airfields were unusable because the landing strips were a sea of mud. Running off the rocky surface of the desert, the torrential rain-water poured into wadis where soldiers were sleeping and drowned them in their beds. It was a macabre situation; men were drowned in the middle of a desert which had seen no rain for more than half a century. The panzer crews were ordered to take cover in their vehicles and there they stayed until the rain clouds rolled away. Then they had the laborious task of digging their half-submerged vehicles out of the rain-soaked, clinging sand. While the panzer regiment was occupied thus, a hundred kilometres or more to the east the Eighth Army, under Cunningham, was already streaming across the frontier wire.

In the final days before both armies opened their offensives the collection and interpretation of last minute intelligence details became a paramount consideration. The torrential rain already referred to, and the low cloud ceilings which accompanied it, meant that the Luftwaffe's photographic reconnaissance planes could not fly their customary missions. Had they done so their photographs would have shown long columns of AFVs and soft-skins rolling through the gaps in the frontier wire and debouching into Libya. There was also a lack of radio information. In the past British wireless traffic had supplied the Panzer Group with much of its most valuable intelligence, but Auchinleck, on being advised of this, ordered a tightening of wireless procedures with the result that little now came through to the Germans. The Eighth Army was therefore able to move westward for

German troops beating off a British armoured thrust near Segnali. In the foreground is a Volkswagen staff car. To its left a German half-track mounting an anti-tank gun is firing at the advancing enemy. In the middle distance an anti-tank gun is also in action against the British AFVs, which can be seen approaching.

two whole days without being detected. 'Operation Crusader' opened at dawn on 18 November.

The Eighth Army's approach march began with a circuitous journey because Axis troops still held the eastern outpost, and this detour, which took the column to the south of the enclave, was followed by a long drive through the desert. Once inside Libya, the single column of the Eighth Army's formations and vehicles had separated into three as planned: one rolled towards Gabr Saleh, a second wheeled in a north-easterly direction to attack the eastern outpost, and in the deep south the third, consisting of an Indian brigade, began the long march through the desert that was intended to bring it up behind the Axis troops. The Eighth Army's high command was employing a 'bait' tactic of its own design. It anticipated that an attack upon Rommel's eastern force would compel him to strike eastwards with his panzer divisions. En route to the eastern sector these would be met, countered and destroyed by the guns and armour of XXX Corps, which would be halted and waiting in position around Gabr Saleh.

Among the first moves of 'Crusader' on 18 November was the 22nd Armoured Brigade's attack upon the 'Ariete' Division in the Bir el Gobi area, an attack which the Italians first held and then deflected. Meanwhile, the 7th Armoured Division was advancing towards Sidi Rezegh and had met little opposition, unlike the 4th Armoured Brigade which, during the evening of the 18th, was struck by the riposte which Rommel had ordered when the 21st Panzer Division reported that British armoured units were active on its front. Rommel

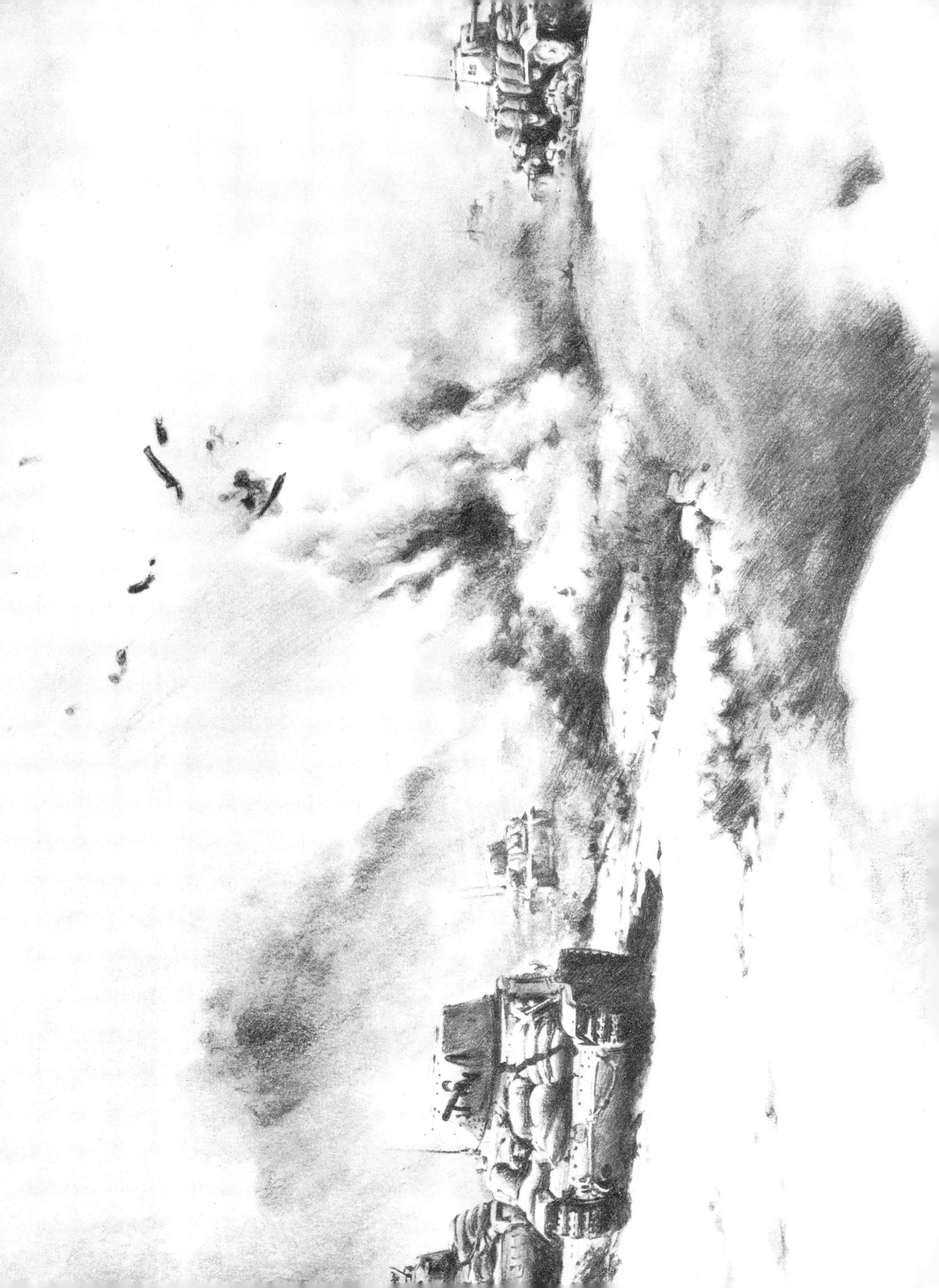

Italian tanks of the 'Ariete' armoured division. The front and sides of the vehicles are covered with sandbags for additional protection against British anti-tank gun fire.

had ordered Battle Group Stephan to carry out a counter-attack, and in its advance it had intercepted the 4th Armoured Brigade. The battalions of the panzer regiment had been deployed in a fan formation across the desert so as to cover a maximum frontage, and when word came that British armour was approaching Colonel Stephan ordered his panzers to deploy into battle formation. The first clashes halted the British squadrons, and in the subsequent fighting they were dispersed and flung back in disorder. The battle ended at last light – late afternoon at that time of the year – and while 4th Armoured Brigade's units moved away from the battlefield and went into laager for the night, the panzers stayed on the ground they had won, where their damaged vehicles were repaired in field workshops.

As late as 19 November, Rommel and his staff had still not been able to determine where the Eighth Army's *Schwerpunkt* would come, and he was unwilling to release forces prematurely. The British had achieved complete tactical surprise with their three-pronged assault and the absence of a definite *Schwerpunkt* reinforced the belief still held by German Corps Command that the Eighth Army's operation was not an all-out offensive but only a 'reconnaissance in force, with which they would deal easily.

During the morning of the 19th Rommel again used the 21st Panzer Division to try to locate and destroy this British 'reconnaissance in force', which reports had placed between Sidi Omar and Gabr el Saleh. Upon receipt of its movement order the division's Kampfgruppe Stephan, now consisting of more than 120 Panzer IIIs and IVs and reinforced with both conventional field-artillery and a battalion of flak guns, moved out on a seek and destroy mission. As a precaution Rommel also ordered 15th Panzer to move forward to a concentration area to the south-west of Gambut. Its task was not merely to support

21st Panzer, were that support to be needed, but rather more to strengthen its sister division when the time came for it to move into the attack. The 15th advanced in a four-column formation, ploughing its way across the desert and raising high clouds of dust which shrouded the formation completely. As it approached the concentration area the division changed formation and took up the tactical arrangement which, as has been explained in an earlier chapter, Rommel had developed for just such situations – a solid square of vehicles extending across the desert for several kilometres in length and depth. Such a formation needed little in the way of flank protection, being so flexibly designed that any unit could be detached and put into action without the need for formal orders or long briefings.

Meanwhile, in its race across the open desert late in the afternoon 21st Panzer had again crashed into the 4th Armoured Brigade, at a point 8 km north-east of Gabr Saleh. However, although this was exactly where the Eighth Army's XXX Corps had expected to clash with Afrika Korps' panzer divisions, according to German reports only one tank unit – the 8th Hussars – was actually holding the ground, the 4th's other two regiments having hared off across the desert to follow up earlier sightings of enemy armour.

The well-rehearsed German units prepared for action, the 88s being unlimbered and forming a short gun line. While the light Stuarts of the 8th Hussars, one of the cavalry regiments of the 4th Armoured Brigade, were still some distance away the panzers carried out their standard 'bait' manoeuvre, racing forward as if to attack but then wheeling away as if in retreat. The 8th Hussars charged in pursuit at high speed, to get as close to the 'retreating' enemy vehicles as possible. It was essential that they got in close, since only by reducing the distance between the British squadrons and the panzers could the battle be fought on anything like equal terms. The Hussars' charge had almost reached the 'retreating' panzers of Battle Group Stephan when the German gun line opened up, and the oncoming Stuarts immediately suffered losses. They wheeled, reformed, and came on again, only to have more vehicles destroyed. The survivors pulled

A German 88 mm heavy flak gun moving across a battlefield in Cyrenaica to take up a new firing position. It is passing knocked out British soft-skinned vehicles.

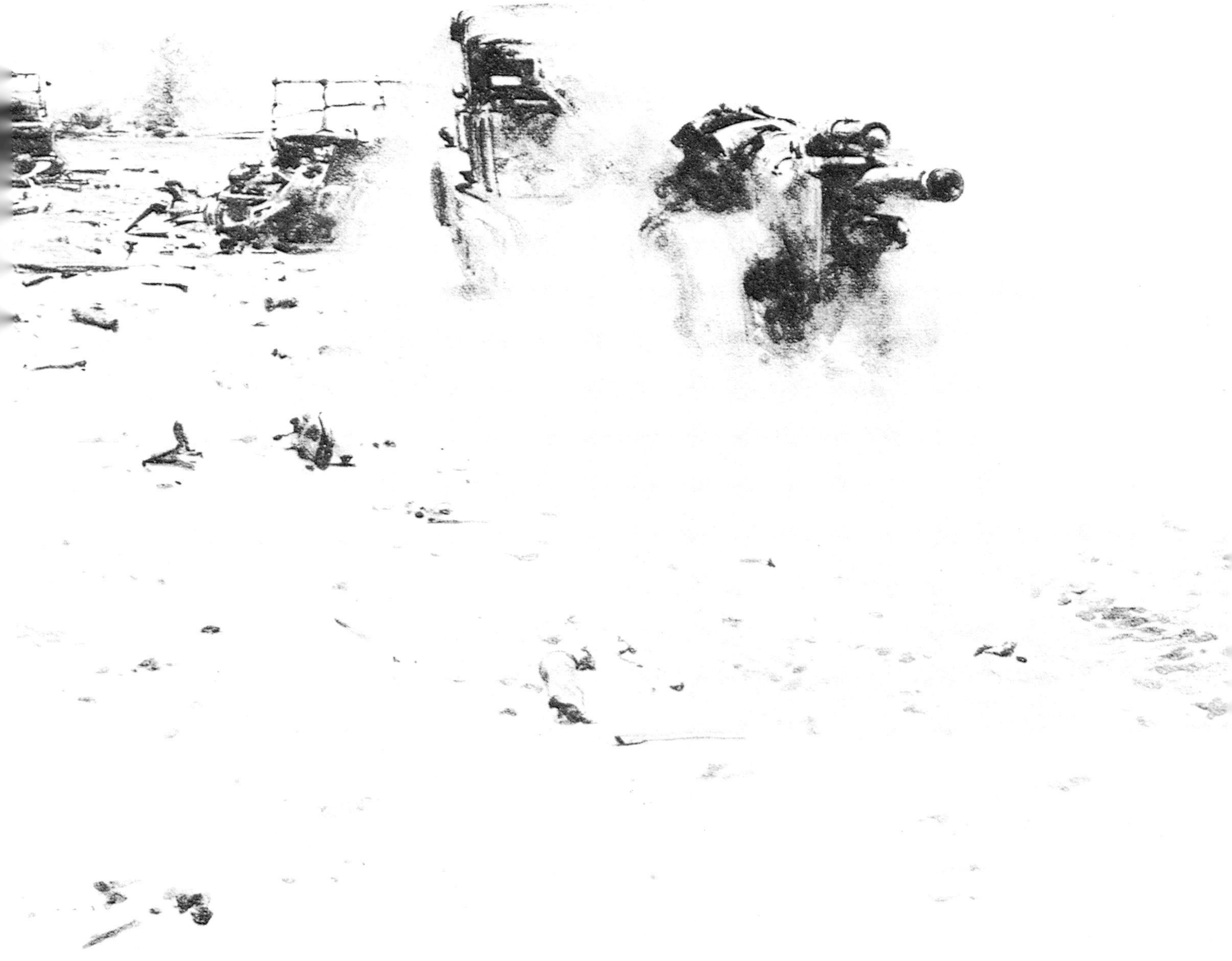

Caesar made this drawing at El Alamein.
It shows a German heavy gun in action,
which has just survived a near miss.

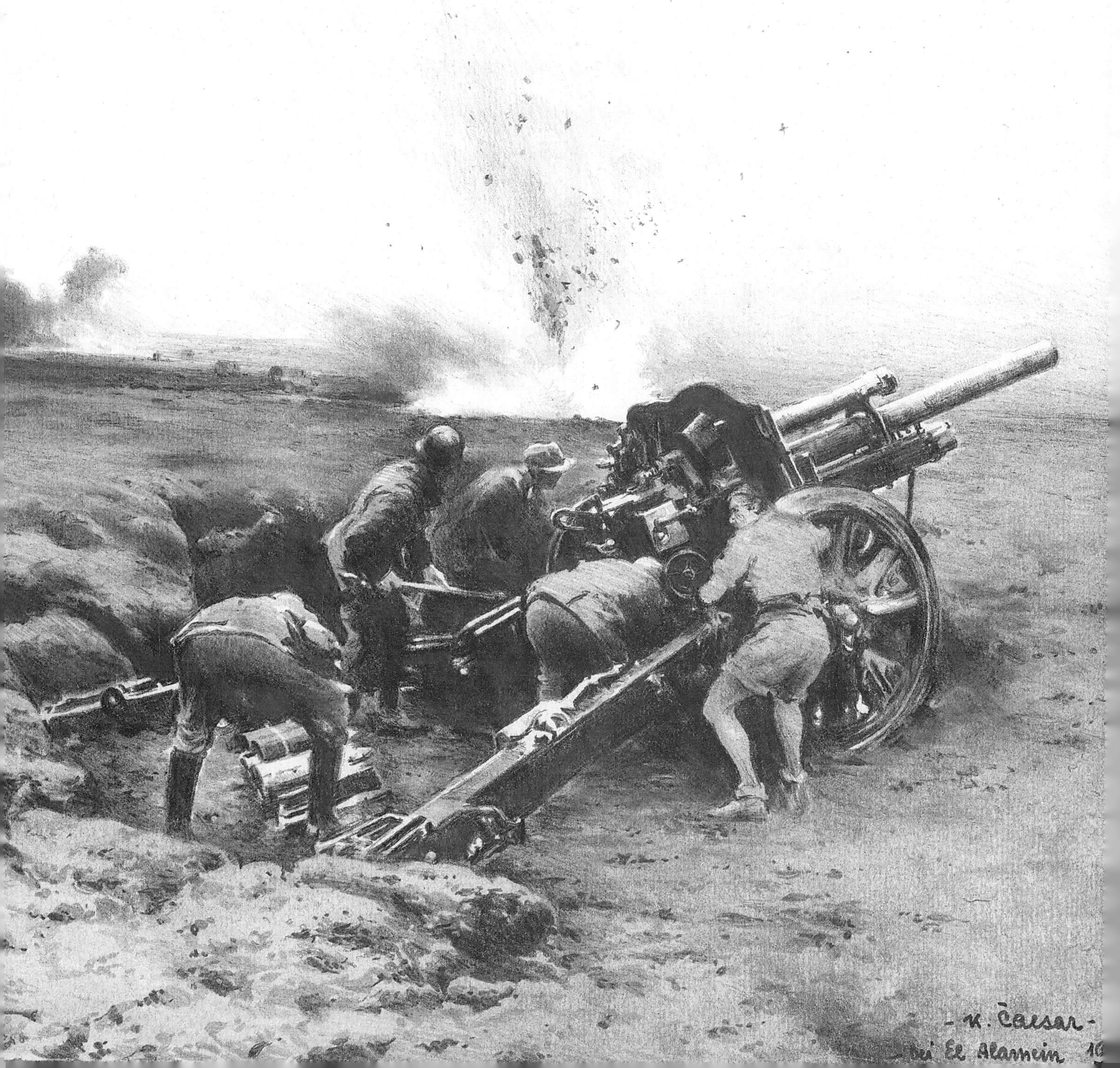

back, not in retreat, but to regroup once more. Determined to win at all costs they charged for a third time, and for a third time were repulsed. The battle had opened in mid-afternoon, and the Hussars did not break off their attacks and move back to laager until just before last light. Forty-two of their tanks had been 'killed' in those few hours of combat, while the 21st Panzer Division had lost just three. Rommel, who had been on the battlefield, noted with approval how Battle Group Stephan dealt with the British tank attacks. It was a vindication of his training and his tactics.

The Eighth Army's tank regiments had driven away from the battlefield during late afternoon because it was their standard practice to break off a battle well before nightfall so as to drive to their supply echelons for food, fuel and ammunition. It will be appreciated that this post-battle drive placed an extra burden on British tank drivers. Already tired from the strain of fighting, they had to take their tanks back to laager and to the workshops in which battlefield damage could be made good. Panzer units, by contrast, stayed on the battlefield, thus sparing their drivers the strain of an extra drive, and also allowing their recovery crews and workshops to deal with battlefield damage on the spot, tasks which the workshop personnel often carried out under floodlight. At the height of the afternoon's battle at Gabr Saleh, German recovery crews had actually gone out under fire and had brought in some of the knocked out Stuart tanks, determined that British recovery teams should not retrieve them.

Late in the evening of the 19th, von Ravenstein proposed to Crüwell, the General Commanding Afrika Korps, that both panzer divisions be amalgamated into a single force. Rommel, to whom the proposal was put, gave Crüwell a free hand but did add the caveat that it was important for this combined force to destroy British units operating in the Bardia–Tobruk–Sidi Omar area before they grew powerful enough to threaten the Axis ring around Tobruk. He was well satisfied with the progress of operations in the area of the fortress.

The morning of the 20th brought the familiar problem to the vehicles of 21st Panzer of fuel tanks running dry. This situation had

Alongside the wreck of a British 15 cwt truck, the crew of a German heavy machine-gun – an MG 34 on a tripod mounting – go into action in Cyrenaica.

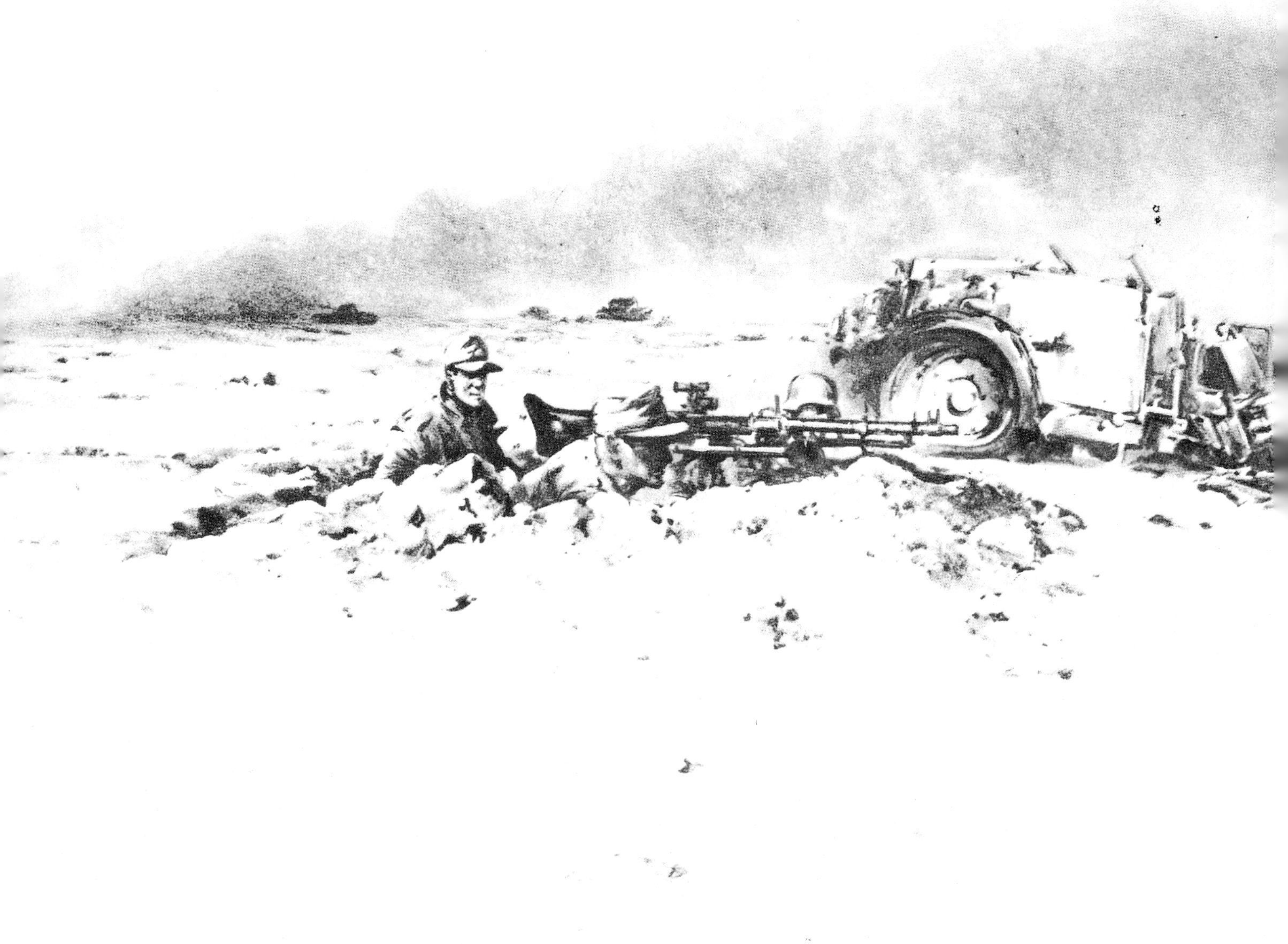

arisen because the British armour at Sidi Azeiz had begun a fast withdrawal and had been pursued by the panzers as far as Sidi Omar, thereby draining their fuel tanks and leaving the machines stranded in the desert. And there they had to stay until the Luftwaffe flew in supplies. During the time that the 21st was halted, 15th Panzer had come forward and had reached the area of Gasr el Arid. During the course of a wide encircling movement it too struck vehicles of the 4th Armoured Brigade near Gabr Saleh. In the ensuing battle, which again lasted until nearly nightfall, the 15th claimed to have destroyed fifty-five of the 165 tanks which had been sent against it.

During the evening of 20 November orders were issued from Eighth Army HQ to open a general advance to relieve Tobruk. The intention was for the Tobruk garrison to break out on 21 November and make contact with the main element of the Eighth Army. British units began to move towards the fortress from the south and the east, their new orders from Cunningham radically altering the Eighth Army's original battle plan. It no longer intended to smash the panzer force and then to go on to relieve Tobruk. Now the plan was to lift the siege before going on to destroy the enemy's armour.

Units involved in a battle often overestimate both the strength of the enemy forces attacking them and the damage which they believe they have inflicted upon those forces. General Cunningham had received optimistic reports that his armour had driven off the Axis formations, and thought that the small unit actions which had taken place at Gabr Saleh constituted a major victory over the enemy's panzers. He further believed that these operations had been the decisive clash which he had anticipated, and was deluded by false reports of other minor successes into believing that the Eighth Army had won the day. It was this misplaced confidence which led him to change the operational plan, unaware that Afrika Korps' panzer divisions had not yet been seriously engaged.

For his part, Rommel, having now accepted that he faced a major British offensive, decided to attack the rear of the Eighth Army's main body which was now moving towards Tobruk, and issued orders that this

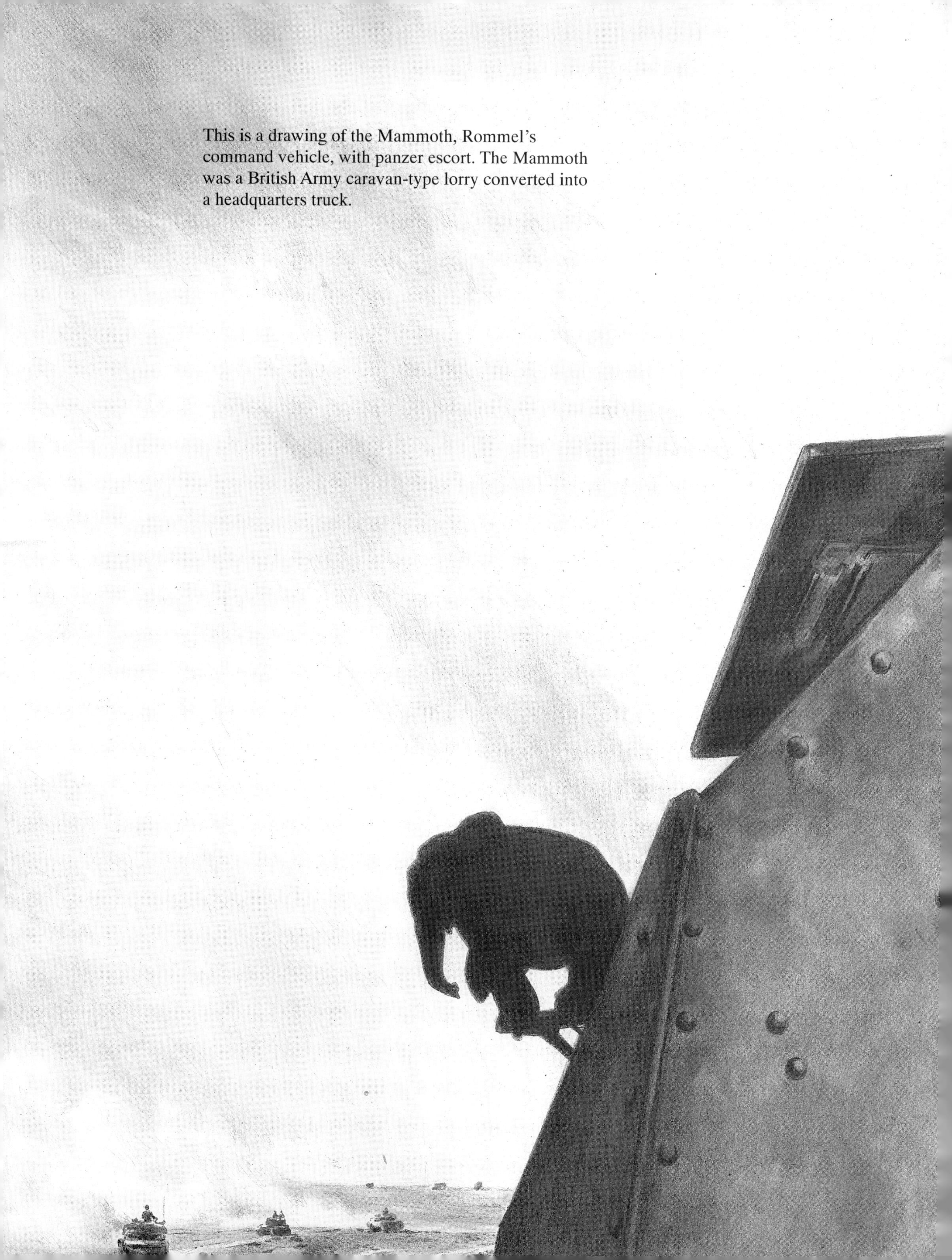

This is a drawing of the Mammoth, Rommel's command vehicle, with panzer escort. The Mammoth was a British Army caravan-type lorry converted into a headquarters truck.

assault was to go in during the afternoon of the 21st. During the night of 20/21 November he realised that the Eighth Army's concentration for a decisive operation around Tobruk placed his forces in a dangerous position and sent off a further signal: 'Situation critical. Move with utmost speed.' He was right to be concerned. The break-out formations in Tobruk had begun to undertake their sortie towards El Duda, a place only 7 km to the north of the heights at Sidi Rezegh, where the 5th South African Brigade was already in position and towards which two brigades of the 7th Armoured Division were hurrying. The battlefield situation then became unbelievably complicated.

It is hardly surprising that confusion was felt on both sides. During 21 November, a situation had developed whereby, on a north-south line across nearly 40 km of desert, from the south-eastern corner of Tobruk and extending into the open desert to the south-east of Sidi Rezegh airfield, the units of both sides were intricately mixed. The Tobruk garrison, which had opened its break out, was being confronted by German and Italian formations which were facing both north and west, fighting to contain and force back the sortie. At the back of these Axis units were other formations from Panzer Group Africa, facing southwards, which were under attack from part of the 7th Support Group, which was itself part of the 7th Armoured Division. To the north of the Sidi Rezegh airfield was the remainder of the 7th Support Group and other elements of the 7th Armoured Division, both of which were facing north and south, fighting hard against divisions of the Afrika Korps which were advancing northwards with the 4th and 22nd Armoured Brigades in vigorous pursuit. On the tactically important Point 175 to the east of Sidi Rezegh there were detachments from the German 36lst Regiment, while to the west stood the whole of the 155th Regiment.

Supply convoys searched in vain for their parent units amidst the whirling haze. It was confusion piled upon confusion. Much of this arose because of the difficulty of identification. A rapidly approaching cloud of dust would indicate the arrival of vehicles, but were they friendly or hostile; were they soft-skinned or armoured? Over much of

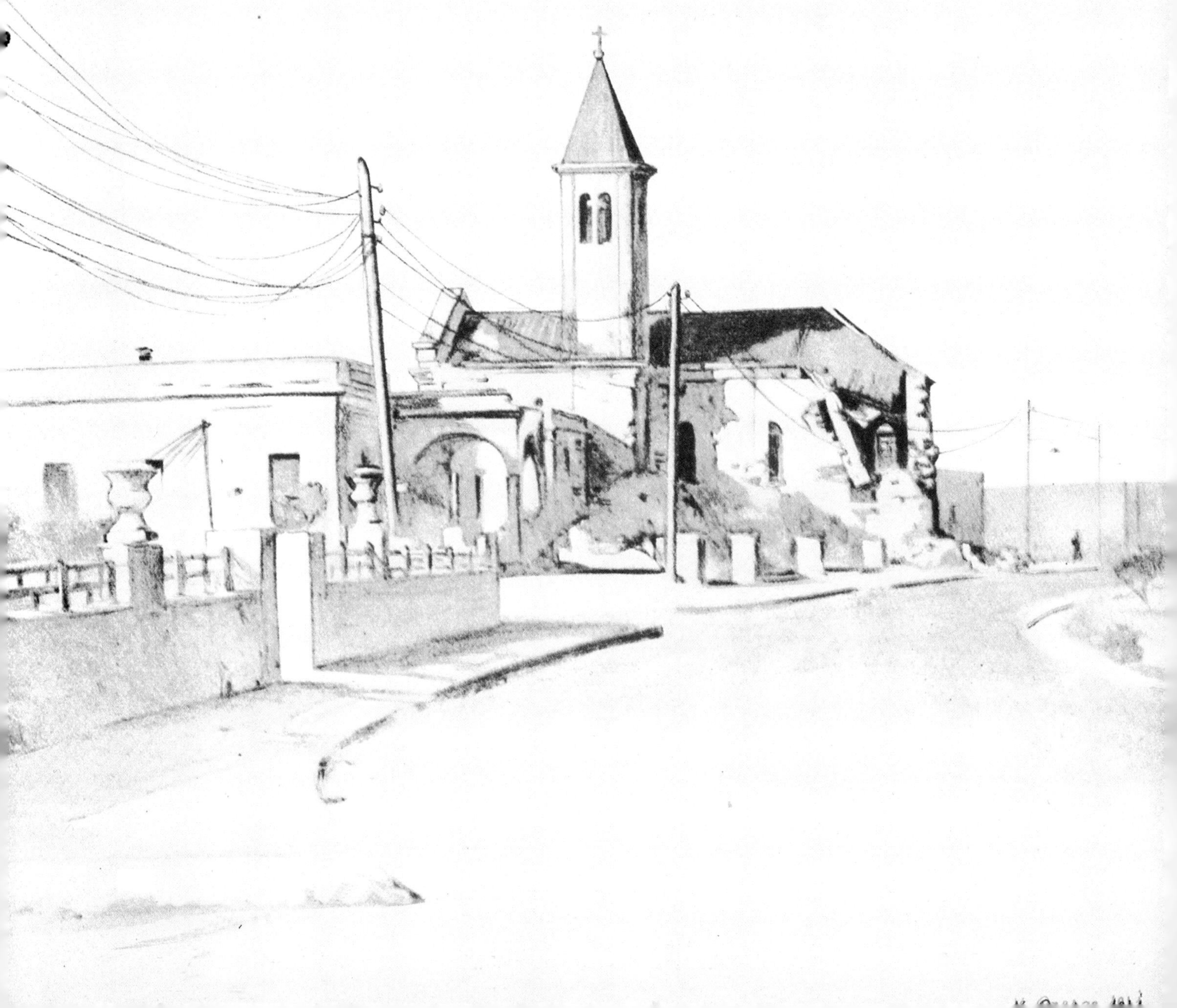

The ruined church in Bardia, behind which was the little house which once served as the quarters of the General Commanding Afrika Korps.

the battlefield hung opaque curtains of sand of such density and so all - concealing that within and beneath them units blundered into and clashed with other formations only dimly made out in the swirling dust. Wireless orders were succeeded by counter-orders giving the panzer formations new objectives. This often meant that, advancing along the new thrust lines, they would again crash into and fight against 8th Army units they were convinced they had already destroyed. None knew who the troops on either flank were, or which units were ahead, or which were at the rear. Victory went to the side which was quickest to identify that the vehicles in the approaching dust clouds were the enemy, and engaged them successfully.

In the Tobruk sector the break-out forces' actions had cut a six-kilometre wide corridor through the encircling Axis ring. Though the break out had succeeded it had been costly in men and machines. The 7th Armoured Division's 6th Royal Tank Regiment, which should have fought its way to the perimeter exit, was almost destroyed in close and bitter fighting as it advanced towards El Duda. Worse was to come. Both brigades of the 7th Armoured Division were hit in turn and severely mauled. The advance of the Eighth Army's relief force towards Tobruk then ground to halt, thwarted chiefly by the 90th Light and 'Bologna' Divisions. One battalion of the 90th Light's 361st Regiment – which, it will be recalled, was composed mainly of Foreign Legionaires who had once been German nationals – did not wait to be attacked by British armour but went out tank-hunting, destroying them with explosive charges and land mines. It was at the height of the fighting, during the late morning of 21 November, that the leading elements of Afrika Korps reached the battlefield and struck into the back of the 7th Armoured Division's two brigades.

Rommel had ordered the panzers to advance, but had directed that their main body was to move northwards, leaving just a minimum force on the ground to pin the British down. The main bodies of the 15th and 21st Panzer Divisions had therefore moved off in a north-westerly direction, in line abreast, with 15th Panzer striking towards Sidi Rezegh and 21st Panzer thrusting for Belhamed. Once contact

A view of the high cliffs around Bardia. In the foreground is a 2 cm rapid-firing anti-aircraft gun, acting in a shore defence capacity. On the far high ground lorries move across the escarpment.

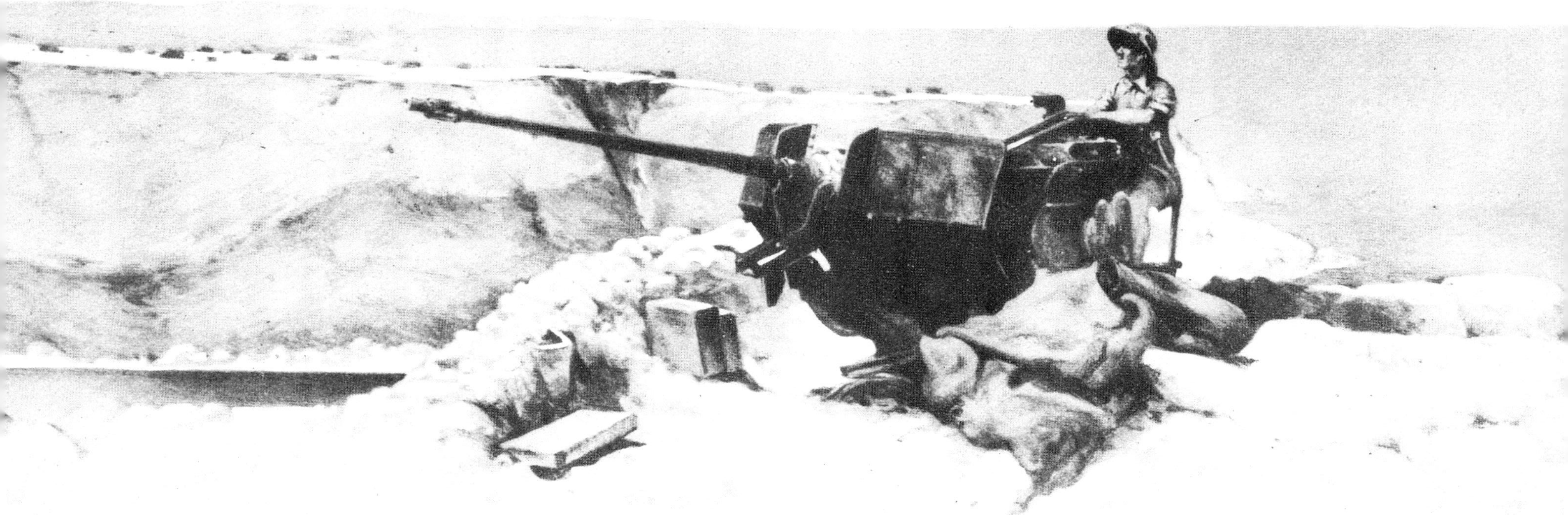

was made with the 7th Armoured Division's brigades, the panzers, firing while on the move, soon inflicted heavy casualties, driving the British regiments back until, by midday, both panzer divisions had gained the high ground to the south-east of Sidi Rezegh. The 7th Armoured Division struck back at the Germans with a thrust into their flank, but was itself struck by the concentrated fire of Afrika Korps artillery and panzers, which deflected it with heavy loss. As the onset of darkness brought the day's fighting to an end both sides knew that a major battle would be fought on the morrow.

The workshops of the 15th and the 21st Panzer Divisions worked hard during the hours of darkness, and the panzer units moved out to do battle while it was still night. The 15th Panzer Division was ordered to move eastward to a position on the deep flank of 7th Armoured Division, while the 21st was to thrust upwards from Belhamed and make ground to the north of Trigh Capuzzo. There was, nevertheless, concern for both formations because, once again, their supply trucks had not reached them. The soft-skin units had not been advised that their parent formations had moved out, and it was 10.00 hrs before they made contact so that fuel tanks could be filled, ammunition loaded into lockers, and the men fed. Rommel waited impatiently, but at about midday the 21st was able to move out to confront the Eighth Army's regiments around Sidi Rezegh, which promptly withdrew and involved the 8th Regiment's 1st Battalion in a running battle which continued throughout the afternoon and into the night.

The situation which had been confused enough during 21 November became more so during the days that followed, with panzer units being sent out and then ordered to return. As an example of this confusion, on 22 November Crüwell sent 15th Panzer off to make contact with the 'Ariete' Division. En route it smashed into the 7th Support Group and scattered it. While still recovering from the shock of battle, it then clashed with the 5th South African Brigade. During the late afternoon it made contact with 'Ariete', positioned around Bir El Gobi, where they were joined by the 5th Panzer Regiment, which Crüwell had sent out in support. Then came a signal ordering the

German formations to return to the Tobruk battlefield, and en route both attacked the South African brigade. This time the South Africans were prepared, and at first held off the German attacks. Eventually, however, weight of numbers prevailed and much of the 5th Brigade was wiped out.

Next the Germans collided with the 4th Armoured Brigade, laagered to the east of the shattered South Africans, with the laager of the 22nd Armoured Brigade on their western flank. With low clouds and neither moon nor starlight, winter nights in the desert are thick and impenetrable, and the commanders of 15th Panzer Division's spearhead group, standing in their turrets, did not see the 8th Hussars' laager in the inky blackness until they blundered into it. There was initial confusion until a white Very signal light, fired off by the commander of the lead panzer, guided the other German units to the spot, by which time 4th Armoured Brigade's headquarters and the 8th Hussars were already in action. But theirs was an assault born of desperation and the desert night was soon illuminated by the fires of their burning tanks.

The advance northwards by 21st Panzer reached Sidi Rezegh airfield, where nearly 200 British vehicles were drawn up ready to open an attack. An all-arms battle developed here, with infantry, armour, artillery and aircraft all engaged, the outcome of this general melee being that the remnants of the 7th Armoured Division and 7th Support Group were shattered. This battle not only put the Sidi Rezegh airfield back into German hands, but in addition helped to thwart the break out attempts by the Tobruk garrison.

Rommel's six-page signal sent out during the night of 22/23 November stated his intentions for the Afrika Korps and Gambarra's Corps di Manovra. They were to carry out an encircling operation on the 23rd and to force a decision at the south-eastern corner of the Tobruk perimeter. When Crüwell received the coded signal he saw that it would take hours to decipher, and realised that he could not wait that long. He therefore determined to operate in the way which he thought Rommel would expect, setting out at 05.30 hrs with a few of his staff

Fort Capuzzo, one of the most hotly contested places in eastern Libya.

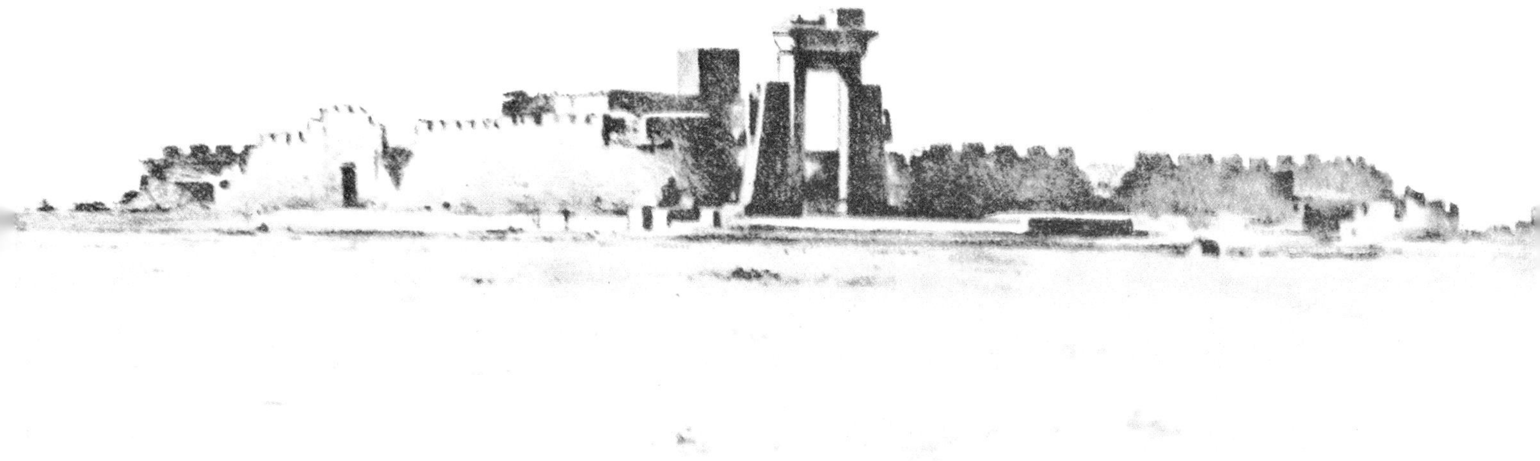

and leaving orders for the rest of Afrika Korps to follow half an hour later. However, these follow-up units were intercepted by the 6th Brigade of the 2nd New Zealand Division, which shot them up and dispersed them. As a result of this short, sharp engagement Crüwell lost his corps staff and all his documents and communications systems. He was nevertheless able to order the Afrika Korps to attack the Eighth Army's rear, emphasising his orders with the words: 'The enemy must be decisively beaten today.' Acting upon the corps commander's orders, 21st Panzer battled hard to knock out the remnants of the 7th Armoured Division at Sidi Rezegh, while 15th Panzer advanced deep into the Eighth Army's rear area. In the Tobruk ring the 'Pavia' Division halted another break out attempt, while 'Ariete', racing through the desert from Bir el Gobi, gained contact with 15th Panzer. Crüwell then regrouped the German and Italian units.

The *Schwerpunkt* of the attack was in the sector held by the 8th Panzer Regiment, with 'Ariete' on the left and the 5th Panzer Regiment on the right. The solid mass of Axis armour drove forward until at length it crashed into a line of anti-tank guns manned by another South African unit, the 1st Brigade. A battle developed which spread across the whole width of the Axis front, with duels being fought between guns and panzers, as well as between the armoured vehicles of both sides. Slowly the great Axis mass prevailed and the British units were compressed more closely between the German and Italian jaws. The solid block of three Axis armoured divisions formed front to deliver the killing blow, and at 14.30 hrs the advance began. At the end of two hours of bitter fighting 8th Panzer had smashed all resistance in its sector, but 5th Panzer had itself been attacked by a thrust which drove it eastwards and out of wireless range, rendering a coordinated assault by the German units impossible. There then followed another confused battle, with panzers being sent off to relieve pressure on German infantry, and other German infantry units attacking to relieve pressure on the panzers. The final attack during this episode was made by a scratch force created by Cramer out of men of the divisional pioneer battalion, carried on lorries and accompanied by the panzers of the regimental defence platoon. Late in the afternoon reports came in that the Sidi Rezegh airfield had been taken and that firm contact had been made with 21st Panzer.

This division had been ordered to halt the British thrust towards Tobruk but, as we have seen, its panzers had been detached to serve with 15th Panzer. It had been left to the divisional infantry and artillery to hold the British drive, and so successful had been their actions that XXX Corps had been unable to make contact with the Tobruk garrison. At the end of the day Afrika Korps reported that between seventy and a hundred British tanks had been destroyed, that the 22nd Armoured Brigade had been totally defeated, and the 5th South African Brigade scattered. Rommel's signal to Berlin at midnight on 23 November reported that his intention the following day was to complete the destruction of the 7th Armoured Division and then advance to Sidi Omar, in order to attack the British forces in the Sollum area of the eastern enclave. British losses had been disastrous, but those to the Axis forces were proportionately even worse, because whereas the British could be re-equipped from their stores in the Canal Zone, Rommel could only be resupplied from mainland Europe. To cite but one example of the reduction of Afrika Korps strength, the 8th Panzer Regiment had lost forty-three vehicles in the day's fighting.

On 24 November Crüwell had reported the destruction of the British at Sidi Rezegh, and Rommel, accepting that the Eighth Army's forces around Tobruk had been eliminated, issued orders for operations in the eastern enclave to be stepped up. Habata and Maddalena were to be taken quickly in order to cut the Eighth Army's supply route, and the attack was then to go on to seize Sidi Omar. To achieve this he stripped Tobruk's encircling ring of most of its panzer forces and put them into the eastern advance. However, the battle for Sidi Omar turned out not to be the quick victory which he had expected; the Eighth Army was prepared for him, in good defensive positions, and fought desperately against the panzer regiments. Then the RAF struck the 33rd Reconnaissance Battalion as it thrust for Habata, scattering it. Determined to force a decision, Rommel ordered

15th Panzer to sweep past Sidi Omar, and then to wheel and attack it from the east. This strike cost the division seventeen of the twenty tanks involved in the operation. When night fell on 25 November it was clear to Rommel that his 'race to the wire' had failed. His forces were too weak to gain the victory, and the evidence of the Axis failure was the reduction in strength of the 5th Panzer Regiment to just twelve machines, only two of which were still 'runners'.

Rommel must have known that the attack to the east would be a high risk operation. He was assaulting an enemy who had short lines of communication and who still possessed a reserve of men, guns and tanks close at hand, while his own lines of supply were lengthening and his forces diminishing in strength. The 26th, a day already filled with difficulties, developed into one of successive crises, chief of these being a massive failure of radio communications. Some units had moved out of wireless range, in addition to which the German radio equipment was beginning to malfunction, and bad weather was affecting reception. These factors added together meant that the Afrika Korps ended up thrashing about, mounting uncoordinated and generally unsuccessful attacks in the absence of firm control. There were minor tactical victories, but not the decisive blow which Rommel had hoped for.

At this moment of crisis, the Eighth Army around Tobruk suddenly increased the tempo of the fighting. Westphal, Rommel's Ia, saw from the situation maps that the encircling ring around Tobruk, which had been stripped of its panzer units, was now too weak to withstand the Eighth Army's attacks at the approaches to the fortress. To compound this dangerous situation, the Tobruk garrison had once again broken out and this time had made firm contact with the Eighth Army. It was a serious crisis, and Westphal tried in vain to raise Rommel on the radio to advise him of the grave situation in which Panzer Group Africa found itself. When his attempts to get hold of him by radio failed he sent out five Fieseler Storch aircraft in succession, each of which was shot down.

Acting in the accepted fashion of holders of his office, Westphal

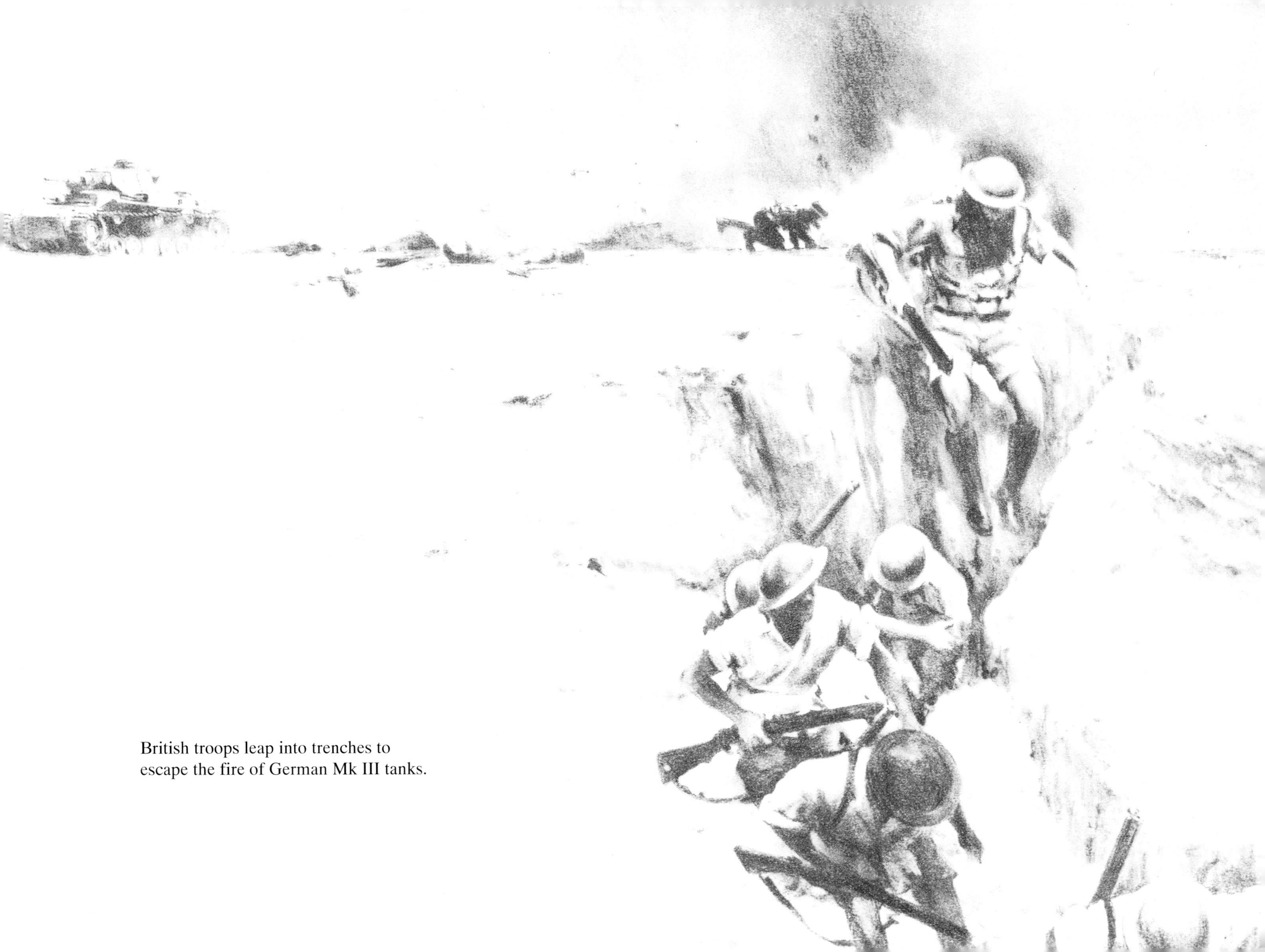

British troops leap into trenches to
escape the fire of German Mk III tanks.

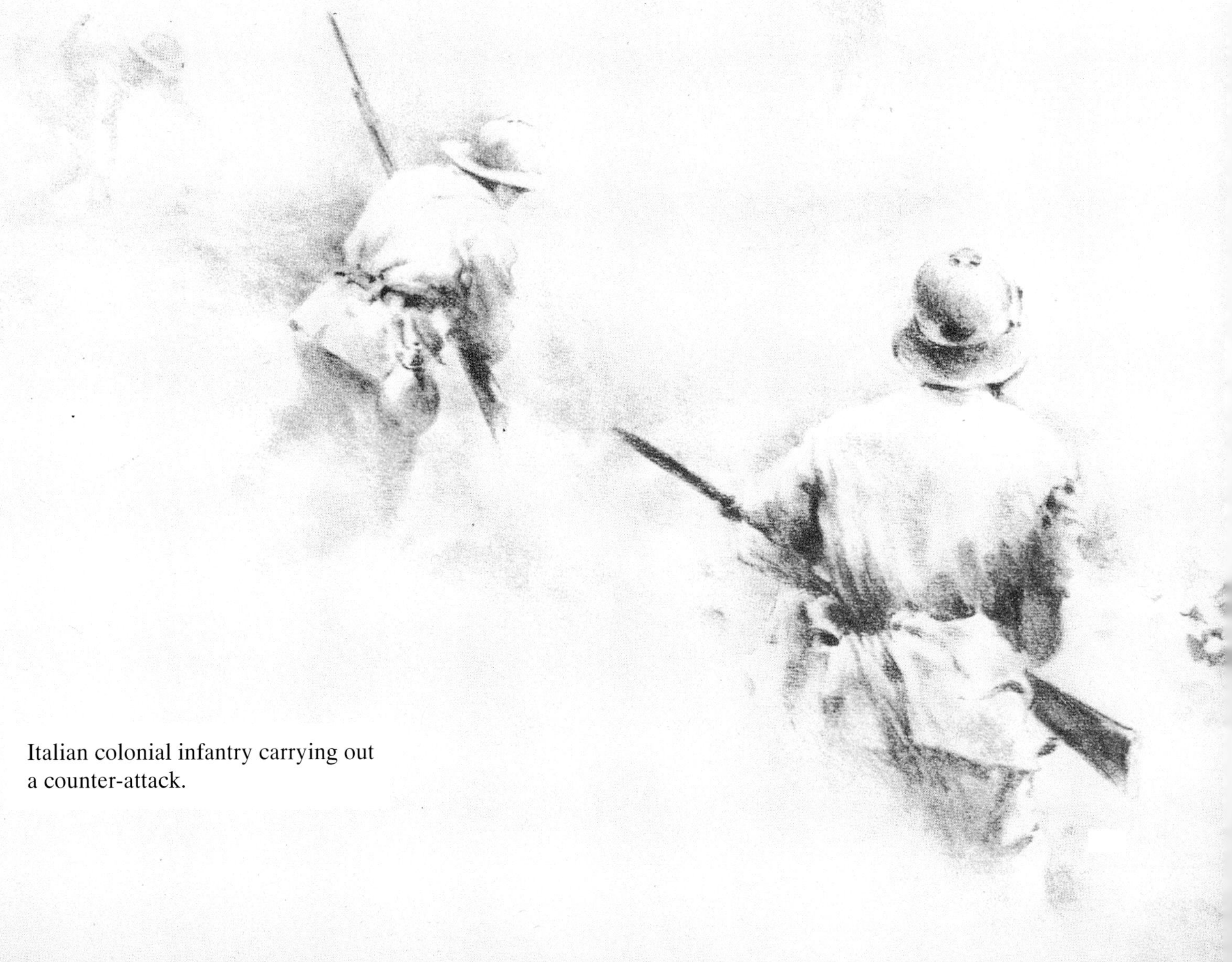

Italian colonial infantry carrying out
a counter-attack.

finally took a decision without waiting for his superior's approval. On 27 November, using the corps headquarters' powerful transmitter, he sent the following signal: 'All previous orders are hereby cancelled. Afrika Korps will return at best possible speed to Tobruk.' The divisions which had been anticipating an attack eastwards toward Egypt, then wheeled round and headed north-westwards towards Tobruk. When Rommel learned of Westphal's signal he was livid with anger and threatened a court martial until he saw from the maps how dangerous the situation had become. He consequently not only approved Westphal's action but recommended him for the Knight's Cross. When Rommel met Bastico at El Adem on 30 November, he told his Italian superior that the offensive had become a battle of attrition which he could not win. On 2 December he reported to Führer HQ on the victories which Panzer Army Africa had gained, although he knew that his efforts had not resulted in the total success that had been hoped for. An entry in his diary reads: 'Afrika Korps' thrust did not succeed, chiefly because there was no co-operation by the Italian Corps di Manovra ... The enemy will soon go over to the attack using superior forces.' Despite this gloomy forecast, Rommel still hoped for success in the Bir el Gobi sector, recognising that should he fail to gain a victory here then the only alternative would be for him to break off the fighting and to retreat back to the Gazala positions.

The attack which opened on 6 December depended entirely for its success upon Gambarra bringing his corps to the battle in good time. He did not, and the outcome was unavoidable. Then Crüwell, commanding Afrika Korps, requested permission to retreat in order to save his corps from total destruction, and Rommel agreed. The withdrawal began during the night of 8 December and did not stop at the Gazala position. Rommel reported to Führer HQ on 15 December that Panzer Group Africa would not be able to hold this line, and that a retreat to El Mechili–Derna had to be expected. Despite entreaties from the Italians to hold Cyrenaica, Rommel was adamant; the retreat must continue if the Army was to be saved to fight again.

Throughout the coming weeks the pattern of life for the fighting

German troops attaching a British 25-pdr gun to its Quad, or towing tractor. The gun is in a prepared position and is ringed with sandbags, but the cover still on the muzzle indicates that it must have been captured before it could be brought into action. Caesar's note at the bottom of the drawing says that it was made south of El Adem, *ie* during the Gazala battle of late-May or early-June 1942.

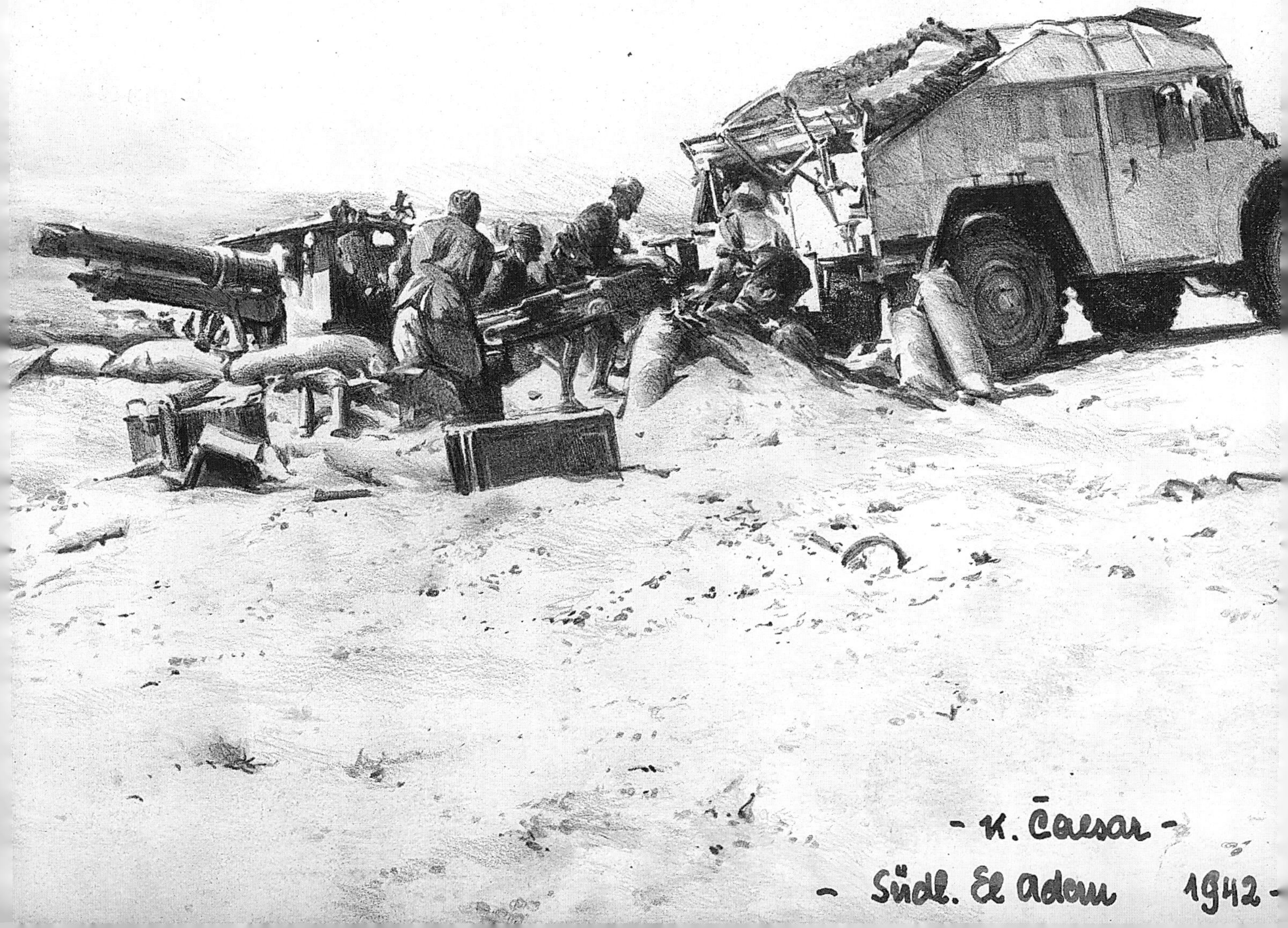

echelons of Afrika Korps was constant. A withdrawal to a point where a stand could be made against the pursuing Eighth Army, then a brisk action followed by a further retreat. By 12 January 1942, Panzer Group Africa was in the Mersa el Brega position. Although its main body had managed to pull back in time, it had not been possible to bring out the units isolated in the eastern enclave, some 700 km distant. They were trapped. Bardia fell on 2 January, and Sollum only a few days later, but Captain Bach at Halfaya held out until 17 January before surrendering. When Halfaya fell there were no longer any German fighting units east of Mersa el Brega.

The Axis forces had been forced on the defensive during December, but that situation changed with the arrival of convoys from Italy towards the end of the month and during January. The RAF had been temporarily driven from the skies, and the number of ships in the Royal Navy's Mediterranean Fleet had been cut back, forcing it to reduce its operations. Japan had entered the war, resulting in the Royal Navy's Australian contingent returning home. Aware of the changed situation which now favoured the Axis Powers, Westphal proposed a pre-emptive strike before the Eighth Army grew too strong. Rommel agreed, and in the early hours of 21 January a new offensive was opened. Battle Group Marcks headed the assault, with Rommel in the lead vehicle of the spearhead. As the advance commenced, a signal from Führer HQ stated that the Panzer Group Africa would in future be known as Panzer Army Africa.

The offensive rolled on, repeating the pattern of the previous year, and Rommel, up with the forward units and able to evaluate the situation, frequently amended the battle plan. An offensive operation which had begun with a string of minor victories then developed to become an outstanding triumph of his tactical skills, his flexibility, and his personal leadership. By 6 February 1942 the Eighth Army had been driven from Cyrenaica, leaving behind it hundreds of trucks and tanks. With the capture of Benghazi after only 17 days of cross-desert movement and lightning operations, Panzer Army Africa stood along the Gazala line once more. Behind the tired but exultant ground troops

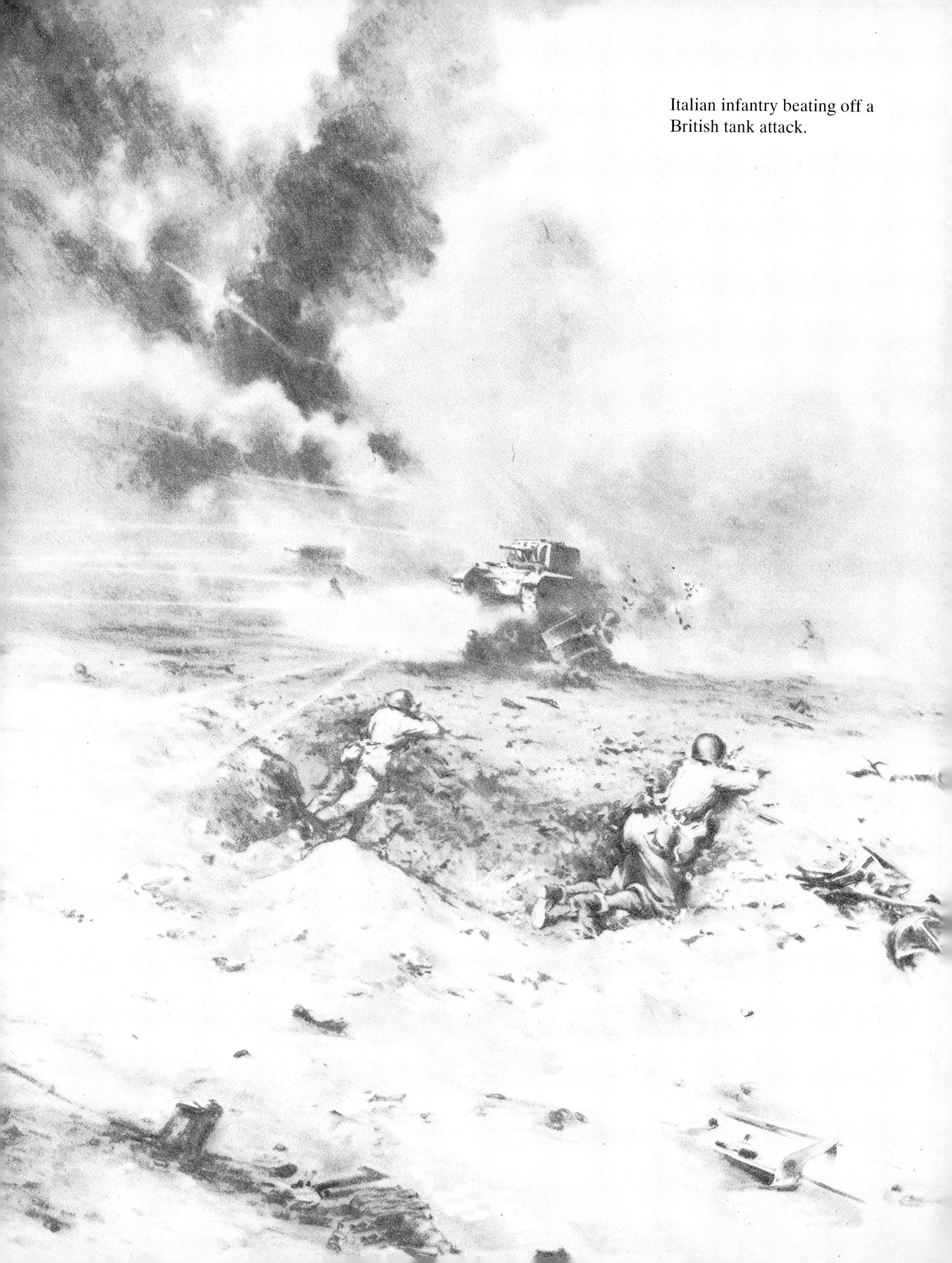

Italian infantry beating off a
British tank attack.

Luftwaffe units moved back to re-occupy the battlefield's forward airstrips. More and more reinforcements came in, and Rommel, now promoted to the rank of Colonel General, began to plan a summer offensive that would this time capture Tobruk and roll on to destroy the Eighth Army.

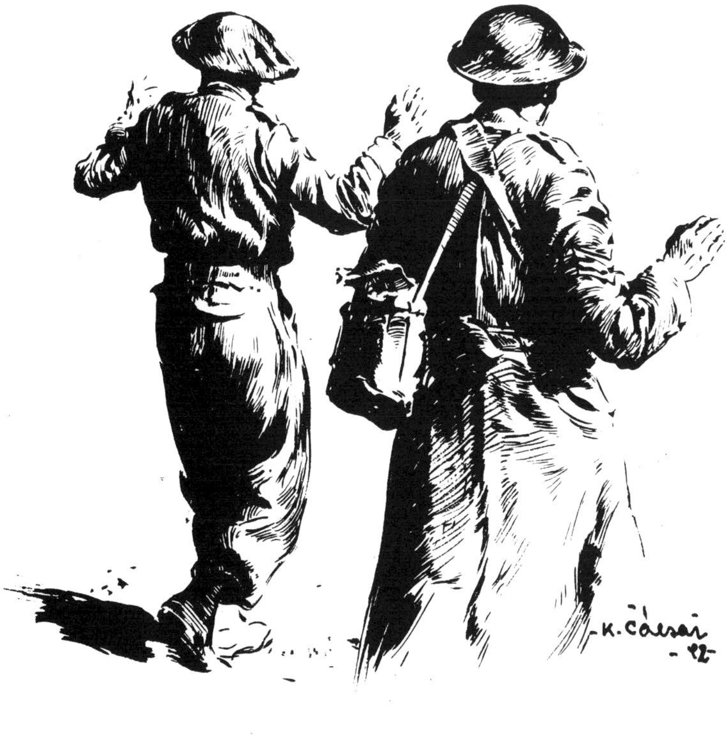

Three German soldiers pushing a staff car through clinging sand. From the sign 'Knightsbridge' it is likely that the drawing was made close to the Trigh Capuzzo some time in late-May or early-June 1942.

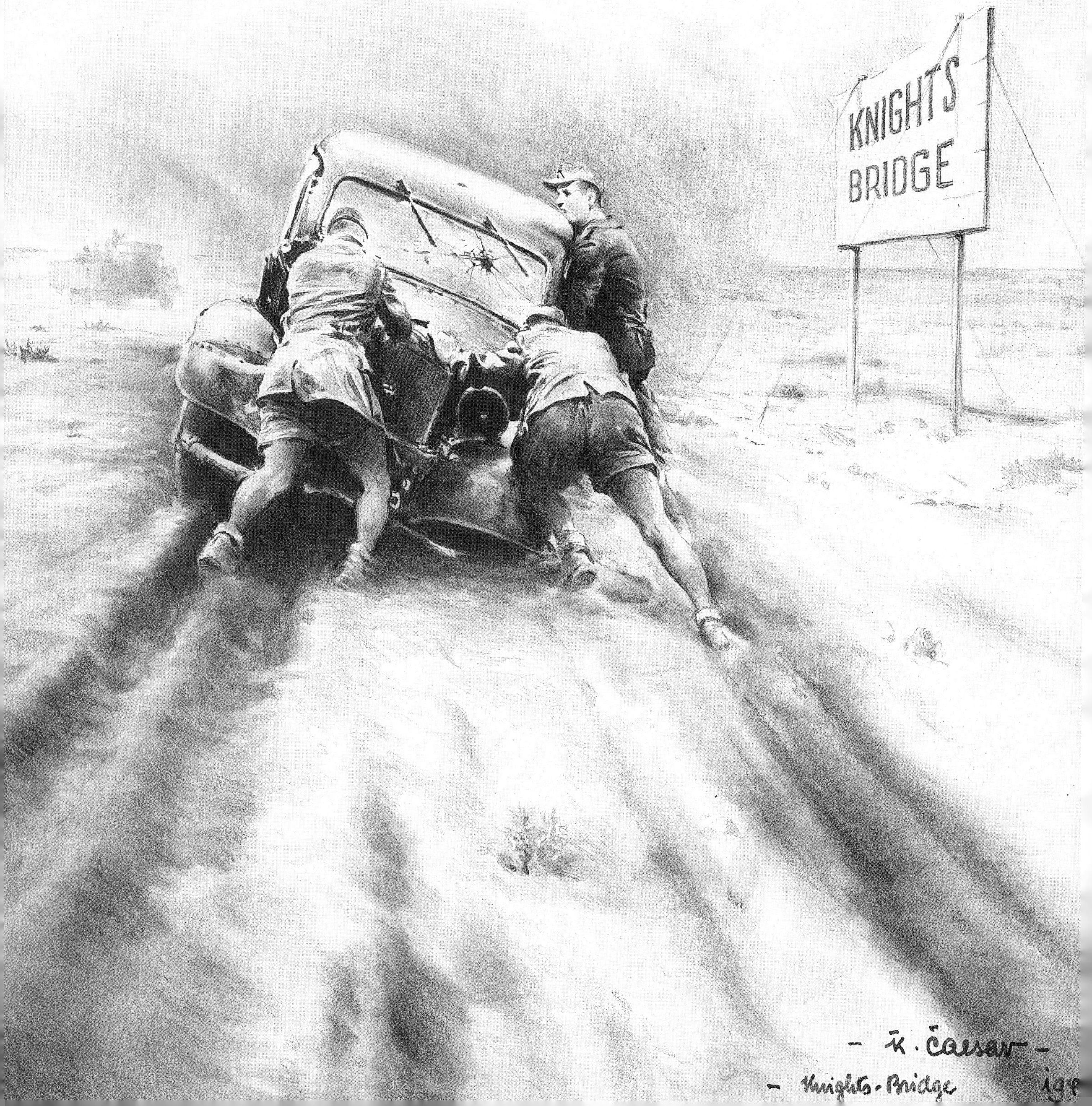

# THE FIFTH CAMPAIGN – MAY TO NOVEMBER 1942

*After a three-month pause in the fighting, Rommel's ambitious summer offensive turns the southern flank of the Gazala line at Bir Hachim. Armoured clashes around 'Knightsbridge' inflict heavy losses upon the British tank regiments and force the Eighth Army to begin a retreat which ends to the west of the El Alamein positions. German attempts to smash through that defensive line are repulsed. Rommel, recognising that his force is too weak to gain a victory, breaks off the battle to await reinforcements.*

*When these arrive he opens an offensive at Alam Halfa which is beaten back with heavy losses. On 23 October 1942, Montgomery opens his offensive at El Alamein which smashes the Axis armies. In order to avoid their total destruction, Rommel orders them to retreat. The Eighth Army pursues the Axis forces across Libya, captures Tripoli, and finally corners the Italo-German armies in Tunisia, bringing the war in Africa to an end.*

The Gazala line to which Rommel's reconquest of Cyrenaica had brought him extended inland from the Mediterranean for about 70 km, and was protected by vast 'marshes' of anti-personnel and anti-tank mines. The Eighth Army's battle line was made up of a series of static, semi-permanent field fortifications known as 'boxes', capable of all-round defence, all of which were garrisoned by infantry and artillery. To the west of the 'box' line there were vast minefields, and to the east British tank regiments were deployed, ready for the clash of armour which the Eighth Army's commander anticipated would take place in the Gazala–Tobruk–Bir Hachim area.

Rommel trained his men hard for the forthcoming battle, taking them through individual training to company level and then battalion exercises, with special emphasis on all-arms collaboration and ending with

A Panzer IV rolling over a destroyed British artillery position in the Halfaya Pass.

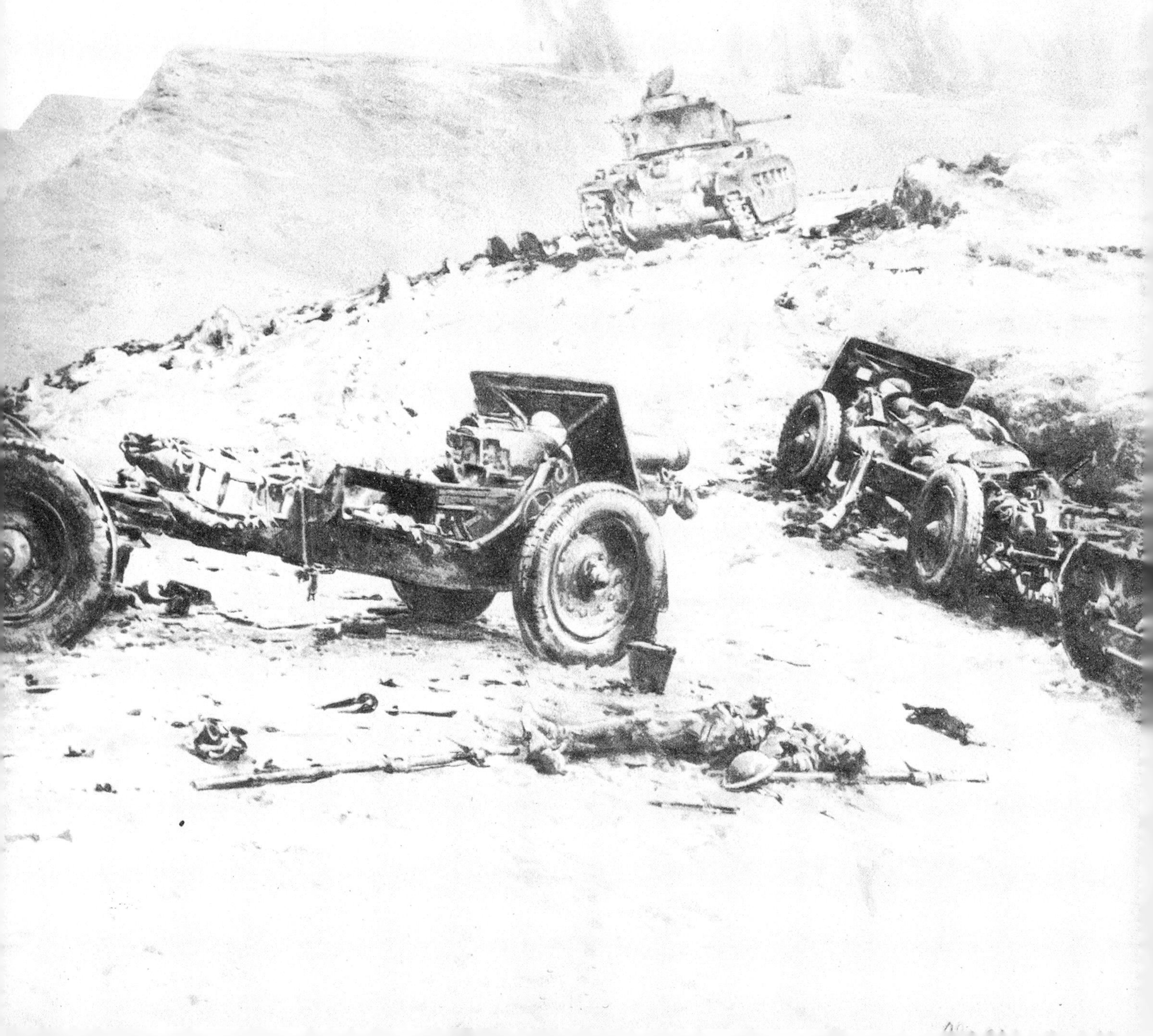

divisional manoeuvres. Although there had been a steady stream of reinforcements, comprising both men and armour, these were not sufficient to replace the losses which had been suffered. There were now 12,000 men fewer on Afrika Korps' establishment, and the most acute shortage was in infantry. The panzer regiments had fared better, but even though the 21st Panzer Division, for instance, had increased its strength to 165 machines, this figure was still seriously below war establishment.

Rommel's plan for the forthcoming battle was to launch a feint attack in the northern sector of the Gazala line using the Italian infantry divisions, who would be supported by elements of the 90th Light Division. This feint would be made against the most northerly 'boxes' of the British line. A few days before the feint attack opened Rommel intended to deceive the Eighth Army into thinking that the Axis panzer strength was being concentrated in the north, by having lorries and panzers drive about to throw up massive dust clouds. He was convinced that Eighth Army headquarters would immediately move the 1st and 7th Armoured Divisions to the northern sector and would position them close behind the infantry/artillery 'boxes'. With the British armour now drawn to the northern flank, he would move his main force southwards.

On the night of D-Day minus 1 he would lead out the whole armoured mass of Panzer Group – now Panzer Army – Africa. This great armada of German and Italian vehicles would pass down the western front of the British minefields to reach Bir Hachim – the most southerly 'box' – before dawn. Here the vast mass of armoured and soft-skin machines would pause to regroup, after which the panzer divisions of Afrika Korps, supported by the 90th Light Division, would wheel south of the Bir Hachim 'box' and thereby turn the flank of the Gazala line. The Italian armoured units were to attack the southern 'boxes'. The Afrika Korps would then deploy for battle and advance northwards behind the line of 'boxes' towards the Mediterranean. On its northward march it would then strike into the flank and rear of the two British armoured divisions, and with those formations defeated the offensive would turn in a north-westerly direction and roll on to take out Tobruk. Another pause for regrouping, and then the main attack force would return to Gazala, where the line of British 'boxes'

A field kitchen near the front line.

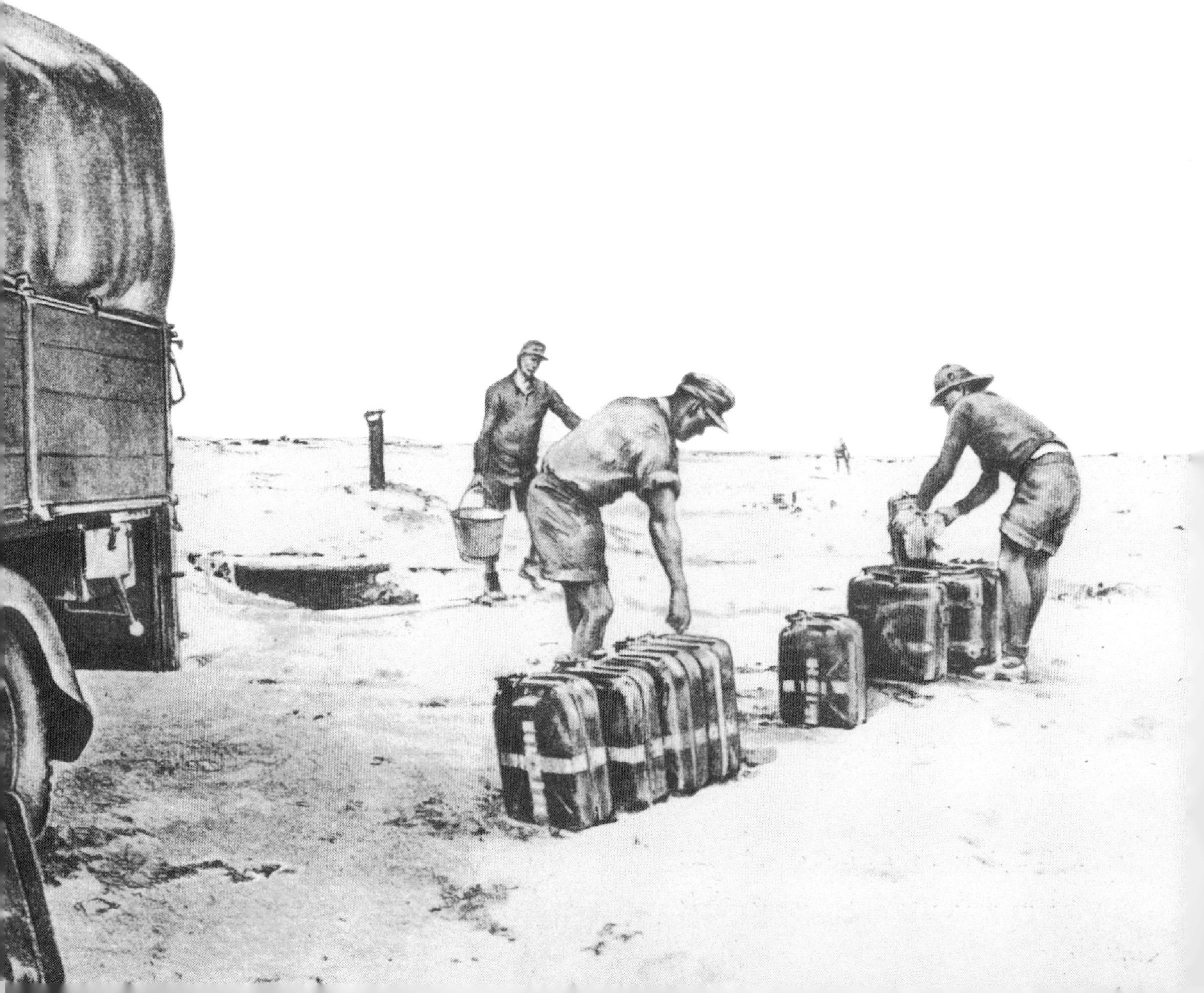

would be attacked and rolled up in succession, leaving the way open for Panzer Army Africa to advance eastwards to the Canal.

This was Rommel's most daring offensive. The opening move would be a long night drive through the desert by the Afrika Korps, the 90th Light Division, and the whole of the Italian Corpo di Manovra. This vast armada of over 500 vehicles would maintain cohesion by driving at the controlled speed of eight miles per hour, and direction would be kept by the vehicles moving on a precise compass bearing.

During the morning of 26 May 1942, the feint attack opened against the 'boxes' in the north of the Gazala line and then, after last light, the main body began its march across the desert. The organisation of this drive had been planned in exhaustive detail. Rommel had long since learned that in desert operations military pragmatism was in many cases no substitute for detailed planning. He had chosen the night of 26 May for the offensive because there was a full moon which would provide good visibility, but to supplement the moonlight, as well as to guide the column, he had also ordered his pioneer units to lay out shaded lamps, the beams from which would be visible only to drivers moving along the *trigh*. This corridor of lamps extended from way up in the north nearly as far south as Bir Hachim. The night-time drive went well and shortly before dawn, just to the west of the Bir Hachim 'box', the vast concourse of vehicles halted, regrouped, and separated into its respective columns before moving towards their objectives. By midday Afrika Korps had driven so far north that it was behind – that is, to the east of – the British minefields. The 90th Light Division, half of whose strength had been committed to support the Italian feint attack, was positioned on the eastern flank, where it had the task of protecting the main thrust of the 21st and 15th Panzer Divisions when they clashed with the British armour.

The advance of Afrika Korps' three divisions had gone quite smoothly, but that of the Italian formations had been halted abruptly at Bir Hachim. The 'Ariete' Division, the most southerly formation of the Italian Corpo di Manovra, had crashed into a 'box' to the south of Bir Hachim which German intelligence sources had neither located nor identified. This was held by the 3rd Indian Brigade, and as the Italian formations swerved northwards to avoid its fire they came under attack from the Free French garrison of Bir Hachim. The Italians, now deeply committed to a battle which they had not expected to fight so early, had to call for help from Afrika Korps. The 21st Panzer Division was deflected from its northern advance and swung southwards to attack the Indian 'box'. Although the 3rd Indian Brigade had no heavy weapons to employ against the panzers, it fought off the first German attacks and was defeated only after bitter fighting. The deflection of 21st Panzer, involving it in a long drive and a fierce battle, led to its vehicles' fuel tanks running dry prematurely, and supplies could not be replenished because no petrol supplies were coming forward. The soft-skin fuel and ammunition columns, which should have followed the panzers, had been shot up and destroyed by roving British armoured units and the staunch defenders of Bir Hachim.

The main panzer group, now east of the British minefields, was ordered to conserve fuel by avoiding battle and withdrawing westwards until they had the minefields immediately at their backs. The Afrika Korps plan was to overcome the fuel crisis by ordering engineers to 'gap' the minefields and then to pass their supply columns through the gaps. The German engineers being all committed to battle elsewhere, orders were issued for Italian mine-clearing teams to undertake that task. They went to work with a will, imbued with the optimism of certain victory.

Reports that the Axis forces had retreated to a position where they had British minefields to the west and British armour to the east elated Eighth Army HQ, which reinforced the armoured units massively in order that its regiments could carry out a thrust which would destroy Afrika Korps. The confusion evident in desert fighting and the similarity to small-unit actions in naval warfare can be seen in an episode which occurred during the afternoon of 29 May, at the height of the Gazala battle.

Before the two panzer divisions had changed direction and drawn back to the protection of the British minefields, 15th Panzer, the more easterly of the pair, was struck in flank by a British tank group which thought it was operating against a beaten enemy, as indicated by the optimistic reports of GHQ in Cairo. It certainly seemed that this was so when they met, struck, rolled over and destroyed the lightly armoured German 'tail'

Two soldiers under a makeshift tent.

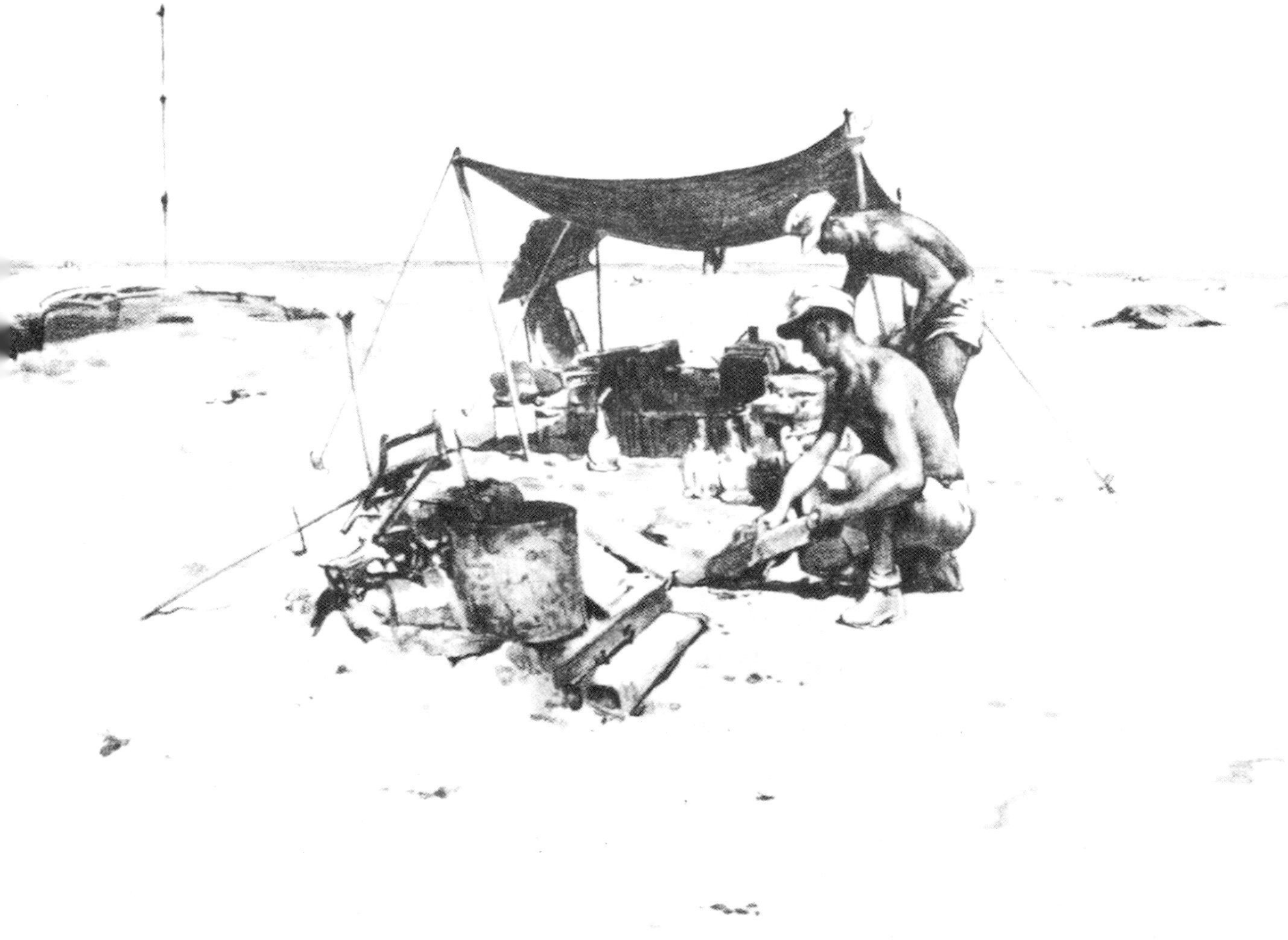

It is likely that this is a drawing of a German patrol group. All three vehicles appear to be *Schwimmwagen* mounting 2 cm flak guns.

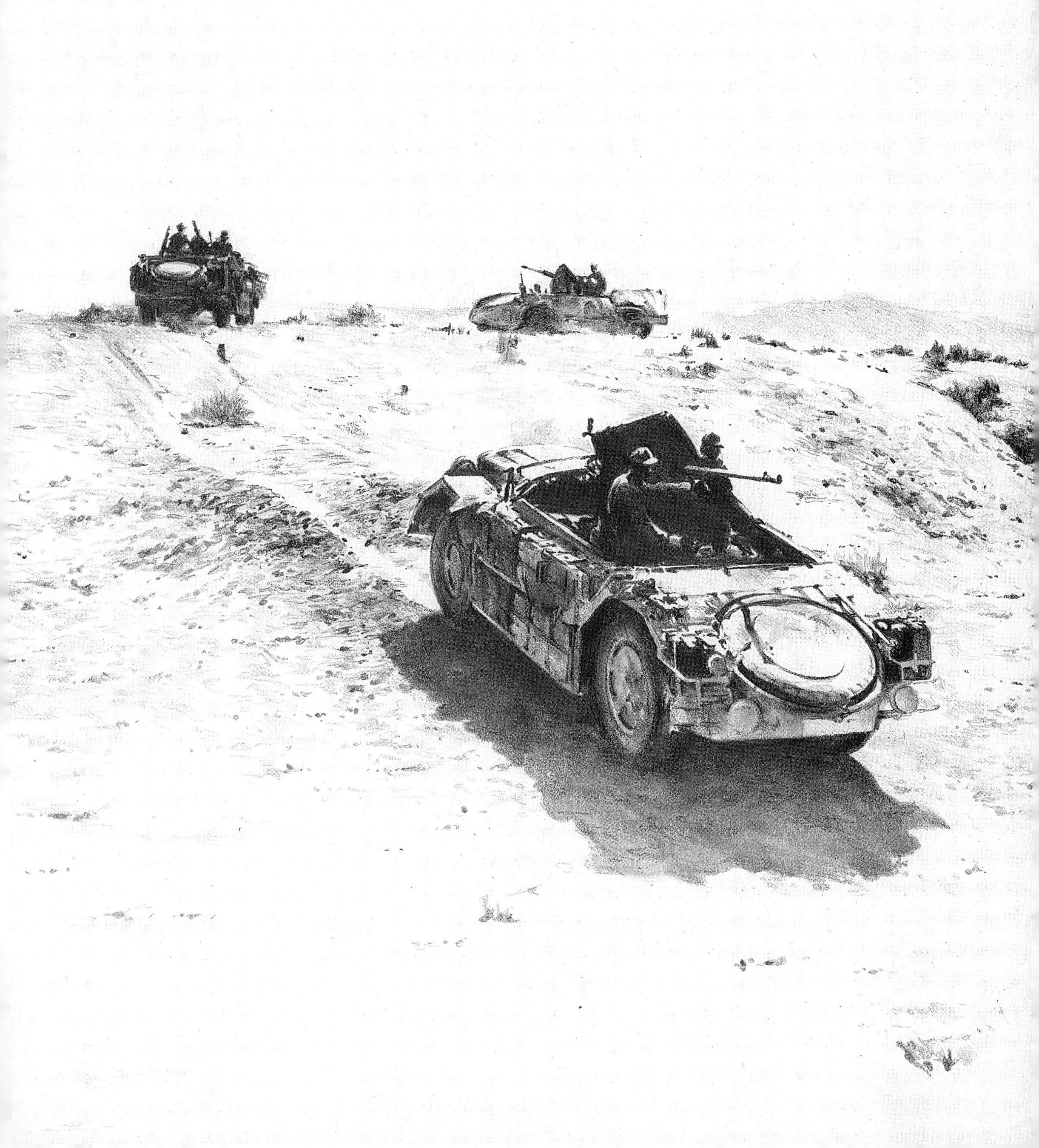

units. The Germans were only able to offer minimal opposition because the division's panzer regiment was at that time still fighting its way northwards towards Acroma. The German soft-skins which survived the fury of the British armoured attack retreated in wild disorder and in their confusion almost ran down General Nehring, the new commander of Afrika Korps, who had brought forward his corps HQ to assess the deteriorating situation. Together with Colonel Wolz, the commander of the flak regiment, Nehring was discussing countermeasures when the two officers were suddenly surrounded by rear echelon vehicles racing pell-mell across the desert in flight from the advancing British tank regiments. The general panic infected the tail units of Nehring's corps HQ and they, too, raced away westwards. Before long only Nehring and Wolz were left in the area.

Not long after this, a flak battery came roaring towards the two men out of the dust clouds. Accompanying it was an irate Rommel. Leaping from his staff car, he confronted Wolz and demanded to know why his guns were not firing. The General then went on to lay the blame for the whole retreat upon the fact that the flak detachments had failed to halt the British armour. Wolz stopped the retreat of the flak battery which had come with Rommel and then, together with Nehring, ranged out across the desert intercepting other flak units. Within a short time a line of 88s, nearly three kilometres in length, stood ready to receive the British charge. This was halted when it came, as were the successive but uncoordinated attacks which ensued, and when the day ended twenty-four British tanks lay broken or burning in front of the gun line. The surviving tanks voided the field and moved back into laager.

Although Eighth Army HQ was optimistic and believed that Rommel's forces were trapped between a wall of Eighth Army tanks in the east and British minefields to the west, this was not the situation as Rommel saw it. True, he was aware of the fuel shortage, but this was a temporary inconvenience, and in his eyes Panzer Army Africa was holding a bridgehead in the enemy minefields and was already gapping those fields. As soon as the 'box' at Bir Hachim had been taken out, and he had driven corridors through the gaps in the Gazala minefields, then the British

German armour overrunning a British battery position.

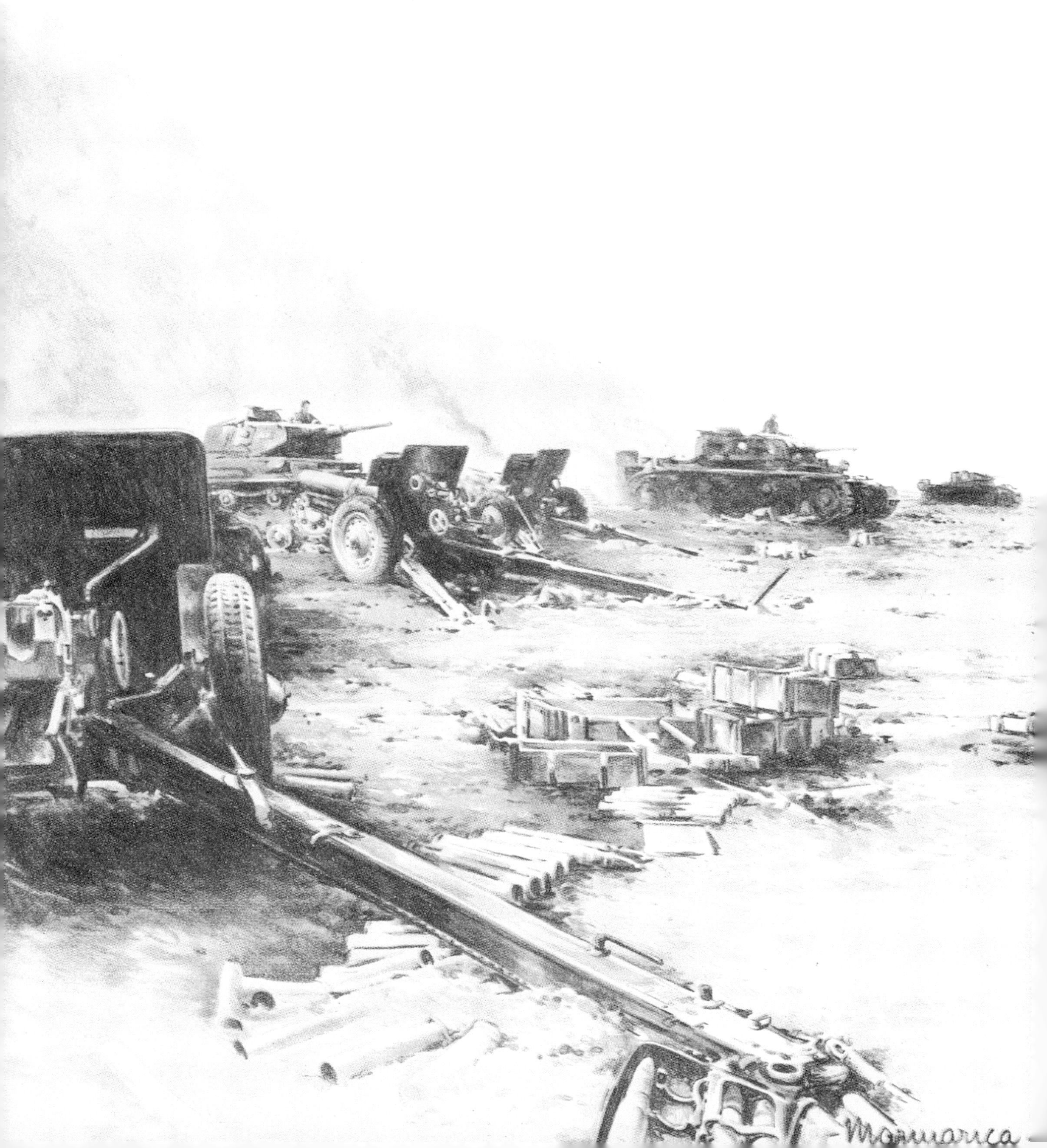

defences would have been torn wide open. He could then carry on with his attack northwards to the sea. Then came the welcome news that the minefields had been extensively gapped and that soft-skin convoys were already refuelling the panzer divisions. These now swung out to resume operations. Then another crisis developed. The British 2nd Armoured Brigade, striking westwards from Knightsbridge, had begun to drive a wedge between the panzer divisions to the north of the Trigh Cazpuzzo and the 'Ariete' Division to the south. Alerted to the danger, Afrika Korps HQ sent out orders for the Axis armoured formations to close in towards the centre. The 2nd Armoured Brigade, advancing with high elan, was struck by the concentrated fire of the three Axis panzer divisions and suffered heavily. Two other British armoured brigades were ordered in to reinforce the 2nd but their assaults were weak and unsupported. Afrika Korps and the 'Ariete' dealt harshly with them too. With the British tank attacks temporarily stalled, the German assault moved on to attack one of the 'boxes' between Gazala and Bir Hachim. This was held by the 150th Infantry Brigade of the 50th Division, and it was essential that it be taken out to ease Afrika Korps' still precarious supply situation. The 'box' was overrun after hard fighting, and then the weight of the Axis blow was directed against Bir Hachim.

When the Bir Hachim 'box' fell the remaining 'boxes' followed in quick succession. Then, on 12 June, the combined power of Afrika Korps' panzer divisions turned back northwards to savage the weakened armoured regiments in a series of swift operations which forced them to begin an eastward withdrawal. This withdrawal soon became a retreat, which degenerated into a rout. A great many British formations did not halt and take up a line west of Tobruk, as the commander-in-chief, Auchinleck, had directed, but continued to move eastwards until they were almost at the Egyptian frontier, where the Eighth Army's commander had ordered them to halt. The 'Gazala Gallop' was being run. The exultant Afrika Korps was in hot pursuit of the Eighth Army, intending to bring it to battle and to destroy it as an effective fighting force. While the main Axis body pursued the British fleeing eastwards, the divisions in the encircling ring entered with enthusiasm into the fight

British Mk II Infantry tanks, knocked out near Fort Capuzzo.

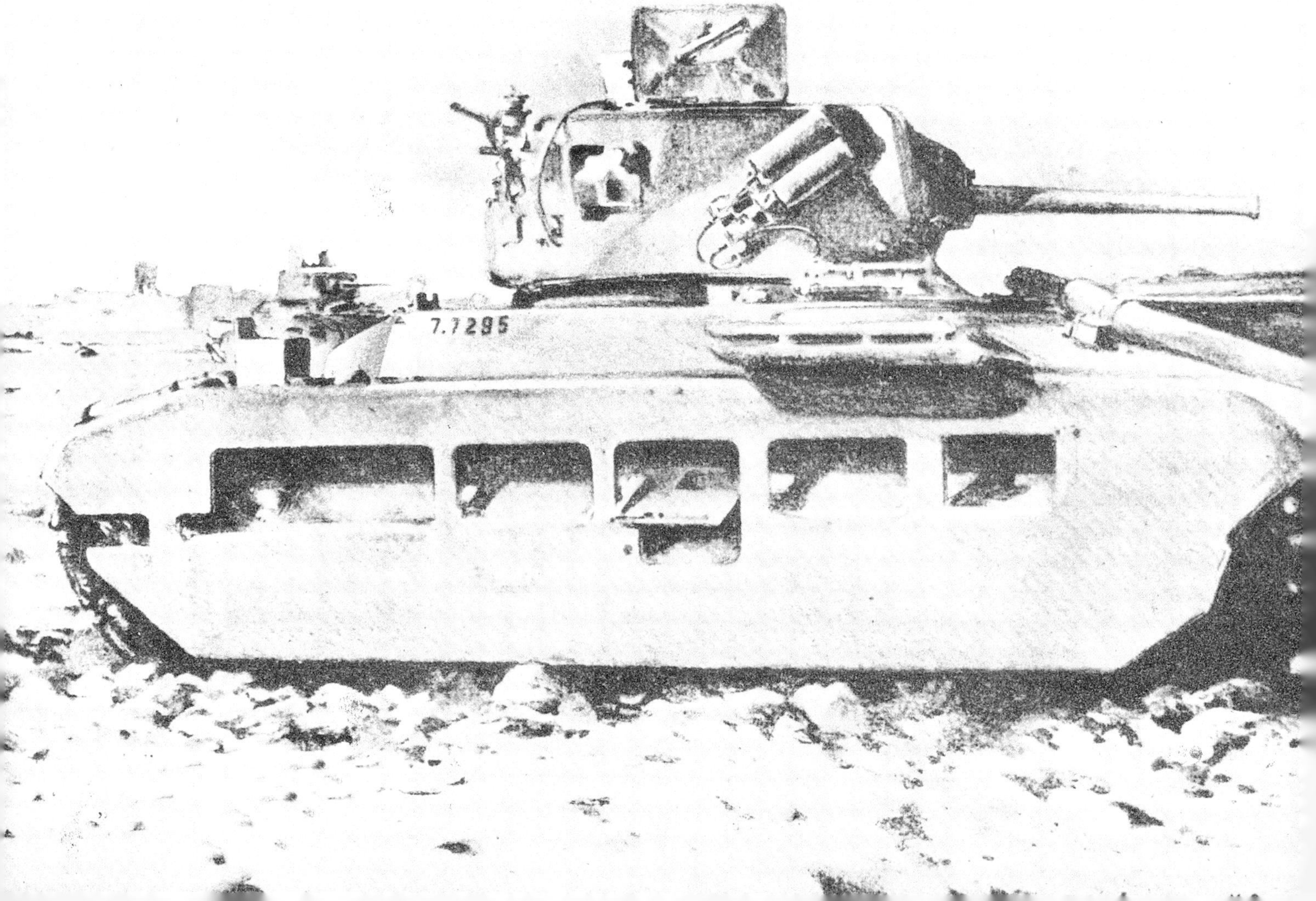

for Tobruk, and by the morning of 21 June had captured it. With its fall, masses of men and supplies were taken. Their imaginations aflame with mirages of Cairo, Alexandria and the Canal, the German and Italian soldiers set out to gain these objectives, fighting throughout the fierce heat of the desert summer.

Three days after taking Tobruk the main body of the Afrika Korps had advanced 140 km in pursuit, and had been able to exploit a gap which had opened up between two British armoured formations. Both were smashed in succession, and these defeats seemed to be the last straw. The central command structure of the Eighth Army began to fail, with orders being issued from Cairo that each corps was to operate as its commander thought fit. Contingency plans were drawn up for Egypt to be evacuated and for the Eighth Army to divide, with one part going up the Nile and the other withdrawing into Palestine.

Those remnants of the British desert army which had emerged from the 'Gazala Gallop' and were still more or less intact, stood at bay with dogged determination. They were all that stood between the Axis and total victory. The ever-confident Rommel sent out an all-arms battle group commanded by Georg Briel, which was to be a spearhead formation which would 'bounce' the British Alamein line and thrust eastwards into Egypt. Rommel finished his briefing to the young commander with the words: 'Very soon, you and I will be drinking coffee in Shepheard's Hotel in Cairo.' On 1 July the Afrika Korps, having advanced to contact in an all-night drive, rushed impetuously into battle, but by the end of the day the 90th Light Division had lost all its artillery without making any impression upon the British defenders. The division's assaults continued throughout 2–3 July, and although slight advances were made the attacks launched by the tired and understrength division gradually faded away. The losses it suffered were so severe that it was reduced to a strength of just 58 officers, 247 non-commissioned officers and 1023 men. Then the 'Ariete' Division was attacked and broke under the British assault. The need to take the Italian division out of the Axis battle line underlined the serious situation facing the newly-promoted Field Marshal Rommel. At the present scale of losses he could no longer continue the offensive. He made the bitter decision to call it off. Some idea of how heavily the Axis forces in Libya had suffered can be gauged from the nightly strength returns to Rome and to Berlin. One of these showed that the two Italian divisions, 'Ariete' and 'Littorio', had been reduced to five tanks, and one and two guns respectively, while the 15th and 21st Panzer Divisions of Afrika Korps had a combined total of only fifty vehicles. The casualties to both sides had so reduced their condition that neither had the men or supplies to fight and win a long battle. Both sides needed to rest and prepare for a new campaign.

Panzer Army Africa was the first of the protagonists to be ready for action again. Its opening attacks went in on 9 July against the Alamein defence line, in which bitter fighting and fierce attacks were succeeded by equally fierce counter-attacks. The battlefield on which the Afrika Korps opened what many thought would be the offensive that would take it to the Suez Canal, was a narrow one, on an east-west axis. This strip of desert, on which the three battles of El Alamein would be fought, lay between the British forward defence line and the Trigh Abd el Rahman in the German rear. On a north-south axis, the British defensive line ran from the Mediterranean to the Quattara Depression, a distance of about 80 km.

The Afrika Korps and the Italian divisions, scenting what they thought was imminent and complete victory, flung themselves impetuously at the gap between the sea and the Depression. Facing them were the tired but dogged infantry of the Eighth Army, only some of whom were veterans, the majority being fresh out from the United Kingdom. The Axis thrusts were not strong ones; indeed, they could not be. The Afrika Korps had been reduced to just fifty-five panzers since its formations had first rushed the Alamein positions and, in addition, the Axis soldiers had been fighting for nearly five weeks without rest. They had long since passed the limits of endurance and it was only confidence in Rommel and the mirages of Cairo and Alexandria which kept them moving forward. Rommel asked them for one last effort. His soldiers responded to the call but suffered such losses in their assaults that within days Afrika Korps' panzer force had only twenty-six 'runners' left on its establishment.

A situation report sent to OKH detailed how badly the formations had suffered. The numerical strength of the divisions, each of which had a war establishment of over 10,000 men, had sunk to just 1500. The last gasp effort for which Rommel had asked had failed; the Axis units were just too weak. With the realisation that his offensive could not succeed, Rommel reviewed the situation. He was determined to hold and not to retreat from the positions which his men had gained. He would wait for reinforcements to arrive from Europe, and when they came he would use the positions he held as a springboard for the final assault. Auchinleck, too, realised that his mainly inexperienced soldiers needed a rest. The 22nd Armoured Brigade was so badly trained that it lost 131 of its machines on 22 July, and only three days later the Eighth Army suffered over 1000 casualties in a disastrous infantry assault. A British appreciation written in July admitted that the Eighth Army would first have to be taught to fight a defensive battle before it could attempt offensive operations. It went on: 'The newly arrived infantry and armoured divisions must be trained for this (the breakthrough battle) as well as for the pursuit.'

Rommel regrouped once again, and at the end of August struck afresh in what he hoped would be a re-run of the Gazala offensive. He proposed to swing round the southern flank of the Eighth Army's battle line at Alam Halfa, to advance and destroy the Eighth Army's tank divisions before going on to strike up towards the Mediterranean. This time the left hook operation failed completely. Montgomery, the Eighth Army's new commander, intended to fight a set-piece battle which would thwart the Axis attack. Both the 15th and 21st Panzer Divisions advanced during the night of 30/31 August, intending to attack the British armour which they could see positioned on a ridge. But that armour was bait, and the Afrika Korps had taken it. In a bloody battle which endured for two days, the Afrika Korps was enticed into a cul-de-sac which then rapidly became a killing ground. German and Italian engineers had had no time to cut broad gaps through the British minefields, and as a consequence there was a build up of vehicles around the narrow entrance gaps through which the panzer units passed slowly en route to their form up areas. While the immobile Axis forces were crowded around these entrances they were

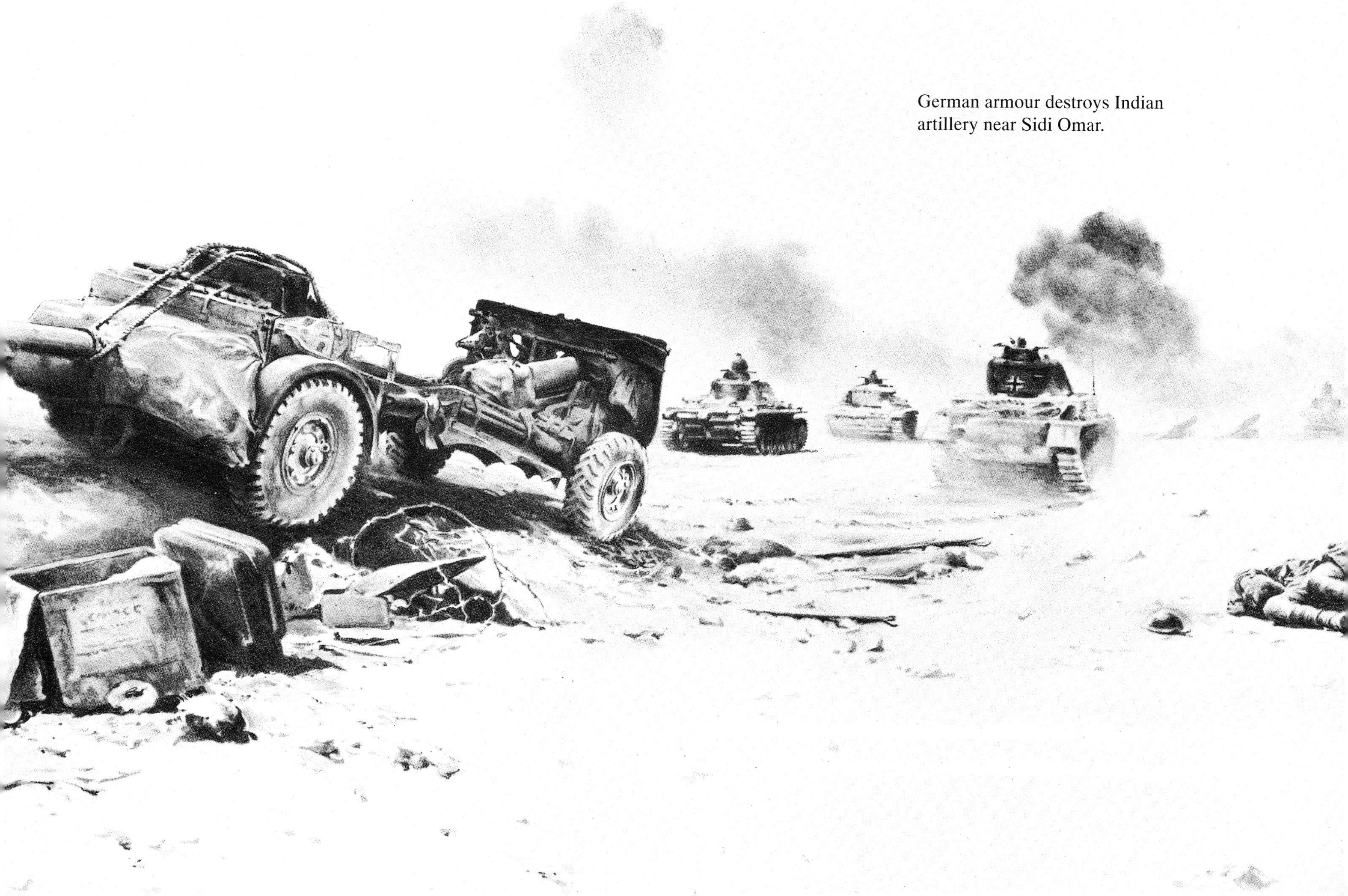

German armour destroys Indian
artillery near Sidi Omar.

struck by a series of aerial attacks by RAF bombers, which shook them badly. The panzer units which had already passed through the gaps could make no progress against the Eighth Army, which was holding the high ground and refusing to be drawn into futile cavalry-type charges. The end of the Battle of Alam Halfa was not in doubt, and during 3 September Rommel acknowledged the inevitable and ordered the Panzer Army Africa to withdraw. The trap in which Montgomery had hoped to catch the entire Afrika Korps did not completely close, but the Eighth Army had won a major battle – Second Alamein, as the Germans called it. The Axis flood, which had reached almost as far as the British Alamein defensive line, had been checked and flung back.

Rommel was aware, of course, that each succeeding day would see the Eighth Army growing stronger while the Axis forces became ever more weak, denied the supplies and men they so desperately needed. His year of victory had ended, but, determined to stave off the inevitable, Rommel prepared a defence of the ground between the British forward minefields at El Alamein and the Trigh Abd el Rahman. During the next few weeks he did receive some reinforcements, and by the end of September had five Italian divisions and one German division holding the front line. In support positions to the west of El Daba was the 90th Light Division, with the 'Littorio' and 'Ariete' Divisions and both panzer divisions of Afrika Korps in the south of the Axis line.

During the evening of 23 October 1942, the long expected British offensive opened at El Alamein. Rommel, who was away on sick leave, flew back to Africa immediately, and although his mastery of the field enabled him to obstruct for a short time the breakthrough operation planned by Montgomery, he could not prevent it developing and ultimately succeeding. 'Operation Supercharge', which finally broke the Axis line, opened during the first week of November. When the Eighth Army attacked in this last operation of Third Alamein, its tank armada of more than 800 vehicles faced just nine German panzers and 100 Italian tanks. Permission for Afrika Korps and the remainder of Panzer Army Africa to retreat was at first refused by Hitler, who demanded that his soldiers fight and die where they stood. But eventually, even the Führer had to accept the situation for what it was, and he gave his grudging consent. The Axis retreat was marked, as the Eighth Army's retreats had always been, by examples of outstanding bravery, most of which went unseen in the swirling desert dust clouds and, therefore, unrecognised and unrewarded. The retreat, punctuated by rearguard actions fought out across the whole length of Libya, continued up into and eventually through the French colony of Tunisia. On 12 May 1943, Cramer, its last commander, sent the signal which reported the death of the Afrika Korps.

Some 130,000 German and 180,000 Italian soldiers were taken prisoner, while 100,000 soldiers of all nations had been killed or died in the entire desert campaign. It was a bitter harvest, but more bitter was the irony that the fuel-oil supplies on which both armies had depended lay undiscovered and untapped beneath their very feet.

In the desert wastes there are now only cemeteries and memorials to mark the fact that between 1940 and 1943 this area had been a major theatre of war, important, indeed unique, because it bordered the Mediterranean, the great inland sea which links the continents of Europe, Asia and Africa.

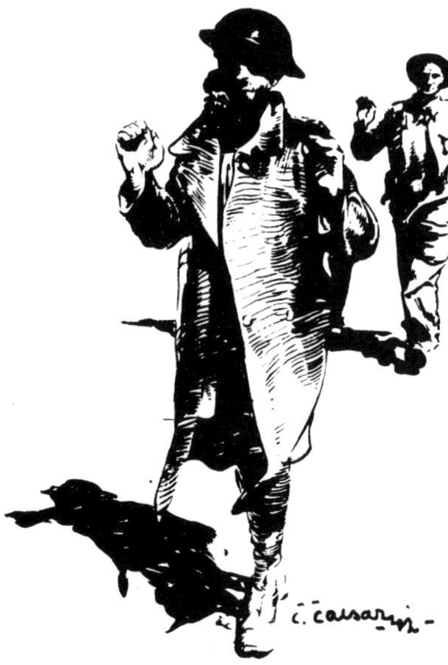